TRULY BLUE

Debbie Fletcher

Hallmark Press

Published by Hallmark Press International
7 Greenway Gardens
Croydon
Surrey
CR0 8QJ

ISBN 978-1-906459-23-9

Printed and bound in Great Britain by
CPI Antony Rowe, Chippenham and Eastbourne

Dedicated

To my Mom and Family

And to Dave Brueton

Acknowledgements

I would like to give thanks to all those who have supported me during the writing of this book and those who have contributed to my adventures following Birmingham City and England over the years. Thanks to my mom Sheila Fletcher for her continued support and unending supply of food for match days, without her none of this would have been possible. Thanks also to my sister Annette Fletcher for her support and company at many Blues games over the years and to the rest of my family including my dad Gerald Fletcher and my brother Neil Fletcher, who has also been to games with me in the early years. A big thanks to my constant companion for many years following Blues – my nephew Stephen Fletcher, and to my niece Nicola Fletcher who has also accompanied me to games.

Thanks also to Stephen Woolley (known to his mates as Stegga) for obtaining match tickets for many games and arranging travel for away games in the later years and for his support throughout. Thanks also to my companions from the early years – Julie Guest, Pamela Beasley, Debbie, Brendon Anderson, Ron, Lee Pitman, Alan, Graham & Craig, Fiddler and many more. Thanks to the girls that I travelled to Germany with to follow England in the World Cup Finals in 2006 – Roxy Fulton, Janine Goss and Carolyn Young. Thanks to my other best mates in Abu Dhabi who have supported Birmingham City with me via live matches at my house – Trish Kennedy and Tracey Rawnsley. Also to Craig

Chisholm and Steve Parr for being a part of my life and enjoying the football with me despite supporting different teams.

I would also like to remember big Dave Brueton who contributed to this book with his suggestion of 'Truly Blue' for the title and who I met up with at many Blues games and was a true friend away from the game also. Sadly Dave lost his life while on holiday in Tenerife but he is still remembered fondly by all of his friends.

I would like to say a very big thank you to all of you that have been involved in my life and added to my adventures over the years. Keep Right On!

Contents

CHAPTER ONE – The Beginning

I remember my first match at St. Andrews and my very first experience of the famous 'Keep Right On' as if it was only yesterday. It was 24th March 1973 and I was eleven years old. I don't really know where my interest in football began, as none of my family were football fans. I can only say that I was born with blue blood running through my veins. I was born a Bluenose!

My dad didn't know anything about football and had no interest in the game whatsoever. My mom didn't know anything about football either, although she is a Bluenose now and always looks for Birmingham's results. Mom has been to a few matches with me over the years, including a Wembley Final and a Play Off Final in Cardiff.

My brother Neil, who is two years younger than me, also had no interest in football either, although he has been to a few games in the late seventies and early eighties with me and he always looks for Birmingham's results. My sister Annette is six years younger than me and I must admit she was probably the only one who took a bit of interest in football at first, although she had a bit of a soft spot for Liverpool. I think that was probably due to the fact that Liverpool were winning everything at the time (in the 70's) and were always on the TV. In fact, I would often come home from school to find Annette sitting in front of the telly watching a Liverpool game. She also had a Liverpool belt, which I think she must have got from Weston-Super-Mare when we visited on a family outing. I have to say though, she is now a very ardent Bluenose and gets to games whenever she can.

If I think back it probably came from my great-granddad on my mom's side who was an ardent bluenose too. Then there was my granddad. I don't remember too much about him as he died when I was still young – around twelve I think. I remember that he used to get out this big teapot in which he kept loads of newspaper cuttings from over the years and would patiently explain the old times to me. My Nan Rose used to tell me how she used to make rosettes for her dad (my great-granddad) to wear to the matches when he used to go down St. Andrews to cheer on the Blues.

Whenever I visited my granddad he always liked to tell me how 'brummigem', as he called Blues, were doing. So began many years of 'joys and sorrows too' – there would be many sorrows though as most bluenoses know! The joys, however, would be memorable and would more than make up for the sorrows.

My best friend at the time – Sue, also started to take an interest in football, unfortunately though her team was Manchester United. Together we used to chat about football and we both longed to see our heroes play and go to a live game. I began planning a way to get to St. Andrews to see the boys in royal blue and due to the fact that there was no way Sue could get to Manchester she agreed to come to the Blues with me.

I lived in Weoley Castle and Sue in Selly Oak, so it meant a three-bus journey for us to get to St. Andrews the home of Birmingham City. A bit daunting for two eleven year olds! Mind you, it was much safer at that time to be out and about in those days – not like now. I was always a bit independent and adventurous and on Saturday, 24th March 1973 Sue and I set of for St. Andrews to watch Birmingham City take on Coventry City in a local derby in the old first division (now known as the premier league).

I don't remember a lot about the journey or the match really but I do remember the atmosphere and the feelings it inspired. When I first set eyes on the stadium I was overawed. It looked so big! I stood on the Coventry road and gazed up the Kop sitting regally at the top of the grassy hill that it sat on. I saw the people that had gone through the turnstiles climbing up the steps towards the entrance to the terraces at the top. I remember paying my money and squeezing through the old turnstiles and climbing the many concrete steps to the top of the old Kop terracing. We had got there early and the terracing looked massive while it was filling up. I thought the pitch looked so green. On the terracing the atmosphere was unbelievable! I was completely overwhelmed. It was fantastic – I was well and truly hooked! The whole stadium looked so big to me, and the noise was incredible.

It was still early but the ground seemed full already and the fans (as always) were in fabulous voice. It was the first time I heard 'Keep Right On' sang, and it was belting out so proudly. I fell in love with the club and the supporters that day. Sue and I were brave little souls and stood at the heart of the Kop, in the middle, just to the left of the halfway fencing and just in front of the refreshments stand at the back. In fact we were so small at the time that the guys lifted us onto a concrete shelf about six inches wide and about a18inches high that surrounded the refreshment stand so that we could see.

I remember looking across the top of all those heads and seeing a sea of swaying blue and white. There were 34, 775 inside St. Andrews that day and it seemed like every one of them had at least one scarf either around their necks or tied to their wrists. At the time the Kop and Tilton were terracing, with the old railway end and the main stand the seated areas. I had a blue and white bar scarf tied proudly around my wrist as this was the style at the time – as I am sure many of you remember.

When Blues scored I remember throwing my arms in the air, whilst trying to keep my balance and catching my scarf on the barbed wire on the top of the refreshment stand! One of the guys had to untangle it for me. I am sure I did that a few times over the years. The fans on the Kop were swaying back and forth like a tide and I loved it when they did 'Knee's up mother brown' and everyone jumped up and down until they all surged forward with a few getting squashed or getting wrapped around the crash bars.

No one seemed to get hurt though and they soon came back to where they had previously been standing, or thereabouts! The odd pie would get dropped and a few drinks spilt but it was all good fun and added to the atmosphere.

Seeing my heroes run out onto that lovely green pitch was such a thrill, as it still is. I was so excited that day and although I don't remember much about the game I remember that I thought Blues played fantastic in their royal blue shirts as they beat Coventry 3-0. I soon caught on to the songs and sang my heart out for the entire time I was there, despite trying to stay on the six inch shelf I was balancing on. I did fall off a few times though but was always caught by the guys beneath us who seemed to look out for us. I came out thinking Birmingham City were the best team in the world. The sound of 'Keep Right On' and 'Shit on the Villa' were ringing in my ears for days afterwards. I was learning fast that we really hated the villa! Mind you, I had already gathered that from school!

Leaving the ground was fantastic too, being amongst the tide of people marching down the steps towards the waiting football special buses that were always waiting to take everyone back to the city centre. I remember the long line of Double Decker buses and how we would all queue to get on one, and when the bus was jammed full then the queue would move on to the next one. The bus would then head for town with the bluenoses singing at the top of their voices and the bus seemed to sway with the singing. All the way back to town I could see the Blues fans on both sides of the road as well as in the road and it was like a continuous sea of blue and white. It was fabulous and I couldn't wait to go back again. That was my pocket money accounted for, forever I think!

Because I was still at school I couldn't go to all the games but I intended to go to as many as was possible. I also started a scrapbook and treasured my one and only football programme that I had so far. As I said earlier – so began my love affair with Birmingham City and it is still going strong many years later!

I'm not sure how many games I managed to get to for the rest of that season but I don't think it was too many especially as there weren't that many games left but I listened for the scores on BRMB radio when I couldn't make it. Blues did well that season and we finished in tenth place in division one with Liverpool winning the championship and Arsenal coming second. Blues had beaten Liverpool 2-1 at our ground and had only narrowly lost at Anfield 4-3, so quite a good season for us really. We didn't get to play the Villa as they were in the old second division that season so I had to wait a while longer to get my first taste of that special derby day atmosphere.

I didn't get to many games the following season as school and pocket money continued to prevent me but I listened to the games and went to St. Andrews whenever I could. That following season Blues finished 19th in division one with Leeds Utd winning the championship. Oh yes, and the big and mighty fell, with Manchester United being relegated to the second division.

The following season 1974-75 was similar with me only getting to a few of the games. Mind you, I was still only 12; in fact I was 13 by the end of the 1975 season and was side tracked somewhat by Donny Osmond and Co! Blues finished in 17th place with Derby County winning the championship. The hardest part of the season was our heartbreak at the hands of Fulham in the semi final of the FA Cup. After a 1-1 draw in the first game we went on to lose in the last minute of extra time in the replay at Maine Road. We should never have lost that game and at 13 years of age that was probably my first sorrow as a Bluenose. Certainly not my last though.

The FA Cup meant so much to the fans – more than now I think. I remember each season when the draw was made for the 3rd round. I would listen to it live on Monday lunchtime with such excitement. It was always my dream to be at Wembley to see Birmingham run out onto that famous pitch in the FA Cup final. It still is my dream to be honest. It felt even bigger than the champion's league final is now to a young bluenose.

The following season 1975 – 76 saw Blues play Villa for the first time in my memory. As I was still very young and I was finding my feet as a teenager I did not get to many games and spent most of my time out with my friends at disco's or the local youth club in Selly Oak called '870'. I was getting involved in lots of activities with the youth club such as canoeing and such and was also discovering boys at the local Disco's. The Disco's were real fun back then, and I still remember us all having to have the back of our hands stamped to prove that we had paid. I used to go to the local Disco at Gabby's in Weoley Castle – which was part of a church, and all the local youth used to be there. I can't remember the name of the other one that I went to, which wasn't far from the local school that I went to – Shenley Court Comprehensive. But it was safe to say that I was having fun and probably just a little side-tracked.

I think that is why I don't remember the first game with the villa, which was away, and Blues lost 2-1. Glad I don't remember to be honest, as I have never taken well to any sort of defeat by the villa – luckily I haven't seen many over the years. I couldn't get to the return game at Stans (St. Andrews) but I remember that we beat them 3-2 and it was to be the start of a good run of wins against them. We finished the season in 19th place with Liverpool winning the championship. The following season 1976 – 77 I was a regular, getting to all the home games.

I was growing up fast and my interest in football had gone up a gear and I was really looking forward to the start of the 1976 season. Life was good at the time. I had lots of friends, the pop scene was good and I had a great family life. That was probably another reason I had missed so many matches, the family weekends away. We had a caravan in Brean Sands, which is next to Weston-Super-Mare, and my mom and dad would take us for a trip away most weekends and for our holidays too. It was good fun to go to the seaside and I would often pick up football souvenirs while I was there. I remember buying a Birmingham City comb once! I would always play football with my brother Neil on the beach and in the fields. My sister Annette joined in as she got older too. Any football game being played and I would join in. I would always be found playing football with all the kids in the grove on the grass island in the middle of the grove where I lived in Weoley Castle. I used to love playing and would always come in for my tea with a rosy complexion and cuts and bruises.

The season began with a great 2-2 draw against Manchester United at Old Trafford, and after another good draw against Leeds Utd at home, Blues again beat the mighty Liverpool 2-1 as St. Andrews. I was amongst the 33,000 there that day when Gallagher and Francis scored and the crowd went wild. To beat the champions was brilliant, especially as they had such a good side. As always the atmosphere was electric and the Kop was a constant sea of motion, swaying one way, then the other. I am always amazed at how impressive it sounds when the Kop belt out 'Keep Right On' in full voice. Fantastic!

That great win was followed by a couple of 1-0 defeats, one of which was against our other neighbours West Bromwich Albion, and then we were off to Villa Park for the real derby. I couldn't go to this game so I had to make do with listening to the radio and was thrilled when we beat them 2-1 with goals from Burns and Connolly. It was a brilliant atmosphere in the city after that. Especially at school, where we tormented the few villa fans something rotten. Got to be done though. Part of our job as a Bluenose.

I went to all the home matches that season and it was so much fun. I loved the banter with the rival fans, who used to be positioned at the far end of the Tilton Road End Terrace and they were always given loads of abuse from us, Blues fans. The Blues fans have always had a great sense of humour and some of the chants or shouted comments could be hilarious. I remember at one match, although I do not remember which one it was, there was a funny incident with a ladder that must have been used to make repairs to the roof etc. During the match someone must have got it down from the roof because all of a sudden it was being waved from side to side like a giant scarf as the fans sang 'you'll never walk alone' (which was sang a lot at the time by all sets of fans as everyone waved their scarves). Next thing the police had decided that they would put a stop to any fun that was being had and moved into the crowd to reclaim the ladder. Now that was when the fun started. As the police arrived in numbers at the back of the Kop the ladder was passed hand to hand above everyone's heads down towards the front of the Kop to chants of 'you'll never take the ladder!' Whilst the rest of us laughed and the police raced to the bottom, the ladder was passed back up again to more chants of 'you'll never take the ladder!' This seemed to go on for ages, up and down the Kop the ladder went, to much laughter and singing until the police finally managed to reclaim the ladder to loud boos from all around the ground! It was so funny. Even the players risked the odd glance into the crowd to see what was happening.

I saw some good games that season, beating Derby Count 5-1 at home was a good one, along with a 1-0 win over Portsmouth in the FA Cup third round before being knocked out by Leeds Utd 2-1 in the next round.

However, my favourite game that season has to be my first real derby game against the Villa on 10th May 1977 as St. Andrews. The atmosphere was like nothing I had ever experienced before or since. It was electric inside the ground that day. The singing was top notch and the ground was packed. I was standing on the terracing at the back of the Kop and I was constantly lifted bodily off the ground when the crowd swayed one way or another and at times my feet were not on the ground! There were 43,721 inside St Andrews and they sang their hearts out. As it was a local derby, it was also the largest away following I had seen and the villa fans were given most of the Tilton Road End with lines of police, a strip of empty terracing and high fences separating the fans. I remember Blues singing 'over there, over there – and do they smell..... Like fucking hell!' They also sang the 'chim-chimney song – we hate the bastards in claret and blue'. It was great. The match lived up to expectations with Francis and Hibbit scoring in a 2-1 win. Bluenoses sang 'we're still the kings of Brum' as we poured out of the stadium in high spirits. There was not a Villa fan to be seen outside, just a mass of singing blue and white fans. It would have been impossible to drive a car down any of the streets, as it was just a sea of Bluenoses. They poured into pubs, queued for buses or streamed towards town on foot; it was a fabulous sight. One that I will never forget. There were a few fights in the city centre here and there.

I headed home and stopped to wait at the local shop for the pink Argus to come in so that I could enjoy it all over again. That's three wins on the trot against the Villa now. I picked up the paper and some chips and headed back home to tell mom how we had battered the Villa again. What a day.

Blues finished that season in 13th position in the first division with Liverpool again the champions. It was a good season – a good finish in the league, beating the champions and also doing the double over neighbours Villa. It was also the first season that I went to every home game.

CHAPTER TWO – My first away game

The following season 1977-78 again saw me as a regular at St. Andrews. I loved getting up early on a Saturday morning before a home match and getting ready to go. I used to arrive early at around one o'clock and would always be amongst the first people to go in. Lots of other people would flood into the ground too and the singing would start in earnest.

The season didn't start very well with a string of defeats and Blues only scoring one goal in 5 games until we beat Middlesborough away 2-1 in September followed by a 3-0 win over Newcastle. Then in October we took on the Villa again on their own patch at Villa Park. I could not get to this game but I was thrilled that our run remained intact and Blues came out 1-0 winners. That was now four wins in a row against them. I was gutted that I missed it but over the moon that we triumphed yet again.

In November 1977 my granddad died and I went to stay with my Nan for a while to keep her company and to help her cope with being alone after spending the whole of her life with my granddad. My Nan's house was also in Weoley Castle and not too far from my own home. It meant that I would now have to catch a bus to school each day, which I caught right outside my Nan's house. She would see me onto the bus every morning and off to school. It was also closer to a new disco that I had recently started going to so that was handy too. On the weekends I would walk up the big green hill that led to Weoley Castle Square and onwards to see my mom.

On 3rd December we took on the newly promoted Nottingham Forest and I remember to this day thinking how dirty they played. They kicked us off the park and came out 2-0 winners. I'm surprised we had a player left walking after playing them. Forest did well that season too with their very physical side and won the championship. Then on the 2nd of January we took on the might of Manchester United at Old Trafford. I listened to it on the radio as the goal alerts started coming in on BRMB radio. I think it was Tony Butler the DJ at the time and I remember clearly when the music was stopped for him to announce that Birmingham City had gone 1-0 ahead at Old Trafford with Trevor Francis (the King of Brum – as he was known) scoring against the reds. I prayed that we could hold on and win although I knew the odds were against us as Manchester United were a decent team and very rarely got beat at Old Trafford. So, when the news came through that Manchester Utd had equalised I was not really surprised. The DJ returned to the song that had been playing and only a few seconds later the music was again stopped to announce another goal at Old Trafford. I listened with dread and then utter surprise as he reported that Birmingham had knocked the ball straight from the kick off to Trevor Francis who had run straight down the other end and scored 2-1 to Birmingham! We held on to win 2-1 at Old Trafford and for me it was one of the highlights of that season and one that left a smile on my face for weeks, especially as my best friend was a Manchester Utd fan.

It was a really good January for me. On the 7th January we played Wigan Athletic in the FA Cup and at the time they were a non-league team. We thrashed them 4-0 and the atmosphere in the ground was great as it always was for the FA Cup. Blues completely outplayed them with the fans singing 'you should have stuck to rugby'.

I raced home from school on the Monday lunchtime to catch the FA cup draw. I waited nervously by the radio and then I heard it. Derby County versus Birmingham City. That's it, I thought, I have to get to this game, this has to be my first away game. I began trying to talk my mates into coming with me and eventually a couple of them agreed. I was so excited and off we went to the ticket office to buy tickets for the away end at the old Baseball ground in Derby.

However, before the FA Cup game, and three days before my sixteenth birthday Birmingham pulled off the shock of the season. Blues were playing away against the mighty Liverpool at Anfield and the reds had not lost a game at Anfield for four years. All that was too change as Blues came out half time and stormed into a 3-0 lead, scoring 3 goals in 13 minutes in front of the stunned Kop! I was running round the room at home listening on the radio. I couldn't believe it, but began to feel nervous as they came back at us with a vengeance. Liverpool pulled 2 goals back but we managed to hold on for a historical 3-2 win! I rushed out at five to six to the local shop to get a copy of the Argus which I knew got in about six o'clock. What a headline 'Kop That', and what a score line – Liverpool 2 Birmingham City 3! I read it about ten times and then stuck it in my scrapbook. What a fantastic birthday present.

I had met my first serious boyfriend around this time too. His name was Graham and he was from Harborne, which is not too far from where I lived. It was a bus journey away mind. He was two years older than me and had a car, which was really cool of course. Especially as he would pick me up from school much to the envy of all the other girls. He was a Bluenose too, although he didn't go to the games that often. He had a really fab car that was painted like the Starsky and Hutch car, which was really cool at the time. Also the trend at the time was to have names at the top of the front windscreen, so as our relationship progressed 'Graham 'and 'Debbie' were proudly displayed at the top of his front windscreen. I now appeared really cool at school. He was really good looking too. However, no man has ever prevented my going to the blues and I was really looking forward to the Derby game.

Finally the day of the Derby game arrived. It was Saturday, 28th January, four days after my birthday and I was so excited. I met up with my friends and we set off for New Street station to catch one of the many football special trains that were travelling to

Derby that day. The train station was starting to fill up with Bluenoses and we joined the queue for tickets for the special. That was when it all went wrong. It was announced that the Derby Co v Birmingham City game had been called off due to bad weather! I was devastated. Especially as the game would now be played midweek on a school day. The other girls were upset too and said that they would get their tickets for the game refunded, as they would not be able to go. Me, on the other hand, was determined to go still – even if it meant bunking off school and going on my own. I had looked forward to this for so long that I could not give up.

I told my mom when I got home and when she saw how determined I was she said I could come out of school early to go to the match. She was really worried about me going on my own though, and I reassured her that I would be okay. The replay was now on the 1st February – midweek.

I ran all the way home from school that day and got changed in record time. Mom had arranged for my Nan to take me to town to the station and to put me on the train! So off we set, my Nan and me. We arrived at the station and purchased my ticket for the special with no problems. Football fans were not allowed to get on the specials through the station, we had to queue outside the station at the side door where the police would keep an eye on proceedings. As we walked to the queue my Nan spotted a group of girls and to my embarrassment, took me over to them and asked if I could stay with them as I was alone and would they look out for me. It was nice of my Nan and I made friends with them and stayed with them for the trip. It was a massive queue by the time the doors were opened and we surged through and onto the waiting football special. There were a few football specials on that day and the one I was on was packed with singing fans. The bluenoses were sitting everywhere, on the seats, on the tables, in the luggage racks and standing in the aisles. It was brilliant. 'Wembley – Wembley' was being sang loudly thoughout the journey along with 'Keep Right On', 'Shit on the Villa' and other favourites.

The train pulled into Derby station and immediately everyone streamed off en mass. The noise was deafening in the confined space of the station as the bluenoses sang 'the brummies are here!' at the top of our voices. People just stopped in amazement and watched the flow of fans as we swarmed up stairs and out of the station to the waiting police escort. The police were waiting in numbers and immediately moved to the front of the fans and to either side and led us towards the ground in some sort of order. It was non-stop singing – it was great. I have always thought that away games are better for the atmosphere of the visiting Blue army and this day was when it all began for me. I was as overwhelmed as all the people we passed who stopped what they were doing in amazement to watch the blue army as it passed by in full voice. We passed the odd Derby fan too and they immediately came into verbal abuse from the blue army. It was an invasion. I was so impressed.

The ground was a bit of a disappointment. It was a right shed. It was smaller than St. Andrews and just looked tatty and old. We were led into the away end, which was on the one side and included the corner, which contained a massive floodlight in the middle of it. A bit crap I thought at the time. Our end was the lower terracing underneath the stand with the top stand jutting out over the top of most of us. Our end was packed and due to fact that I am not that tall, it was difficult at times to see some of the match. The blue army sang our hearts out, and I thought that we outsang the home fans. Could have just been me being blue eyed thought! The Derby fans were in good voice too and the game was exciting.

Into the game and I could smell smoke. The blues fans started singing 'Derby County's burning down!' to the tune of London town is burning down, and I looked behind us to see that the refreshment stand was on fire! Never a dull moment following the blues eh.

The match was always going to be close with Derby just shading it and beating us 2-1. When blues scored the Bluenoses went wild and I got an accidental punch in the face – what a day.

I was okay though and still managed to jump up and down to celebrate the goal. Shame we lost though. I have always loved the FA Cup, as most fans do, so I was feeling a bit disappointed on our walk back to the station. We had the usual police escort back and at one point the Derby fans taunted us with a rendition of 'were going to Wembley – your not', but they soon ran when some Bluenoses broke away from the escort and chased them down the road to lots of cheering from the rest. We continued to sing though, and stormed into the station and onto the waiting football special in full voice. The train journey back was fun with everyone singing and we got back into Birmingham late in the night. I had to ring my dad and explain why I was out late and get him to come and pick me up from the station. I don't think he was too impressed to be honest, but I had enjoyed my first away game immensely despite our defeat and was really looking forward to my future away travel. I was hooked.

Not long afterwards on 25th February we played the Villa again at our ground. I was able to get to this game and once again the atmosphere was fantastic. There were 33,679 at St. Andrews that day and the majority came out happy. Another win for the blues. Birmingham City 1 Aston Villa 0. Five in a row, which is exactly what the Bluenoses sang as well 'we beat the Villa, we beat em five times' to the tune of the Muppets. It was a brilliant day, we were still the kings of Brum - as the fans sang, and I reckoned that if we played Villa every week we would win the league! I came home very happy that night.

I was due to leave school in the summer after my exams and was being encouraged by the careers advice people at school to apply for jobs. They mostly told you what jobs you should be doing around this time and told me I would make a good medical secretary. This was because I could type and I wanted to be a doctor – which girls weren't really encouraged to do then. So I applied for jobs along with everyone else who was leaving that year and I got one in a locum doctors organisation working in the office. I was due to start at the end of April and would have to have time off to go back and sit my exams. This meant that I did not get my summer holidays off like the rest of my mates.

Before I started work I was off to my second away game before the season finished. On 15th April I set off with my mates for Leicester to watch Blues play Leicester City at their old ground Filbert Street. Once again we got the football special, which was again packed with Bluenoses sitting everywhere, drinking cans of beer and singing at the top of their voices. It was great. Blues always take a lot to local games such as this and the atmosphere was really good. It is always great to be part of the Blue army when they arrive at local train stations. When we arrived in Leicester there was a mass of blue and white taking over the station. Again the police were there to meet us and gave us an escort to the ground. The walk to the ground was fun, with lots of singing as usual and we were led straight into the away end. Inside the ground we sang our hearts out and watched Birmingham thrash Leicester 4-1! It was great on the terraces when Blues scored and everyone jumped on each other and the crowd swayed towards the front. Especially as it happened four time that day for us.

The journey back to the station was much more fun than after the Derby County game. It makes a big difference when we have won, and we celebrated all the way back to the station, on the football special and when we got back to Birmingham later that day. I headed home from New Street station, picking up fish and chips and a Sports Argus on my way. Mom was pleased to see me in such a good mood. I really enjoyed that season as we had some very good results and finished in 11th place, whilst once again doing the double over archrivals Villa.

My childhood was officially over though and I started my new job at the end of April.

CHAPTER THREE – Wembley Stadium

It was in the same year – 1978, that I made my first trip to the twin towers of Wembley.   On Saturday, 16th May 1978 I set off for London to see my first England international at the home of football. It was a really nice day and I was out of bed bright and early and I excitedly ran around the house, eating breakfast and getting ready for the trip ahead. I had my new England scarf all ready and I was soon on my way to New Street Station to catch the train to London. England were playing Northern Ireland in the home championships that were a regular thing at the time. This was when England, Scotland, Wales, Northern Ireland and Republic of Ireland all played in a competition each year in a sort of mini league. It was eventually stopped due to trouble between rival sets of supporters. Emotions would always run high in these games, especially between England and Scotland. I think it came to a head the year when Scotland fans invaded the pitch at Wembley, taking away the goal posts and tearing up most of the pitch to take home with them.

The train was full of England fans on their way to the game and everyone was in good spirits, downing cans of larger and singing England songs. It was great. It was strange for me to be amongst fans wearing red and white rather than blue and white but I easily became part of them and have continued to proudly wear the white and red of England ever since.

Everyone who has ever walked down Wembley way will have his or her own memories and they will stick in their minds forever as do mine. It was fantastic getting off the train and seeing the seething mass of white and red swarming down Wembley way as one towards the great twin towers in the distance. The sight was magnificent. I didn't much enjoy coming out of the station though. It was through an underpass, which was jammed with fans and a bit claustrophobic to be honest, and a little frightening. But once we were out and onto Wembley way it was great. The noise and the singing was amazing. Wembley looked so impressive as I got close and I wandered around the stadium, stopping at various stalls to buy food and of course a programme. I remember buying sausage and chips in a tray and eating it as we walked around, watching everyone and looking for our entrance. It was a carnival atmosphere and I was really enjoying it.

I found my way to an entrance and pushed through the turnstile into the long corridor/tunnel that runs all around the inside of Wembley, underneath the terracing. There were more stalls inside selling food and drink including beer in bottles. I remember that a bottle of skol was really expensive at the time and the only choice of alcohol you were given. I know I was only sixteen but I admit to drinking the odd alcoholic drink on occasions. After all, I did have an older boyfriend (eighteen!) so I would go out to local pubs with him, but that's another story.

My ticket was for the lower terracing just behind the goal, so I made my way up the steps and out onto the terrace. What an awesome view inside Wembley itself. It looked massive and the sound inside was amazing, even though it was still early and the stadium was only half full. There was a real buzz around the place and the fans were already in full voice.

As kick off time got closer and the stadium filled up the noise level went up another notch and the singing was brilliant. I have always loved Wembley, it had such a great tradition and it certainly lives up to its reputation. I don't remember much about the game, probably because I was so overwhelmed by the occasion. I seem to remember that it finished 0-0. I remember the white shirts of England and the green shirts of Northern Ireland running around on the green of the pitch. After the match finished, when we had applauded our boys off the Wembley turf we headed back down the steps and joined the sea of fans swarming out of the ground and back up Wembley way towards the local train station. There was a bit of a crush going through the subway that led to the station, which I have to admit I found frightening. I thought I was going to get crushed and was glad to get to the other side still in one piece. However, I was soon safely back on the train and on my way back home to Birmingham feeling tired but satisfied with the fabulous day I had had.

My second England international was a couple of years later when we took on Russia at Wembley. Again, the atmosphere at Wembley was fabulous but this time we were outplayed by the Russians and they beat us 2-0. I was on the upper terracing this time, which did seem further away from the pitch, but it was still a good view. The terracing behind each of the goals was further away from the pitch at Wembley, whereas at Birmingham the fans are much closer to the pitch. I remember the England fans singing our hearts out but in the end we applauded the Russians off the pitch because they had played so well against us. I was disheartened by the result but I still enjoyed my day out at Wembley as I always did.

After the game my friend and I decided to hang around for a while to give the crowd time to leave so that we were not involved in the crush to get into the station again. So we wandered around the tunnel inside Wembley and that is when we saw Trevor Brooking. Brilliant! He is a real England hero and we went over to speak to him and get his autograph. He was really nice to talk to and he signed our match programmes for us. I was over the moon and it really made my day. I headed back to Birmingham happily after a great day out, despite the result.

And so it was back to the domestic football scene and the 1978 – 1979 season. I had settled into my new job nicely, I had got engaged to my boyfriend Graham and I was looking forward to the coming season. I had bought my first car around this time too, it was a white Austin 1100 and I really loved it. Probably just because it was mine to be honest. I had not passed my driving test yet and had only just got my provisional driving licence. The only driving experience I had was that of driving my boyfriend's car around the country lanes at the back of Bartley Green reservoir. I had also learned to drive a little when I was young when my dad used to let me drive his car on the beach. My dad had lots of different cars and I used to love driving them on the beach. Usually it was just steering when I was small. My favourite of my dad's cars was our green Zephyr four with the wings at the back. It was great; the front seat was one long seat like a sofa. It definitely had character.

The bodywork of my Austin 1100 wasn't too good and wouldn't last long, so soon afterwards I bought another (cheap) car. This time it was a dark green Austin 1100. My dad used to be a mechanic, among other things, and along with my boyfriend Graham they both changed the engines around, as the bodywork was better on one and the engine on the other. I remember them using a sort of winch to lift the engines and change them over. Brilliant. I never did get to drive them much though, due to the fact that I hadn't taken my test and I sold them not too long afterwards. It was impressive to own two cars for a while though! I would have to make do with being allowed to drive Graham's car now and again.

It was off to St. Andrews again for me in August for our first home game against Middlesborough, following a 1-0 defeat away to Manchester United in our opening game. I was hoping that we would have a good season with our new manager Jim Smith, who had taken over from Sir Alf Ramsey in the March. Sir Alf Ramsey had retired due to ill health.

The season started off badly and continued badly. In fact it was a nightmare of a season with Blues only winning a handful of games. The highlight of the season was when we played Manchester Utd at St. Andrews – first against bottom. At the time Blues were bottom without a win and Manchester United were undefeated. Manchester Utd predictably went 1-0 ahead but then a miracle happened and Blues turned on the style and completely outplayed the reds and came away 5-1 winners! I think it was probably the shock result of the season.

I travelled across the city to Villa Park only to see us lose to the only goal of the game. It was the first time I had seen us lose to the villa, and I must admit I took it very badly as I always do. I wasn't impressed with Villa Park on my first visit there; but then again I wouldn't be really due to my intense dislike of them. At the time the away end was just open terracing behind the goal at the witton end with no roofing. The new stand was not built then. The bluenoses sang throughout and the away end was heaving with swaying blue and white clad supporters. It was great. I am sure we outsang them, and each time 'shit on the villa' rang out (which was a lot!), it seemed to echo around the ground.

And so I headed home with a heavy heart. I went quietly to my room and didn't talk to anyone for days.

I didn't get to any other away games that season. I seemed to have quite a busy social life that year but it didn't prevent me going to most of the home matches. I was heartbroken when we got relegated at the end of the season. I had every confidence that we would come back though – or so I hoped. In the early days of supporting Birmingham I was always quite optimistic. This was way back before I realised that at Birmingham City, everything is done the hard way!

Around this time Graham and I had decided to get married on the 12th May – FA Cup final day and we were planning a holiday to the Isle of White by way of honeymoon. To cut a long story short we decided we were way too young to marry but still went on our planned holiday to the Isle of White after the end of the football season. I remember it was cup final day – I think it was Manchester United v Arsenal, which turned out to be a memorable match with the final score being 3-2 – although I'm not sure which team won. We had been listening to it on the way and on the ferry over to the Isle of White. I had a nice relaxing holiday with Graham and was re-charging my batteries ready for the coming season.

Once again I was really looking forward to the next season even though Blues would be playing in the old second division. I am always like this – I always look forward to a new season. I still think that the atmosphere at the first home game of each new season is something special. There is always that special buzz in the air and the atmosphere is always alive with hope for the new season. Everyone is always happy and there is so much optimism around.

The first match of the season was at St. Andrews and was against Fulham. What a start we made, Blues were 3-0 up at half time and cruising. But, like I said, Blues like to do it the hard way or not at all and completely buckled in the second half. Unbelievably we conceded four goals and lost the game 4-3! The problem with Jim Smith's attacking team was that as much as we could score a lot of goals we could also concede a lot too. It was a very attacking team though and very entertaining. This was also the day of the first heart transplant in England and I remember the newspapers reporting that the man who had the transplant was a Fulham fan and when he came round after the operation, his first question was how had Fulham got on. Good job he didn't come round at half time eh!

Birmingham had a good FA cup run in early 1980. As you know by now I love the FA cup and the atmosphere that surrounds it. In the third round we saw off Southampton at home 2-1 in front of over 24,000 people. It was really exciting and we were all hoping for a home draw in the next round. Once again I sat listening to the radio in my lunch break at work as we were rewarded with a home draw against Middlesborough. Blues were having a good season and had already beaten one first division side so I was hoping for a good result against the Boro.

There was 29,152 people packed into St. Andrews that day and I stood on the corner of the Kop and Tilton terraces to watch Blues beat Middlesborough 2-1. I had taken my sister Annette with me to the match and we stood on the corner of the Kop and the Tilton so Annette would have a good view. When Blues scored the winner I was so excited that I jumped in the air and knocked a guy standing near me, off his crutches which he had been balancing on at the time. Annette laughed a lot and has always remembered it! He was fine, by the way.

It was brilliant to be in the fifth round of the FA cup and when the draw sent us to white hart lane to play Tottenham Hotspur I was really excited. So on the 15th February 1980 I set out clad in my blue and white, to new street station to board the train bound for London. We went early, which meant getting the normal intercity train to London and not the football special. With drinks and sandwiches packed, we settled comfortably on the train and began chatting avidly about our chances of getting to Wembley this year.

We arrived early and got on the underground to seven sister's tube station. This was my first experience of the London underground. It seemed really noisy and busy but the tunnels and the underground maps of the various lines that ran throughout London intrigued me. On arrival at seven sisters we headed up the stairs and out of the station and onto the main road that led up towards White Hart Lane. We decided to walk up to the ground to have a look around and then go for a drink as we were very early. The pub on the way up the road looked good, so we decided to head back there after a look round the ground. It is always good to visit different football grounds, as most fans know. White Hart Lane looked interesting, and after locating the away end we then headed back to the pub.

As we were really close to the ground we left it till late before we left the packed pub to head up towards the ground and that turned out to be a big mistake. As we approached the ground we saw thousands of Blues fans standing outside the away end singing and drinking. I thought they were just waiting to go in, but when I got closer I discovered that the ground was full and the turnstiles had been closed! I was gutted! There were 50, 000 people inside and at least 3,000 blues locked out. After travelling all this way, no one was going anywhere, and all the blues fans remained outside throughout the game singing and listening to the noise from within. Whenever there was a goal scored someone inside would shout out to us all who had scored, although it was easy to know when Blues scored because we heard our end erupt and we could see the Bluenoses inside the ground jumping around – so we all celebrated outside too! Everyone was jumping up and down, jumping on each other and running around celebrating when we scored our goal. It must have looked strange really with so many of us outside.

Unfortunately, Blues lost the game 3-1, and at the final whistle the fans started pouring out. There was already lots of police around due to the fact that there was a lot of football violence at this time, but I don't think they were helped by the fact that a milk float passed the Blues fans as the Spurs fans came out of the ground. It really kicked off and there were milk bottles flying everywhere. I don't think the spurs fans knew what hit them really (apart from the milk bottles), and the police were just as surprised. I decided to leave them to it as glass rained down everywhere, and headed back to the tube station to head back to Euston to catch the train back to Birmingham.

I couldn't believe that after travelling all that way, I had not even got inside the ground. Paying at the turnstile had its advantages but I wouldn't be making that mistake again. It was my own fault though for staying in the pub too long, but I didn't anticipate the amount of fans, especially blues fans that travelled to the match. Blues have always had good away support though and it is always great fun to travel with them. It was still a good day out though despite not getting inside the ground and Blues losing. Over the years I travelled a lot and got quite used to the regular away travellers. It became like a second family.

At the time we played Spurs we were 5th in the second division and in serious contention for a promotion spot. Unfortunately for Blues fans the club decided to sell Trevor Francis to Nottingham Forest and he became the first player to be sold for a million pounds. A lot of the bluenoses were gutted but I must admit, as much as I liked Trevor I was beginning to think that we had seen his best years so perhaps it wasn't such a bad time to let him go for a very decent sum of money indeed. Could Blues invest it wisely though? Although Francis did play well for all the teams he played for after Blues I still maintain that we had his best years and he didn't quite play the dazzling football that he graced St. Andrews with during his time at Birmingham.

A few weeks later on 11th march, we entertained Chelsea at St. Andrews and at the time we were fourth in the league and pushing for promotion. Chelsea were also pushing for promotion and were higher than us, in fact I think they were top and were doing extremely well, and we knew it would be a tight game. I went with my boyfriend Graham and we decided to stand on the corner section between the kop and the tilton for a good view. There were nearly 30,000 inside St. Andrews and as always the atmosphere was fantastic, especially as it was a top of the table clash and Chelsea were perhaps the favourites. There was a lot of trouble outside the ground that day and after the game. What a treat we were in for on the pitch though. It was unbelievable as Blues dished out some fantastic football and completely outplayed Chelsea and finished the day with a 5-1 win! Brilliant. Just before the end though as we were celebrating and singing, a load of Chelsea fans who had left early came in the back of the Kop corner and started attacking a load of young Blues supporters at the back. As soon as the Blues realised what was happening, the fans charged towards the Chelsea lot that had snuck in and they ran.

The game soon finished and everyone was well pleased with the result – except of course the Chelsea lot. A gang of Chelsea had waited outside on the Coventry Road for the Blues fans to come out. As the Blues fans ran into them, they started to run away up the Coventry Road to escape, but the quick thinking Blues fans already had a group of fans blocking their exit and took revenge for the attack on the youngsters, before the police arrived in numbers.

I remember that Graham and I decided to head back to his local pub, the Scarlet Pimpernel in Harborne to celebrate with a few beers. I liked the Scarlet Pimpernel because the front room was round, which I thought was kind of cool at the time. As we walked in the pub in our Blues colours, everyone was keen to know how Blues had got on and when we told them that Blues had beaten Chelsea 5-1; no one would believe us! They really thought that we were having them on. Birmingham City were now top of the Second Division!

That season it went right to the very last game of the season against Notts County at home. I took my little sister Annette who was only twelve at the time and we stood on the Tilton, towards the Kop corner where the atmosphere was electric and the view was good. Except when it got packed and we were both on tiptoe! There were 33,863 inside St. Andrews and Blues needed at least a draw to get promotion to the First Division. It was buzzing and the singing was continuous. I remember during one rendition of 'knees up mother brown' when one bloke had his pie accidentally pushed into his face as everyone fell forward. Quite funny really.

I don't remember much about the match but it finished 3-3 and Blues were promoted! The scenes inside the ground at the end were fantastic. The crowd surged forward and onto the pitch to celebrate with our heroes, jumping up and down and carrying the players high on their shoulders, minus most of their kit, which was now being collected as souvenirs. The stewards were now all around the pitch trying to keep people from joining those already celebrating on the pitch. I held Annette's hand and led her towards the front of the Tilton in the hope of getting on the pitch to join the fun. Because the stewards were stopping people getting on the pitch, a crush was now developing and I kept a tight grip on my sister's hand, as she was only small and disappearing amongst the sea of people. However, the stewards realised what was happening and started pulling people onto the pitch, which relieved the crush and enabled Annette and myself to get onto the pitch. It felt fantastic to step onto the soft green of the pitch for the very first time. We both thought it was great and headed towards the mass of fans that were gathered in front of the main stand where the players had found their way up to executive area and were waving and celebrating with the fans. As the champagne corks popped and everyone celebrated, some fans climbed onto the roofs of the executive boxes, which began to buckle a little, but the party went on.

It seemed like the celebrations on the pitch went on for ages before we all headed home to share the news with our loved ones. My sister, Annette, was most definitely a Bluenose now and would be forever!

CHAPTER FOUR – Away days

I had a good summer of 1980, happy in the knowledge that Blues would start the new season in August back in the First Division. I had turned eighteen in January, had been in full time work at the same company for two years and was intent on going to every game of the coming season, home and away.

I had been on a summer holiday with Graham to Cala Millor in Majorca. It was my first holiday abroad and apart from realising that I was coming towards the end of my relationship with Graham, I had a really nice time in the sun. I did manage to get sunstroke on my first day though, after falling asleep on the beach with no sun tan lotion on! It was a cloudy day and I mistakenly believed that I would not catch the sun at all. I was quite unwell and looked like a little old lady for a few days; I was so burnt and wrinkly. Not very romantic, but Graham and I made the most of it and had a nice time. I really enjoyed the flight and being somewhere completely different. I remember thinking that I would love to live in the sun one day.

It was around this time that I went to join Birmingham City Ladies FC. I really enjoyed being with the ladies team but because I was always at the Blues matches it proved too difficult so I eventually stopped playing. Birmingham City Ladies were a top team in the league (local league) and had two sides, the first team and the second team. I was new to ladies football and was not good enough for the first team who were very impressive indeed and always won their games. However, I was to go back and play for them a few years later.

The season started with a good 3-1 win over Coventry City at home and as usual for the first home game of the season, which was a local derby, the atmosphere was great inside St. Andrews and I enjoyed every minute. Four days later Blues were away at Nottingham Forest and it would be my first trip to the City Ground in Nottingham. I travelled by the football special again, from New Street Station, which was, as usual, packed with Bluenoses. There was the usual singing and chanting, with fans sitting on tables, and standing in corridors drinking beers. I would sing and chat with various people as we journey onwards, watching the countryside passing by through the windows. It was great to hear people's stories of the games they had been to and the journey's they had been on. I would vow to travel and follow the Blue boy's wherever they went. I think the journey is the best part of following your team away from home, there is so much fun to be had.

When the train arrived in Nottingham Station, the Bluenoses poured off the train and headed towards the waiting police escort, singing at the top of their voices. It was so loud, and announced our arrival, as it was meant to do, in dramatic style to all those within earshot! We were met by the police, and the hundreds of us that had just disembarked, were surrounded and escorted towards the ground. It seemed like a long walk along various roads before we saw the ground. I remember crossing a large bridge and looking at the floodlights of the City Ground on one side and the floodlights of the older looking ground of Notts County on the other side. I know I saw Trent Bridge cricket ground at some point too, but I can't remember where. I remember that they are all close together though. The City Ground was on the edge of the river and the waiting Forest fans were singing songs threatening to throw us in the river. They were immediately answered by the travelling Bluenoses with several gestures inviting them to try! The ground itself was interesting, as I thought most grounds were around this time. I always loved going to a new ground, and still do in fact.

I've been to the City Ground lots of time since, but I think this first time that the away fans were situated along the side of the ground, close to the pitch. The singing at away matches is always great, and so it was today at Forest with the Bluenoses giving the Forest faithful loads of stick. There was loads of Blues there and we sang our hearts out for the Blues. I thought the ground was slightly better than Derby but not as good as St. Andrews. I bought a programme, as I enjoyed collecting them, as well as reading them during the game, and it cost twenty-five pence! Football was affordable to the normal supporter in those days.

Despite Frank Worthington scoring for Blues, we lost the game 2-1, but being Blues fans we were never too down. Keep Right On, rang out loudly as the game finished and we clapped our lads as they came over to applaud us for our support. Blues had played well, and fought hard, so we had no complaints as we filed out towards the police escort that would lead us back to the station to get the football special. As was usual around this time the Blues faithful were kept inside the ground for about 15 minutes to allow the home supporters to leave the ground first. The weather was nice, so the walk back was pleasant with lots of singing and the odd fight breaking our as a few Forest fans would turn up to taunt us and a few Blues would break away and join them for a scuffle before the police intervened. Then we were back at the station and onto the train back to Birmingham. The singing and chatting carried on all the way back home with everyone in good spirits. We were happy to be back in the First Division and still full of hope.

It was a good day out really, and as usual when I got back to Birmingham, I picked up the Pink Sports Argus, fish and chips and headed home to tell my mom about my adventure. I was already looking forward to the next game, which was a big one against the mighty reds from Manchester and St. Andrews three days later.

28,661 turned out to watch Blues draw 0-0 with Manchester Utd, and as was always the case when the red boys were in town there was a bit of trouble. Windows were broken in some shops in town as the mob come through the shopping centre at the top of new street station and the trouble continued outside the ground.

The ground outside the Kop stand at the time was wasteland and was covered with bricks and stones, which always provided ammunition for the Blues fans if they were attacked by visiting supporters. The atmosphere inside was great and I was very happy with the result. As usual the Blues fans sang 'cockney scum – get out of Brum!' because, as everyone knows most Man Utd fans don't come from Manchester. One of my favourite songs at the time (as well as Keep Right On and Shit On The Villa – my personal favourites!), was 'you're going home in a fuckin ambulance!'. I don't know why, I just thought it was really funny. I also quite liked 'come and have a go if you think you're hard enough!'

Blues then beat Bristol City in the first leg of the second round of the league cup 2-1 at home and then it was off to Southampton for me. This was the furthest trip so far for me and I was really looking forward to heading to the south coast, especially as it was August, and the weather was really nice. So, off we headed to the station for the long trip south. Mom had made me some sandwiches for the train journey and we had purchased a few cans for the trip too. I can't remember how long the journey was, but it was relaxed and as always, the train was full of bluenoses. It wasn't a football special because of the fact that it was a long journey and not as many fans were expected to travel. Blues fans, however, had different ideas and the train was pretty full. Everyone was in good spirits and we arrived in plenty of time and made our way to the ground. We popped into the pub just outside the ground for a couple before the game, and it was full of bluenoses in full voice. Great!

We left the pub in good time to get into the ground which, I have to say, did not look very impressive from outside. It was the old Southampton ground known as The Dell. What an awful ground it was too. Inside was even worse, I remember thinking that it was the worst football ground I had ever been inside, or for that fact would ever be inside (until Swansea that is!). The main problem was the fencing. The away fans were given half of one end of the terracing behind the goal and apart from being really small the fencing was really big and everywhere you stood the view seemed to be obstructed. There was also a floodlight in the end as well, which also obstructed the view. As an away fan, I have to say the end they gave us and the view was crap. Their main end was strange too; it sort of sloped from one end to the other. One side was much higher than the other was and it looked really odd. The ground was so small that there was a block of flats that could clearly be seen inside the ground and the people living there must have had a great view on match days. They could clearly be seen watching the game from their windows. Mind you, at least the grounds had character about them in those days. The Blues end was packed, especially as it was so small, with no roof on either. Luckily, though, the sun was shining, because if it had been raining, we would have all got soaked.

The game got under way and despite Frank Worthington scoring for us again, Blues lost 3-1. It didn't stop us bluenoses from singing and giving the opposing supporters some stick though, and we left the ground a little downhearted but still optimistic. Once again the players came over and applauded the Blues faithful for our support and we applauded their effort in the game.

It was around this time that I was looking for someone to travel to the games to, because my friends were all doing their own thing and my boyfriend wasn't into going to all the games, especially the away games. I wrote a letter to the Blues programme asking if any female fan was interested in travelling to the away games with me and I soon got an answer from a girl called Pam. We became very good friends and began travelling to all the games together. We also started travelling to some of the games with the Blues Supporters Club Coaches.

A few days later, I decided to make the trip to Bristol for the second leg of the league cup game with Bristol City. Again, it was another new ground for me to go to. I don't remember a lot about this trip, but the ground itself was okay and we held them to a 0-0 draw, which meant that Blues were through to the next round because we had beaten them 2-1 at our ground, and so went through on aggregate. I was really excited because I love the cup and was always dreaming of seeing Blues at Wembley! It was funny because it was the smallest crowd I had ever been in. There were only 7,000 in the ground, and a lot of them were Bluenoses. The draw for the next round was made a few days later and Blues were rewarded with a home tie against Blackburn Rovers at Home. I thought we were in with a good chance of progressing.

Liverpool were up next at St. Andrews and the ground was buzzing with atmosphere, as it always was when the scousers were in town. Liverpool had a really good team at the time, as everyone knows and Blues did really well to come away with a 1-1 draw, Frank Worthington again on the score sheet.

Then I was off on another trip down south; this time to see Blues take on Brighton and Hove Albion. I was really looking forward to this because Brighton is a seaside town. We set out on the long trip south very early and in doing so, arrived in Brighton with time to look around and see the beach. It was great, we were really excited on the trip, and had sandwiches and various extras's that my mom had put together for the long train journey. By the time we arrived in Brighton station we had finished off the lot, plus the beers we had packed. Brighton station is a bit different because all the trains finished there; it's sort of like all the railway lines just ending at a wall. It has a nice sort of character about the place. There were a lot of people around though, and we headed out and down the road towards the beach and the pier. The beach was quite nice, with pebbles at the top but the sea was quite a long way out when we got there. I could see the old Victorian pier that was now abandoned and cut off, now that the connecting walkway had collapsed. It must have been very impressive in its heyday. We walked onto the beach and when we turned around to look at the town, I noticed that someone had spray painted – 'BIRMINGHAM CITY' in rather large letters on the sea wall. I had a bit of a giggle at that. Obviously some Bluenoses had arrived before us! Then we had a little look around the shops before calling into a small pub for a pint before catching a bus with 'Hove' on the front, and heading towards the ground.

Brighton's ground was quite open, but the weather was nice and there were quite a few Bluenoses present. Even though the ground was a bit small, it had character and I quite liked it to be honest. Probably because it was a seaside town, and I have always liked being by the sea. The Blues faithful sang our hearts out as usual and we came away with a respectable 2-2 draw, so everyone was happy. There were a lot of police waiting outside the ground for us, and the police insisted on putting everyone on the many coaches that were outside waiting! Despite insisting to them that we had come on the train, the police were having none of it and insisted on putting us onto a coach! It took us ages before we were able to get off again and head back towards the train station. It was a good laugh though.

The following week we entertained West Brom in a local derby at St. Andrews. I always enjoyed these games, the yam yams as we call them always talk funny and they are always great to take the piss out of. They are called yam yams because they always say 'yam coming out' or 'yam coming down the pub' etc! It is great to sing the yam yam song to the tune of the dam busters with both arms outstretched and waved around like an aeroplane – great! The atmosphere was buzzing and the game ended in a 1-1 draw. Not what we wanted but at least we didn't lose. It is always a disaster losing in a derby because you have to live with having it shoved down your throats till you meet them again and gain revenge.

Next up were Blackburn Rovers in the third round of the league cup at St. Andrews and on a cool night, Blues went through to the next round by a single goal scored by big Joe Gallagher. We were on our way to Wembley – or so I hoped. The draw for the next round was made a few days later and my prayers were answered when we were drawn at home. Ipswich Town were the team we drew and I was quite optimistic that we could beat them and progress to the Quarterfinal for the first time in quite a while.

The next match meant a journey to Norwich, another place that would be a new experience for me. This seemed like the longest trip so far to me as it took such a long time to get to and involved a lot of travelling through the countryside. It was a very pretty and pleasant trip thought. The ground was okay and we popped in the pub on the corner, not too far from the ground for a couple of pints before the game. It was a small pub with a good atmosphere, and there were a few bluenoses also in there with the same idea, enjoying a pint. Inside the ground there were plenty of Bluenoses, despite the distance, and all were in good spirits on the terraces singing loudly. It was quite colourful with all the yellow and green of the Norwich City fans, and we took great pleasure singing 'I can't read, I can't write, but that don't really matter, cos I'm a Norwich City fan and I can drive a tractor!' Quite fun really. It was a good game too, and ended in a 2-2 draw. A nice trip out, but a long journey home when you are tired and weary. I was really enjoying my away travel this season.

Next up was a nice local trip to Wolverhampton for the local derby with Wolverhampton Wanderers. I was really looking forward to this, especially as the atmosphere at local derbies was always brilliant. You can't beat a bit of rivalry. As it was only about twenty minutes by train from the city centre, we had a few drinks in town before the setting off for the match. Around this time we would drink in the likes of Edwards No 7, Boogies and others around that area, as they were 'Blues' pubs. Other times we might pop into the midland hotel, the Yard of Ale etc. Or sometimes we would just go into the station bar, inside new street train station. Anyway, we set off on one of the many trains that passed through Wolverhampton, and enjoyed a short but sweet journey on a train packed with Bluenoses. When we arrived at Wolverhampton, the police were waiting and we set off on the short journey to the Molyneux ground, half of us on the pavement and the other half in the road. There seemed to be thousands of Blues and it wasn't long before some Wolves fans appeared and attempted to attack the Bluenose before being chased back up the road. This happened a few times before they gave up and fled in various directions. I could see the ground and the floodlights in the distance.

This was my first time to Molyneux and I was thoroughly enjoying it. The ground looked impressive, and we were led onto the terracing for the away fans that was behind the goal next to, or part of a grassy bank to the one side. We were given a fair amount of terracing though, and soon proceeded to fill our end and the singing and chanting began in earnest. As it was a local derby there was a lot of singing and banter from both sets of supporters, which always adds to the occasion. Our end was a mass of blue and white and I remember looking around at all the gold and black of the Dingles (wolves' fans!). I had my programme proudly tucked into the back pocket of my jeans, as everyone seemed to do at the time, and took up a good position on the terrace. The atmosphere was electric, but unfortunately Blues lost by the only goal of the game. This in turn, let to quite a bit of fighting outside, although most of it was just wolves fans confronting the departing Blues fans, only to get chased down the road again for their trouble. I just watched it all in wonder, laughed a bit, and headed back to the station with the others. It wasn't long before I was back in new street station and heading towards the bus stop to board a bus back to my mom's to pick up my usual fish and chips and the pink sports Argus.

The following two games were both at home and the first of these saw us entertain Arsenal at St. Andrews. Fifteen and a half thousand saw Blues beat Arsenal 3-1 with goals from Lynex, Worthington and Dillon. A great game and fabulous atmosphere inside the ground. Unfortunately our next game bought massive disappointment as we lost at home to the Villa by the odd goal of three, 2-1 in front of 33, 879 passionate fans. It was a great atmosphere as it always is for the big derby, but the vast majority of people went home disappointed, well, gutted would describe it better! I really hate losing to the Villa! There was silence as the Bluenoses streamed out after the match. The Villa fans were nowhere to be seen as they had done their usual disappearing act. There was the odd fight on the way back to town and in and around town as we headed for our bus back to Weoley Castle. Needless to say, I never bought the sports Argus that day!

The following Saturday saw us head to Manchester to see Blues take on Manchester City at Maine Road. We were being driven to the station by Pam's dad and as we were driving along the Bristol

Road I remembered that the tickets for the match were still at home so we had to turn around and go back to fetch them! Good job we hadn't gone too far really. Once we had arrived at New Street station, complete with tickets, we soon found our train and settled down for the journey north.

When we arrived we were unsure which way it was to the ground so we asked a couple of blues fans the way. They were Julie and Debbie, who over the coming games became good friends. Julie and I are still very good friends and still meet up today. So we all headed off together towards Maine Road for the game. Outside there were loads of police on horseback and I found it very difficult to get passed them as they made a line, squeezing all the away fans into the turnstiles. It wasn't very nice with the horses slobbering everywhere and I thought I would get crushed by one of them. It put me off horses for life, I can tell you!

There were the usual hostilities between the two sets of fans outside the ground and once inside the chanting continued. Both sets of supporters were standing on the terrace along the side of the pitch, with us Blues fans having one third of it and the corner and the Mancs having the rest with a large fence and a line of police separating us. The four of us stood together on the terracing and before long a bit of missile throwing commenced and I was very narrowly missed by a flying object that actually brushed my hair as it sped past, hit a crash barrier and bounced back landing at my foot. It was a cylinder type object with a three-inch spike poking out of it – very, very dangerous! If it had been an inch closer it could have done some serious damage to me. I was all for lobbing it back at the Man City fans as they had thrown it in the first place, but Pam picked it up first and took it to a nearby policeman.

It was a big ground and the side terracing reminded me of our own Kop at St. Andrews, although not as good of course! I did like Maine Road; it was a nice ground to travel to. The atmosphere inside was good and the Blues were having a good old chant and singing the usual war songs and giving loads of stick to the neighbouring Man City lot. Keep Right On rang out loud and clear as usual and the fans swayed like a big blue wave. It was great, and to make it even better Archie Gemmil, the little Scot, scored the only goal of the game giving us a 1-0 away win. The Blues end erupted in a massive celebration and we taunted the Man city fans with chants of 'one-nil, one-nil!' It is brilliant when we win away, it seems to give you that bit more satisfaction.

The next home game saw us draw with Stoke City 1-1 in another local game, and as usual the atmosphere in St. Andrews was electric. There was lots of singing and banter between the two sets of supporters, especially as Stoke had bought a good few fans due to the fact that they didn't have too far to travel. As usual it was a very enjoyable day following the Blues.

And then it was back to the League cup and we took on Ipswich Town at St. Andrews. It was a brilliant atmosphere with loads of Bluenoses singing 'Wembley, Wembley' and 'Kay SA RA SA RA, whatever will be, will be, were going to Wembley' while waving their scarves that were tied around their wrists, in a circular movement. It looked great. A few tractor boys had made the journey, but of course were completely out sung by the jubilant Bluenoses. Our boys did not let us down either, and Blues won by two goals to one. Fantastic! We were on our way to Wembley and we were looking forward to the draw for the next round. Blues were in the Quarterfinals!

The next game on the 1st November was away at Middlesbrough, and unfortunately I could not make this trip which Blues won 2-1! Everybody loves an away win so I was gutted that I missed it but happy that we won on opposition territory. Two goals from Frank Worthington gave us the three points and we were all enjoying life back in the first division. This was soon followed by a home match against Crystal Palace and I did get to this game and enjoyed the atmosphere at St. Andrews as Keith Bertschin scored the only goal of the game to give Blues a 1-0 win. I liked Keith Bertschin, he would try to head everything that came near him, and in fact we would joke that if he took a penalty he would try to head it in from the spot! We all went home happy that evening and I was in really good spirits as I picked up my Sports Argus from the shop on the square and I was happily looking forward to the next home game coming up against Nottingham Forest. I didn't much like Forest since the first time I saw Blues play them when Forest had just been promoted and they literally kicked us off the park. Bring in on, I thought.

And so on 11th November, I headed to St. Andrews and joined the 22,433 to watch Blues beat Nottingham Forest 2-0 with two goals from Frank Worthington, who was having a fabulous season for Blues. The atmosphere inside 'Stans' was great from the off with loads of singing and chanting and swaying up and down the terraces. St. Andrews, as always, was a very good place to be.

A few days later on 15th November, I set out for my first visit to local neighbours Coventry City. I was really looking forward to this as Coventry is not far from Birmingham on the train and it was a lovely sunny day. Blues were 9th in the first division at this point in the season and Coventry were below us in 13th so it should be a good game. I set off early to get the local train which ran regularly to Coventry and was soon disembarking at Coventry station. As expected the train was jam packed with Bluenoses who were also keen to get there early. So off we headed out of the station and after asking directions headed in the general direction instructed and also following the majority of Bluenoses also heading towards the ground. We had a nice walk by a park and it was so warm that I had taken my cardigan off and carried in over my arm. Somehow, however, I managed to lose it by the time I had gotten back to the station after the game!

We found the ground okay and it looked quite nice from outside with lots of early Bluenoses milling around drinking beer from cans. With that idea in mind we headed for the nearest off licence and obtained some cans before heading back to the ground and consuming them sitting in the sunshine outside watching more fans arrive for the game. As kick off approached we paid our money and squeezed through the turnstiles into the ground. I bought a programme, which cost me thirty pence, and it was a nice colourful programme with Sky Blue v Birmingham City across the front cover. It had a picture of a Coventry player in the sky blue kit that used to have the black and white lines running down each side of the front of the kit into the shorts. I bet a lot of people remember that kit, I do. I think it was the kit they had on when I went to my very first game a few years back. There was an advertisement inside the programme for the new madness album called 'absolutely madness'. I wonder how many people remember that?

Inside the away fans were on the terracing behind the goal up to the corner and as the end had no roof on we were basking in the sun. I quite liked Coventry's ground, Highfield Road, it had a bit of character, and the Blues fans singing rang out loud and clear. However, despite Alan Curbishley scoring for Blues we lost the game 2-1. It didn't stop us singing though and we poured out of the ground at the final whistle and headed back to the station down but not out. We still had lots to play for.

Tottenham Hotspur were the next visitors to St. Andrews and 24,817 turned out to see Blues win 2-1 to clear our hangover from the Coventry game. We were back on track. I was standing on the Tilton terraces and had a perfect view of a 30-yard screamer by Alan Curbishley that flew in to the top corner, right in front of the Tilton. The ground erupted and I ended up a few yards away from my original spot after we had finished celebrating. It was a fantastic feeling winning again and the result against spurs was a good one.

The following Saturday I was off to Liverpool to see Blues take on Everton at Goodison Park. This would be my first trip to Liverpool and my first to Everton's ground. I set out early once again and boarded the train at New Street to Liverpool Lime Street. We soon arrived in Liverpool, another station with lots of character about it, and we got a local train to somewhere near Everton and walked down the street by Stanley Park towards the away end at goodison. There were lots of fans milling around the ground outside and as we approached there was a bit of trouble between Blues fans and Everton fans just outside by the pub known as the Blue House. The police soon came between the rival supporters and led the Blues fans into the nearby away end. I followed them inside and we were on terracing behind the goal, and there were already quite a few Bluenoses inside happily singing and chanting. I was impressed with Everton's ground, one side seemed to be quite high and although it looked a bit old it did have a certain character. I remember some girls dressed in old-fashioned dresses passing our end with baskets of Everton mints, which they proceeded to throw into the crowd for the fans. Needless to say the Blues fans immediately returned them with amazing accuracy!

Everton were currently seventh in the first division with Blues not far behind in tenth spot so a good game was on the cards. Blues have not got a good record against Everton at Goodison but we played well and came away with a 1-1 draw. The Blues fans sang our usual songs and came away quite happy with a point. On our way back to the station I looked across at Liverpool's ground just across Stanley Park and thought about our quarterfinal tie at Anfield in a few days time. That was going to be the big game and I was really looking forward to visiting it soon in the League Cup Quarterfinal.

I remember listening to the draw when it had been made live on the radio and saying to my mom, 'that's it now; we are out of the cup!' Liverpool were a top team, I think the best in the country at this time, but I was starting to feel a little optimistic. The good thing about cup games is that they are one off, and on the day upsets can happen. My fingers were firmly crossed!

My boyfriend Graham had decided that he would drive us up to Anfield for the game as he had also got cup fever and wanted to see the game. He still had his spitfire sports car, which meant that only the two of us could go as it only had two seats. The game was on Tuesday night, 2nd December and Graham picked me up from work early and we took the country roads up to Liverpool, not the motorway so that we could stop somewhere nice on the way up. I rang my mom from work to tell her not to make me any diner as I was off to Liverpool for the cup game. We arrived in Liverpool with time to spare and parked the car on the middle section of the duel carriageway not far from the away end, just next to Stanley Park. Lots of cars were already parked up on this grass section so we figured (wrongly I add) that it would be okay to park here too.

So, with the car parked we headed to the pub on the corner, near the anfield road end, called The Arckles. Inside the pub there were Bluenoses and Liverpool fans and everyone seemed to mix okay and the atmosphere was friendly, even though it was the Blues fans who were singing quite loudly. We had a few drinks and then headed across the road and into the away end. Blues had half of the anfield road terracing behind the goal, with fencing, half way along separating us from the Liverpool fans. The atmosphere was fantastic and the ground was packed. Thousands of Blues had made the trip amongst the 30, 236 that were inside that day and they sang their hearts out. There was a lot of rivalry between the supporters inside the ground and a few missiles flew backwards and forwards between the two lots of supporters in the anfield road end. We were standing near a crash barrier and a girder that supported the roof, and at one point a bottle that had been thrown our way hit the girder and smashed and some of the glass fell onto us. When I put my hand to my head there was a bit of blood, but not too much to worry me or make me miss the game! Liverpool seemed to be getting hit just as hard though and a few casualties were taken out of the crowd and led away. One person from the Liverpool contingent had to be carried on a stretcher high above the heads of the crowd and passed over the iron fences onto the pitch to the sound of 'one-nil' from the Blues lot. It was packed on the terraces and the fans swayed and sang, it was great.

Blues went into the game with the incentive of knowing that we were the last team to beat Liverpool on their own ground. It turned out to be a really good game but we were to rue our missed chances as Liverpool took theirs and were rather lucky to beat us 3-1. I took heart from our performance as I really felt that we were robbed and should have come away with a win. Liverpool looked relieved to snatch the third, just five minutes from time. The Bluenoses were not dejected due to the fact that we had played so well, and totally out sang the Kop. Blues had even sang 'where's your famous Kop?' and 'you're supposed to be at home'.

Graham and I headed back across the road and back into the pub for a quick drink before we headed back, and to allow the traffic to die down a bit. We got talking to some Liverpool fans who were quite honest and said they thought that they were lucky to beat us and that we were the better team on the day. I found their honesty quite refreshing and remember it to this day. Their fans went up in my estimation that day. Their keeper Ray Clemence had made some first class saves and it was good to see that the Merseyside press praised Blues performance and admitted that we gave Liverpool a fright. In the team talk in the following home programme at St. Andrews the manager Jim Smith, praised the marvellous following of Blues supporters who encouraged the team and were a credit to the club.

After a couple of drinks we headed back to the car only to find that the local constabulary had put a bloody parking ticked on our car plus several others that had been parked on the grass. I am convinced it was only the away fans that got the tickets though! There was no sign saying you couldn't park there. Oh well, that just about completed our night so we set off home to Birmingham out of the cup but proud of our performance. There is always the FA Cup in January to look forward to.

December turned out to be an awful month with us losing the next three games, at home to Leicester 2-1, followed by a horror show at Villa Park where we went down 3-0 to the Vile in front of over forty thousand fans. I remember standing on the Witton Terrace 3-0 down in tears and when Graham suggested we left before the end I looked at him aghast. I would never leave before the end no matter what the score or who we were playing. I would always support the Blues to the end. I was absolutely gutted though.

Next up was another home defeat to Ipswich Town 3-1, followed by an away trip to Leeds on Boxing Day, which I missed. Blues did come away with a 0-0 draw though and our run of defeats came to an end.

Blues ended December with a good win over Sunderland at St. Andrews 3-2. Tony Coton, our goalkeeper made his debut in this game as Jeff Wealands had been injured in the Leeds game. He made history by saving a penalty in the first few seconds of his career. We were back on track.

Blues had been drawn at home against Sunderland in the FA Cup 3rd round, and so had the strange prospect of playing the same team on successive Saturday's at home. However, the FA Cup is the big one and I was really excited about this game. I arrived early kitted out in Blue and White and in good voice. The atmosphere in St. Andrews was electric and chants of 'Wembley, Wembley' rang out around the stadium. Everybody had recovered from New Year hangovers and were out to enjoy the occasion. Blues were really up for the fight but the game finished 1-1 which meant a replay would be required up at Sunderland in a few days time.

I went out drinking with my mates not long afterwards to a club in Five Ways, and we got talking to a few of the Blues players who were also drinking in there. I think it was called Faces then. I had a right laugh talking to Mick Hartford (Blues player) who is from Sunderland. He offered to put us up at his mom's if we wanted to stay overnight for the replay. He was a really nice bloke I have to say. It was different back then, when players were often seen out on the lash, especially after a game when they would go out celebrating.

I had seen a bit more of the other girls we met at the Manchester City game, Julie and Debbie. Julie has been a lifelong friend and we have been to many a game together and had many adventures together. Although I have lost touch with Pam and Debbie, Julie and I remain friends and I see her at games still, when I can get home. It was on the supporter's coach that we booked for the replay in Sunderland on 7th January 1981 and all four of us travelled together, probably for the first time. We set off early due to the distance and when we arrived in Sunderland, the coach parked up not far from a beach. It looked nice, and had a small fair but it was a bit cold to be honest. We didn't care though, because we were so excited about the coming cup match.

The ground was okay and had a lot of character about it. The Blues fans were on the terracing on the corner of the ground next to the Sunderland fans, who were in good voice for the cup-tie and all around us was a sea of red and white. Our end however, was a sea of blue and white and as usual we were in very good voice singing 'Wembley, Wembley!' at the top of our voices. Once the match got underway the atmosphere was electric and just fewer than 30,000 witnessed a great game. Keith Bertschin and Tony Evans scored for Blues and we won 2-1 to set up celebrations for the travelling Bluenoses despite the fact that it was very late and we were knackered. We were through to the fourth round of the FA Cup. And boy, did we celebrate! The coaches were extremely lively on the trip back to Birmingham! We already knew who we would be playing in the next round as the draw had been made and we were relishing a local derby away at Coventry City in round four.

Next up was a trip to London and to white hart lane to see Blues take on Tottenham. This was a ground I had already been to the previous season for a FA Cup game but had been locked out along with thousands of other Bluenoses so this time I was going early and was looking forward to actually seeing inside the ground this time! So, we set off early and boarded the Euston train armed with beers and more sandwiches made by my lovely mom as usual. I always looked forward to discovering what my mom had packed for me and what she had put on my sandwiches as she was very imaginative and it was always something different. Mind you, despite my protests she would still occasionally pack me cheese and onion sandwiches, leaving me with onion breath for the day! What a fab mom eh!

So, we arrived in London and disembarked at seven sister's tube station with plenty of time to spare. This time however, we only stopped briefly in the pub, downed our beers in record time and headed up to the ground. This time we gained entrance into the ground and I was able to look around another football ground with lots of character. I must admit I really miss the terraces. There was such a fabulous atmosphere on them which some people will never be lucky enough to experience now days. I count myself extremely lucky to have experienced this fantastic period in football history. Bring back the terraces and we will bring back the atmosphere. By all means keep some seats for the prawn sandwiches, but give us back the terraces and we will bring back the atmosphere!

I liked White Hart Lane when it had terracing, particularly the 'shelf' which was terracing in sections. The away end was behind the goal with the terracing at the front and seats above and behind us. At the time the home fans were in the seats above us and we were occasionally treated to a beer shampoo. I guess it all goes in one way or the other though, and it was their beer! There were not as many people inside the ground as there had been for our previous cup-tie against them last year with only 24,909 present. As usual though the Blues contingent were in good voice and 'Keep Right On' rang out loud and proud. The game wasn't too bad but unfortunately ended in defeat by the odd goal with Blues going down 1-0. Oh well, there is always next week, so we set off back to seven sisters tube station trying to remain optimistic.

Luckily I missed the next game which was away to Ipswich. I say lucky because we were hammered 5-1 with Frank Worthington getting the only reply for Blues. This was closely followed by a home defeat against Southampton 3-0, which I was present to witness. Not to worry I thought, it is the cup next week. And so, on my nineteenth birthday, after opening all my lovely birthday presents, I headed off nice and early to Coventry for the fourth round FA cup match. It must go well I thought it's my birthday. However, no one listened to my script and although it was a great day out, Blues were knocked out of the cup 3-2 with Ainscow and Worthington scoring for Blues. The away end was packed and it was great celebrating each time we scored. That was the fun of being on the terraces, it was brilliant celebrating goals, everyone just jumped on everyone else. You made lots of friends at the games and it was so much fun.

The following week I was heading off to Manchester for my first visit to Old Trafford, the home of the mighty Manchester United. The football special was packed and everyone was on good form, singing, chatting and drinking beers all the way to Manchester. The banter was great and everyone was looking forward to the game, and a few beers in the city. Unfortunately, most of us didn't get a few beers as we were met by the local plod at the local train station and marched to the ground. Old Trafford looked very impressive from the outside and we decided to have a wander around to see what their end was like. It was soon made clear that this was not the best idea we had ever had when someone barged into Pam and she promptly threatened them with violence from me! Thanks, but due to the fact that we are heavily outnumbered, I'm heading back to our end and the girls soon followed. We did witness the arrival of the team coach however, and as Brian Robson got off, I have to say it was like being at a pop concert as loads of girls were screaming over him! What on earth was that all that about?!

Inside the ground it was very impressive. The away end was behind the goal and it was jam packed with Blues fans by the time kick off approached. The Manchester United fans to our left were separated by a section of empty terrace and fencing and were trying to incite us by waving 'Brummie Reds' banners. Personally, I thought this was something to be ashamed of rather that flaunting it in such a manner! As kick off approached the Manchester United team came running out of the tunnel onto the pitch and were met by a really loud rendition of 'who the fucking hell are you' from the Bluenoses. We all found this really funny as we had only just been promoted to the first division and Man Utd were a well-known top team. It was one of those moments in football that you never forget. Priceless! There were 39,081 inside Old Trafford, but from all the singing you would have thought that it was Blues that were at home. It was great; we sang our hearts out for the entire game despite losing 2-0. Our players came over and applauded our efforts and we applauded theirs in return. The

Blues end was packed and everyone headed towards the exits, which were at the end of a concrete tunnel leading away from the terrace. However, the gates had not been opened and a crush developed in the tunnel with those at the back unaware and still trying to push out. I was getting crushed and couldn't breathe then everything went black. Next thing I remember I was lying back on the terracing in the ground with a policeman looking rather worried looking over me. Luckily he had seen me as I was about to slump down and he had been able to get to me and drag me back into the ground. What a horrible feeling it had been getting crushed and I was haunted by it for quite a while. Didn't stop me being back amongst the crowd at matches though.

As we were making our way back towards the local station a large gang of Man Utd fans came running towards us and chased us back to the station. As we ran down the stairs in the station there was one of those old trains with loads of doors along it, waiting on the platform. We had been getting a bit worried because it seemed like we were cornered by a much bigger group than us, but then all the doors of the train opened and hundreds of Blues poured off and piled into the Man Utd fans causing most of them to leg it out of the station. Brilliant! That was a close call. The rest of the trip home was uneventful, but even in defeat we sang and enjoyed the trip. Another great day out following our beloved Blues.

The following week our losing streak came to an end with a great home win over Brighton at St. Andrews. I was amongst the 13,691 that witnessed Alan Curbishley and Tony Evans score against Brighton in a 2-1 win. We were back on track and I thought that we were doing very well considering it was our first season back in the top flight. Then on Valentine's Day it was off to Anfield again for a league game against the mighty reds of Liverpool. I always like going to Anfield, it is always a good day out and I always enjoy it. It is a great ground but I think it was much better when it had terracing and had much more character. I don't think the Kop is as impressive now it is all seated. Back when it was terracing it used to sway like it was alive on a match day and added to the atmosphere.

Once again we got the train to Liverpool and our train was diverted to the local station where we disembarked and headed for the Arkles Pub on the corner of the ground. It was a great atmosphere inside the pub, which was full of Blues and Liverpool fans that were chanting at each other in a friendly manner. A few beers were downed and then we made our way into the away section of the ground. The atmosphere was brilliant and the Blues fans were in full voice as 'Keep Right On' filled the stadium. Blues always took a large following with them and the away sections were always packed when Blues were playing.

What a great game it was too and goals from Alan Ainscow and Tony Evans sent the Blues fans wild as we came away from Anfield with a very good 2-2 draw! We celebrated all the way home even though we were chased through the car park before reinforcements arrived enabling Blues to run back at the Liverpool fans. It was a great day out and I couldn't wait to get home and pick up my pink sports Argus with our result splashed across the front page.

This good result was followed up the next week when we took on Norwich City at St. Andrews. I was once again inside a buzzing St. Andrews as Blues ran out convincing 4-0 winners with Tony Evans scoring two and Alan Ainscow and Archie Gemmill getting the others. Brilliant! And then it was off to neighbours West Bromwich Albion and a venture into the Black Country. I love travelling to away derby games; there is so much banter on the way and inside the ground. After a few beers we arrived at the ground which seemed to be swarming with Blues fans. I couldn't see many West Brom fans and we headed through the wasteland area towards the away end of the ground. Blues had the entire end and it was highly charged inside. The usual derby songs were being sung, including our version of 'I do like to be beside the seaside' which ends with 'fuck off west brom' being echoed around the ground. Both sets of supporters were up for the game. It was a pulsating game too, with Alan Ainscow again scoring and Frank Worthington also scoring to send the Blues contingent into raptures as we came away with a 2-2 draw. I have always wondered how the West Brom fans get home because although their end of the ground empties, you never see any of them outside. Where do they get to? It was always the same.

Next up was another local derby, this time at St. Andrews and the return game against Wolves and we owed them one. Revenge was sweet as 20,005 witnessed a passionate derby game with Frank Worthington the hero, scoring our winner! The banter was brilliant and the sea of blue and white sang for the entire game before heading home extremely happy. Bragging rights were again ours until next season.

The blues of Manchester were up next and promptly dispatched 2-0 at St. Andrews before an away trip to Stoke City. We queued outside New Street Station before boarding the packed football special to take us to Stoke. This was to be another new ground for me and I was really looking forward to it. The football special was rocking on the way up to Stoke and once again I got stuck into the wonderful sandwiches my mom had made for me along with a mini pork pie and crisps. Soon we were disembarking in Stoke and after announcing our arrival with a loud rendition of 'the brummies are here!' we were escorted to Stoke City's old ground – known as the Victoria Ground. Our end was behind the goal with the seats behind us. The ground was a fair size and had a certain character about it too. The Blues fans already inside the ground were already in full voice and it sounded like we were at home. Despite the passionate support of our supporters the game ended in a 0-0 draw and we were soon on our way back to the station after our mandatory twenty or so minutes of being locked in the ground. I was already thinking ahead to next week's trip to London to take on the Gunners in their own back yard.

Saturday morning and another hard week of work over with, I got up full of hope and excitement and ready for the trip ahead. Once again I was on the Euston bound train tucking into my packed lunch and downing the obligatory beer or two and discussing our season of ups and downs back in the first division. Every now and again another Bluenose or two would stop to chat and share their opinions on the Blues and often the carriage would burst into song. This happened with increased frequency once the beer was flowing. Very soon we were arriving in Euston and everyone had their own plans about what they were doing first and which pubs they were visiting pre match. We got on the underground with loads of the Blues fans and headed towards Highbury to have a look round and find a nice pub for a pre match drink. I like Highbury; it has something about it and has a lot of character, although they don't call it Highbury library for nothing. What it has in character it certainly lacked in atmosphere. No problems though, because us Bluenoses bring enough atmosphere with us. We were standing on the terraces in the clock stand, of which we had been given half of the end. With about fifteen minutes till kick off our end was packed and swaying whilst giving the Arsenal fans stationed on the terrace to the right of us, lots of banter.

The match got underway and although we played well and Frank Worthington scored we lost 2-1. It never stopped us singing though and the players as usual came over to our end to applaud us for our passionate support. Oh well, back to the station and off back to Birmingham for fish and chips and match of the day later.

A few days later and winning ways were resumed when we saw off Middlesbrough at St. Andrews 2-1 with Tony Evans and Kevan Broadhurst scoring. I had another great day amongst the excitement at St. Andrews and went home content and happy. It was off to London again at the weekend, this time a trip to the Palace – Crystal Palace. It seemed a bit funny heading off to London once again but I was looking forward to visiting another new ground. I wasn't disappointed as Selhurst Park was also a bit different and we were on the terracing on the side and to the corner of the ground. Blues fans were in full voice and enjoying the banter with the home supporters. The match, however, proved to be a bit of a disappointment and we ended the game losing 3-1 and the train home was somewhat quieter than it was going. I think a lot of the Bluenoses had stayed behind for a night on the town to make up for the disappointment we had just suffered.

I missed the next game, which was away at Sunderland. Blues lost 3-0 but I tried not to be too disheartened. We would bounce back. Unfortunately we didn't and in our next match, which I was able to get to, we lost 2-0 to a strong Leeds United side at St. Andrews. Blues were still doing very well back in the First Division so I was still pretty happy. Next up was another trip to Leicester City, I ground I had previously visited, but I liked going to Leicester as we always took a good following to these derby games. I wasn't disappointed either, as we packed out the special trains and filled the away end at Filbert Street and sang loud and proud for the entire match even though we lost by the odd goal 1-0.

Saturday 2nd May and the last game of the season. It was a nice sunny day and 12,863 turned up at St. Andrews to see Blues draw 1-1 in a game with Everton to finish the season. The atmosphere in the ground was great as everyone was determined to enjoy their last fix of football for a few months during which time we would miss our boys in blue. Blues had enjoyed a good season back in the First Division and finished in a very respectful 13th position. I had enjoyed the season and I had visited lots of new grounds, made lots of friends and had many joys and sorrows along the way. And, I had next season to look forward to!

CHAPTER FIVE – Joys and sorrows

Once again I had enjoyed a good summer before the start of the 1981-82 season although I had missed the thrill of the football season. Birmingham City had been on a trip to Holland for their pre season tour, which I had been unable to go on, and they had drawn all their games over there. I was still working for the same company and had enjoyed brief romances with a cockney electrician by the name of Mark and then a very short romance with a guy with a lovely American car with left hand drive and white leather seats. It was fun for a while then I got back to enjoying life out and about with my mates again. I was really looking forward to watching the Blues again and the excitement and hope that a new season always brings. Can we win something this season? I was always optimistic at the start of every new season and still am in fact.

The fixture list was always greeted with excitement when it was published in the papers around June time and would be studied thoroughly by us football fans right up until the start of the season. This was what our life was planned around! I would look firstly for the Villa, followed by the big teams such as Liverpool and Manchester United, and then I would look for the dates for any local away games such as Leicester, Stoke etc. I would also plan nice trips to the seaside for games against any teams on the coast – especially the south coast. They were always a good day out, along with trips to the capital. Everyone enjoyed a day out in the pubs for the London games. I would always look for the Christmas away games, as this was the time when all the Bluenoses would go in fancy dress! Brilliant!

The 1981 season was to get underway with a trip to Liverpool to take on Everton at Goodison Park. It was a lovely sunny day as I popped into the cake shop that my mom worked in on the way to get the bus to New Street Station to catch the train. My mom would always ask where I was off to that day, after telling me off for going out with my hair wet. 'Liverpool today' I replied. Have a nice time she would say, as she handed me sausage rolls and cakes for the journey. After a pleasant journey to Liverpool on a train full of Bluenoses, beers and food, we disembarked at Lime Street Station and headed off towards Everton. As usual there were loads of Blues outside the away end and they were already enjoying banter with the Evertonians as the local police tried to intervene.

Inside the ground I was quite optimistic. Blues won a corner and after I jinxed them by remarking to Julie that we never score from a corner – sure enough the ball was in the back of the net! We had scored – brilliant! The Blues end erupted and we were swept one way and then the other. However, Blues had not read my script and we lost our first game of the season by 3-1. Oh well, there is still a long way to go I thought. On the way back to the train station we were cutting through a piece of wasteland when some scousers started throwing stones at us! We soon chased them away as they were only about 7 or 8 years old – cheeky sods!

A few days later and I was back at St. Andrews amongst the fantastic atmosphere that a first home game of a new season always brings. It is impossible to describe, but those of you who have experienced it will know. The game itself was against Ipswich Town and ended in a 1-1 draw. This was followed by a fabulous game against Nottingham Forest at St. Andrews. What an entertaining game with plenty of goals as Blues ran out winners by 4 goals to 3. I thought what an attacking side we now had – if only we can tighten up the defence a little we may even win something this season.

Next up was a trip up north to Middlesbrough, and what a trip this turned into! Upon ringing the station the day before I had discovered that there was not a direct train to Middlesbrough that would get us to the game in time so we would have to change twice to get there and five times to get back. And it set out at 6.30am. We would also have to leave the game 5 minutes early in order to catch the last train back! What a bloody pain eh! It meant I had to leave the house at the ungodly time of 5.30am, and half asleep, with the packed lunch my mom had prepared the previous night, I headed for New Street Station. There was lots of Bluenoses on this early train, although everyone looked tired and we started on breakfast as soon as the train pulled out. I can't remember where we changed at on the way, but I have a feeling it was Sheffield as I remember a load of Sheffield Wednesday fans milling around. It was a long journey, with us discussing our chances and wondered how we would find the ground when we arrived as there were not enough of us to get a police escort and we were early. In the seventies and eighties almost all football grounds had four large floodlights that could easily be seen for quite a distance so we presumed that once we got out of the station at Middlesbrough we would be able to see the floodlights and head in that direction.

This plan usually worked quite well, however, at Middlesbrough it didn't! As we came out of the station all we could see were floodlights in loads of places. I presume that these were the docks, anyway, we had to set about asking people for directions and as everyone knows, this is not always a good idea when in enemy territory with a brummie accent! We got away with it until we reached the ground when the enemy asked us the time – retreated and returned with about 200 Boro fans that proceeded to chase the 50 or so of us waiting outside the ground. Luckily as the Bluenoses turned round and bravely ran back at the 200 Boro fans, the police arrived and saved the day. I must admit though, the Boro fans did look surprised when the small group they were chasing turned round and ran at them like lunatics. They looked like they were about to run when plod showed up.

Once inside the ground I looked around to survey my surroundings. Aryesome Park looked quite old to be honest, but it did have a certain character. The away section that we had been put in was a corner terrace and the crash bars were not the usual iron bars but were concrete. It was certainly different and as more and more Blues arrived we met other Bluenoses that we were now familiar with due to our regular travelling. We were soon chatting and joining in the singing and banter whilst waiting for the game to begin. I always enjoyed a laugh with the lads and today was no different as we sat on the terracing in anticipation. I saw Lee Pitman as usual and we got chatting whilst we awaited kick off. Before long the Blues were on the pitch and Keep Right On rang out from our section as we sang our hearts out for the lads.

Despite our loud support we were losing 2-1 with ten minutes to go and as much as it pained me, I knew we had to leave to head back to the station to get home. This is the only time I ever left a game before the final whistle and will remain so. So, off we headed at a bit of a run, to the station to start on our six-train journey home. Never one to be too downhearted we sang a bit on the train before arriving at our first port of call – Darlington. Once in Darlington station we obtained beers for the rest of the journey along with sandwiches etc. The rest of the day passed in a blur of train journeys and stations and banter with various fans as we passed through their territory. I called my mom from York Station and explained that I could be late home, if I got home at all! 'How did you get on?' she asked as usual. 'Drew 1-2' I answered, knowing that she wouldn't take much notice. 'Nice' she said, it always gave me a little laugh.

As we were waiting in Sheffield we had a bit of a run in with the locals but plod soon arrived and put a stop to it. There were quite a few of them too. Apart from the result it wasn't a bad day out really, although it was very long and by the time I got home I just collapsed into bed.

The following week St. Andrews was buzzing with enthusiasm for the game against Manchester City and the blues faithful were rewarded with a very entertaining game as the Mancs were swept aside by Blues and we came away with a 3-0 win. Great, back to winning ways I thought. There was however, a tricky trip to Highbury to take on Arsenal in a few days, to overcome.

Packed lunch and beers in a carrier bag, I boarded the Euston train with the girls for our trip to the Arse! We soon got into the mood and after downing a few beers we joined in with the singing and chatting. Sometimes we would move about a bit on the train, sitting on tables and laughing with the lads. Everyone was looking forward to the match. Before long we were sitting in a pub outside one of the local tube stations enjoying a pint with other Bluenoses and a few locals and banter was flowing as usual. Inside the ground the Bluenoses were in full voice, which was a good job really as Highbury always lacks atmosphere from the local supporters. Blues more than made up for it though but ended up watching our team lose narrowly 1-0.

Next up was the big local derby with our neighbours from Aston at their place and after a great afternoon of singing and giving the enemy loads of abuse we came away with a creditable 0-0 draw.

I went to nearly all the home and away games this season, with a few of the away games being at grounds that I had not visited before. One of these was a trip to Stoke in October to watch Blues play Stoke City at their old ground – I think it was called the Victoria ground. As it was local British Rail had put on the usual football specials and the girls and I travelled on one of them loaded up with our usual packed lunch and beers. When we arrived in Stoke it was really cold and I remember rows of terraced houses as the police marched us up towards the ground. No chance of escaping the police escort and getting to a local pub, I thought. We passed a few Stoke supporters who gave us the usual grief, only to be answered with energetic hand gestures from the travelling Bluenose!

Inside the ground we were situated on the terracing behind the goal with more Blues fans also in the seats behind us. Stoke had a nice ground with character about it and quite a bit of atmosphere from the home supporters as well as the travelling Bluenoses. Local derbies are always loud and passionate between rival supporters and this game was no different and despite losing narrowly 1-0, it was quite enjoyable for the banter.

At the end of November I visited another new ground – this time across the border in Wales and the Home of Swansea City. I don't remember a lot about the game, which we lost 1-0, but the ground soon replaced Southampton's in my affections as the worst I had visited. The facilities, the toilets in particular were appalling. I think that Swansea had not long come up from the lower divisions and the ground reflected this. Despite this, I enjoyed visiting a new ground and the usual singing and chanting of the travelling Bluenoses.

In January we were off to Ipswich for a third round FA Cup replay at Portman Road. It took hours to get there only to see Blues get knocked out of the cup 3-2. Not a bad ground to visit though and after I exchanged pleasantries with a female Ipswich fan through the fence (offering to carry on outside afterwards although she failed to show), we headed back to Birmingham.

At the end of January I was again heading off to Manchester for a game with Manchester City. We arrived in Manchester and the most memorable part of the day was when I was the only person inside Maine Road insisting that we would still come back and win when we were 4-0 down. Ever the optimist eh! The girls looked at me as if I was a compete nutter! Mind you, Blues did get 2 goals back and the game finished 4-2. I was mauled by a horse on the way out, as the police tried to keep the Blues and Manchester City fans apart. They are bloody massive and they scared the life out of me. I don't like horses to this day thanks to the Manchester police.

I went in the seats for the first time this season too. It was away at West Ham United and Julie, Debbie and I gave in to Pam's wishes and agreed to sit in the seats. We had met up with some of the lads on the Euston train and Brendan had taken us to a Pub by one of the tube stations for a pre match drink. Then it was off to Upton Park, which is nicely situated in what appears to be somewhat like the 'Eastenders' market. Once inside we appeared to have been seated with the West Ham fans and this proved very trying for me as I was sitting next to a girl who was very vocal in supporting West Ham. This was okay until she started criticising our players and at that point I stood up and words were exchanged before the police spotted the disturbance and got hold of the four of us and led us towards the pitch much to Pam's embarrassment. The away end had spotted this and were singing 'City aggro' quite loudly which amused the life out of me! We were then marched around the pitch towards the away end to cheers from the Bluenoses. Quality! We were then put in with the cheering Blues contingent to a round of applause and we joined in with the singing and banter. Quite a good day out really – and we came away with a 2-2 draw. There were a couple of west ham girls making hand gestures to us through the opening in the fencing, but they declined our invitation to come over and join us in our end.

As I said, I got to nearly all the home and away matches this season and after a nice outing down south at Southampton, and a nice trip to Tottenham, it was soon coming towards the end of the season with Blues in serious danger of relegation. We needed to be winning more games and on 1st May I made my first trip to Meadow lane, the home ground of Nott's County. Although Nott's County's ground was near to Forest's ground it was far smaller and older looking. It looked even stranger once inside. Blues were situated on the terrace behind the goal and the opposite end of the ground was very strange indeed. It wasn't like a normal stand; it was just a very high brick wall with executive boxes (of sorts) precariously positioned at the top of the wall. So it looked like there were no fans at that end of the ground. Anyway, I tried not to get too distracted by this and headed to the refreshment stand at the back of the terracing to see what was on offer. There was a very confused guy behind the counter trying his hardest to understand the brummie accent of the lads who were trying to order 'some rocks?' I explained to the vacant looking guy in the refreshment stand that the lads were just after sweets and that they were commonly known at the time in Birmingham as 'rocks'.

There were thousands of travelling Bluenoses and we made loads of noise as our boys went on a scoring spree in front of our very eyes. Brilliant! We all came away very happy after beating Nott's County 4-1 on their own turf.

Blues went on to lose the next two games by the odd goal to Arsenal and Liverpool and after a 3-3 draw away a Leeds United we were away to Coventry City for the last match of the season. There was only one result that could keep us in the first division, and that was a win. Anything less and Blues would be relegated. No pressure then!

It was a lovely sunny day when we headed off to get the train to Coventry, and there were Blues fans everywhere when we disembarked at Coventry Station. It was really hot, and everyone, me included were in football shirts with our arms bared to the sun. It was a lovely walk up to the ground where we obtained beers and sat on walls outside drinking them before it was time to head inside the ground. This time I was sitting in the seats with the Blues fans to the side of the goal and there were 5000 Blues fans inside the ground. The atmosphere was electric with excitement and of course, fears of relegation. It was bloody nerve wracking. I was so nervous I felt sick, but we sang our hearts out and 'Keep Right On' could be heard for miles. It was a party atmosphere as the players ran out onto the pitch, with Blues playing in their away colours of Yellow shirts, black shorts and black socks. There were balloons and cheering as Blues fans wanted to enjoy the occasion as much as possible and hoped it wouldn't be our last in the first division.

The match got underway and as time ticked on without a goal the stress became unbearable. My stomach was in knots, as I am sure was the case with all the other Bluenoses who refused to sit down and stood for the entire game. Time was ticking by and with about five minutes left on the clock it was beginning to sink in that we were about to be relegated. I felt sick. The fans were beginning to get a bit subdued but we kept singing in the hope that a miracle could happen and save us. Just as the tears were beginning to form in my eyes, the ball was crossed into the Coventry penalty area right in front of us and the big yellow and black shape of Mick Harford rose to meet it – GOAL!!!!!!

Unbelievable! The crowd went wild, the noise was incredible and as Mick Harford was mobbed by yellow shirts on his way over to the crowd, the Blues fans were over the hoardings and onto the pitch to celebrate. Only those of us that were there that day can truly know the depth of our feelings. We went mad, jumping on strangers, climbing over seats to get onto the pitch and crying with relief. It took a while to clear the pitch for the game to restart, but there were only seconds remaining. We had to be safe. With Blues fans all around the edges of the pitch at our end, the game managed to restart but before long the final whistle went, 1-0! The Blues end erupted! It was like a home game and we invaded Coventry's pitch in great numbers to celebrate with the players. No one could keep us off and I am sure nobody really cared as we were celebrating in style. I could not believe it, one minute I had thought we were down and the next we were saved, what a feeling. It felt like we had won a championship. The players were carried to the tunnel shoulder high by the Bluenoses, and they looked just as happy as we felt! It was such a beautiful sunny day and it will be engraved in my mind forever. What a fantastic day! This was one of the many 'Joys' that I have experienced being a Bluenose.

Birmingham finished in 16th position in division one and meant that we would be looking forward to playing in the first division again come August. I was relieved and happy and convinced that we could do much better next season.

CHAPTER SIX – Soccer Six Champions - again

That summer I was still working at the same company and had a nice holiday abroad, although I can't remember whether it was Tenerife or Spain that I went to in this particular summer holiday. I would sometimes go out locally with my brother and his mates to pubs such as the Bale of Hay in Bartley Green and the Balmoral – also in Bartley Green. My brother was seeing a girl called Sue, whom he is now married to, and I would get together with them sometimes in the local pubs. Neil (my brother) had a new motorbike and I was often getting lifts home on the back of his bike or we would ride around locally for a bit of fun. I had managed to get my brother to a few Birmingham games with me even though he wasn't a big football fan. I would also go drinking up town sometimes at Sam Wellers, Boogies, and Edwards No 7 etc with the girls. All of them being Blues pubs of course.

The previous season I had had a season ticket but for the forthcoming season I had got a part time job selling the Blues Lottery tickets inside St. Andrews on match days. It meant I would get in free to see all the games and also make a bit of pocket money as well to put towards the away matches that I regularly travelled to. I also got to meet lots of people including the players afterwards. Debbie, my friend also worked as a Blues Lottery girl, and we could both be seen in the main stand wearing our yellow sash with Blues Lottery across the front in big blue letters. I would start early before the game and my patch was upstairs in the main stand, the end next to the away support (on the Tilton). Hence there would often be away support in this area and I would take a bit of stick but I was also very good at giving it back.

I would sell the tickets before the game and at half time but it meant I could find an empty seat or stand in the tunnel and watch the game. Sometimes I would work the executive boxes and this always meant more money as you would work on a commission basis depending on how many you sold. After the game I would work with the others in the executive lounge, which was nice because some of the players would sometimes come in and there was often famous people in there too like Jasper Carrot, Freddie Starr and I also saw Denis Rousos once. Some were better tippers than others were but I won't go into that!

In the Birmingham City v West Bromwich Albion programme on 8th November 1982 the lottery girls were featured and there was a nice photograph of myself, Debbie and another girl in our Blues Lottery sash. Fame at last eh.

Blues had a good group of players at the time and I was looking forward to the season ahead as I always do. Ron Saunders had taken over at Blues after Jim Smith was asked to leave in February after a run of only two wins in fourteen. I was wondering what the change would bring. I had liked Jim Smith's style of attacking play and he had successfully guided Blues straight back into the first division in his first full season in charge. Ron Saunders on the other hand had come from our enemies across the city so I was not sure what to think but ever the optimist, I was ready to give him the benefit of the doubt.

However, the new season started off very badly indeed with only one point from the first five games (a 0-0 draw against Liverpool) and we conceded seventeen goals in four games – 3 against Manchester United, 4 against Stoke City and both Norwich and West Ham put 5 past us. Shocking! But, never mind we were only five games into the season. I was not enjoying my travels so much this season, losing is bad enough but we were leaking goals at an alarming rate. Then, after finally winning a game against Coventry City at home, we had a bit of light relief with a League Cup draw that paired us with Shrewsbury Town.

As the second round was a two-legged affair it meant a nice trip to Shrewsbury for the away leg on 26th October. I was looking forward to this because it was not too far away, a new ground for me and I could imagine it to be a nice little place really. I was proved to be correct, as Shrewsbury is a really nice place to visit. When we arrived by train it was a nice day, meaning no rain, and it was quite different from the big cities that I was used to. There were Bluenoses milling about everywhere as usual, and we made our way towards the ground to see what it was like. Gay Meadow, as Shrewsbury's ground was called, was situated very nicely next to the big river that runs through the town. It was a really small ground after what I was used to but it looked really quaint. I presumed it wouldn't hold too many though, and once again I was right as the Bluenoses more that filled the allocated end of the ground that we had been given. Although Blues were given the entire end behind the goal, the terrace was full of Blues fans in the 5,003 attendance that day. The best laugh was the many Blues fans that had climbed up onto the roof (not very high I might add) and although the voice from the loudspeaker begged them to come down there were still a few that remained up there. I was a bit worried what they would do should they need the toilet thought!

The ground was so small that on occasions the ball would clear the roof and end up in the nearby river where a man was situated in a small boat thing (cant remember what they are called but they are some sort of traditional boat) and he would collect up all the balls. What a fun job. The game ended in a 0-0 draw and as the Blues fans climbed down off the roof, we headed back to a small pub nearby to have a quick drink before leaving Shrewsbury and heading back to Birmingham. It had been a great day out and the Bluenoses had been in great voice as usual inside and outside the ground. They were still singing on the train on the way home.

The second leg was at St. Andrews's three weeks later following two draws and a defeat in the league. Only 7,861 turned up to see Blues progress to the next round by beating Shrewsbury 4-1 with goals from Curbishley (2), Dillon and Evans. I was at St. Andrews for the game though and enjoyed seeing Blues score a lot of goals for a change and the fans that were present sang the usual songs and enjoyed the evening also.

Blues were rewarded with a home tie in the next round of the League Cup that saw us paired with Derby County at home. The last time I had seen Blues play Derby was in the FA cup at Derby's ground and we had been beaten 2-1, so I was looking forward to some revenge and on 9th November we gained that revenge as we beat them 3-1. Blues were into the fourth round, which I found quite exciting and the draw was an away tie with Burnley, which I was also looking forward to, as it would be another new ground for me to visit.

We had started travelling to some games by coach around this time and for our trip to Burnley we took the supporters club coach. I remember thinking what a cold day it was and it was bloody freezing at Burnley. I thought it was the coldest place in the country at the time. The Bluenoses had travelled in numbers as usual and were in very good spirits as we all quite fancied our chances against a lower league side. If you were to look back now though, you would see that our record against lower league sides is not that good really.

Once inside the ground I took in my surroundings. I was very impressed with Turf Moor as it was very similar to our own great St. Andrews in the way that it had a large terraced Kop to one side of the pitch which joined up to a large terrace behind the goal, not unlike our Tilton. The away fans were situated behind the other goal with terracing at the front and seats at the back of the terracing. We sat in the seats for this one and the Bluenoses were in excellent voice exchanging banter with the noisy Burnley fans. It was set up to be a great cup atmosphere. The game itself would have been enjoyable had we not been robbed and to make matters worse at 2-2 one of our own players managed to put the ball into his own net and we lost the game 3-2. I was deeply disappointed as I thought we were very unlucky to lose. It's always bad to get knocked out of the cup but when you feel it is somewhat unjust then it is even worse. I was not in the best frame of mind on the way home but we still sang a little on the coach on the journey.

I was really missing playing football myself during the summer so when I saw an advertisement to join a ladies football club that met and trained just up the road from me I went along to find out more. Unfortunately the team in question turned out to be none other than Aston Villa. I though about it a lot and decided that if it meant starting at the bottom with Villa and getting better so that I could play for Blues then I would bite the bullet. Villa were in a different league to Birmingham City and were nowhere near as good and played in a league that included teams such as Droitwich and Worcester City to name a few. The top team in that league was undoubtedly Droitwich but villa were challenging them quite strongly when I joined. The manager's house was only up the road from my house on long nuke road and that was where everyone would meet before training or to travel to play a match. They didn't have two sides like Blues so at first I would often be sub and I longed to get on and play my first match.

My position was winger or striker but I would sometimes be used in the right of midfield on occasions. I remember my first game, which was a cup game against a good side and we had a couple of our best players out injured. I started the game and was playing as the main striker and I was over the moon when I scored my first goal to put us 1-0 up. I managed to get to a through ball before both defender and the oncoming goalkeeper and poked the ball underneath the keeper and into the net. It was a great feeling as my team-mates all rushed over to congratulate me. The other team came back at us though and we lost the game 3-1 and went out of the cup. Enjoyable afternoon for me though, as I really enjoyed playing for the full ninety minutes.

Speaking of the villa the most memorable game of the season was next up as we entertained our enemy at St. Andrews's two days after Christmas. Although I was still selling the lottery tickets I made sure that I was sitting in the seats with my friends to watch the game as it kicked off. The atmosphere was brilliant; the

Blues were in good voice as well as the Villa fans that had been given three quarters of the Tilton terracing. 'Shit on the Villa' rang out on several occasions along with the 'chim chimney' song and 'you're the shit of Birmingham!' to the Villa fans who answered with that daft song they sing about some bells ringing for the claret and blue. I mean, what's that all about?

Anyway, Villa were obviously expecting to win and by a large margin going on our current form, but Blues were not having any of that and played exceptionally well. When Blues scored the ground erupted as Blues fans tried to scale the massive fencing that caged them in to get onto the pitch and celebrate. It was a mass of blue and white jumping up and down around three sides of the ground. The entire ground seemed to break into a chorus of 'one-nil, one-nil, one nil! Except the silent claret and blue end behind the goal where their keeper was picking the ball out of the net. One of our players in particular, Noel Blake was enjoying it immensely as he had been coming into quite a lot of stick from the Villa fans. Noel Blake had come to us from the Villa but it was well known that he was an ardent Bluenose and it was Blake that scored the opening goal right in front of the villa end!

It got even better as the ball was soon in the net again for number two by the late Ian Handysides and Noel Blake celebrated by sticking his two fingers up at the travelling Villa fans in order to remind them of the score. Quality! Blues players celebrated and the fans sang 'Noel Blake, Noel Blake, Noel Blake, Noel Blake etc' to the tune of the seven dwarfs in snow white, and then 'two-nil' rang out loudly. When the third goal went in we were in heaven. 3-0! It was a mass celebration as the Villa end shrank visibly and the rest of the ground was like a heaving sea of blue and white. All the Bluenoses started singing 'merry Christmas Aston Villa' to the tune of 'your not singing anymore'. What a fantastic day, one that everyone that was there will remember to this day, apart from the villa that is!

And so it was into 1983, and January proved to be a nice month for me. Blues drew Walsall away in the FA Cup and I was planing to hold my twenty-first birthday party at St Andrews in the Supporters Club. Blues would be playing in the new Soccer Six tournament at the NEC on the 25th and 26th January, which was the day after my birthday.

On the 8th January I made my first trip to Walsall's stadium just across the city for the FA Cup 3rd round tie. The ground was very small and the terrace occupied by the Blues fans was heaving as we sang our cup songs along with several renditions of 'Keep Right On', and generally enjoyed ourselves. The game finished 0-0 and a replay was on the cards for the 11th January when we despatched Walsall by a Summerfield goal in a 1-0 win at St Andrews. Blues were in the next round and we drew an away trip to Crystal Palace in the 4th round.

Blues lost the next two games to Manchester United and Liverpool respectfully and then next up was my birthday party at St. Andrews. I had a fabulous time, with all my family, friends and some of my team mates from villa ladies present and it was a great party. Especially as it was held in my favourite place – St. Andrews! Two of my guests – my dads friend Terry's son's, who I had grown up with – Stephen and Michael went to the wrong side of the ground and were enjoying a party in the main stand until they realised that they didn't recognise anyone else there. It was only then that they realised they were at the wrong party and made their way to mine! Some of the girls from the team gave me the bumps while everyone looked on in amusement.

Then it was off to the NEC for the Soccer Six tournament. Blues were the holders of the trophy, having won it in 1982 and we were hoping to remain champions. The seated stadium that had been set up for the tournament was buzzing with fans from various teams and the majority were Bluenoses. Could we win again? I was confident we could as was usual for me! I really enjoyed the atmosphere inside and the players put on a great show. Blues beat Nottingham Forest on penalties in the semi-final and were paired with Ipswich in the final. The stadium was full for the final and the 7,000 full house was made up mostly of Blues fans. We sang and cheered and Blues put eight goals past Ipswich to win the tournament and lift the trophy in front of thousands of cheering Bluenoses! The train journey back was brilliant. The train was packed with Blues singing 'Champions!' and as we disembarked at New Street Station 'Champions!' rang out loudly and was being sung for ages as we made our way out and onto the town to celebrate! A couple of weeks later in the programme v West Ham on 5th February 1983 I was surprised to see Pam, Julie and myself, in one of the pictures taken at the Soccer Six. We were right at the front and my flag was clearly seen hanging on the railings! Brilliant!

Our bubble was burst on the 29th January when I travelled down to London only to see Blues get knocked out of the FA cup by Crystal Palace one-nil in the fourth round. So it was goodbye to the FA cup for another year, and my dreams of going to Wembley.

Around this time my dad worked in an electrical warehouse and one of the companies that sponsored Juventus gave my dad tickets for the European Cup quarter final first leg match at Villa Park between Villa and Juventus. I decided this could be quite good fun watching the Villa lose at home in the cup so I decided to go with my mom and dad and watch from the seats in the then new witton stand. I was surprised when we went into the ground as there were quite a few bluenoses with the ball and world badges pinned to them. There was a lot of Italians too, so it was quite a good atmosphere in our end with all of us supporting Juventus. There were 45,531 in the ground to witness the villa lose 2-1 and I enjoyed it immensely. There was a bit of a delay getting away due to the fact that a villa fan had been stabbed – allegedly by an Italian in the car park.

Blues were doing badly in the league and had lost quite a few games coming towards the end of the season and with six games to go were rooted firmly at the bottom of the league. It looked like a lost cause and relegation after losing the last four games on the trot. However, we had a team that played with passion and I knew we would not give up without a fight. Could we pull off the great escape? On the 14th April I headed off to Highfield Road on a nice sunny day to take on Coventry City. There were thousands of

Bluenoses, even though we had not won away all season, a shocking away record with no wins in 18 away games so far.

The game was a typical relegation battle even though Coventry were in fourteenth position in the league and despite the lack of entertainment the Bluenoses sang our hearts out and 'Keep Right On' rang out loudly. I had just about given up hope when Les Phillips popped up two minutes from time to crash the ball into the net from just inside the box. The Blues contingent went wild and a chorus of 'jingle bells, jingle bells, jingle all the way, oh what fun it is to see city win away!' rang out. At the final whistle we all poured out of the ground still singing and in fact, we sang all the way back to the station and on the train on the way back. The away win was so much sweeter after having had to wait so long for it to come. I do love away wins!

Next up was Everton at home and once again St. Andrews was buzzing with anticipation and hope. It was another tough game as we hadn't beaten the scousers for quite a while. Our current Blues team were determined to fight for their lives though, and once again Blues scored in the 88th minute when Robert Hopkins managed to get his head to the ball after the keeper had saved from Mick Halsall and the ball was in the net! Brilliant another one nil win and there was hope in our hearts once again. With just four games to go we really did need a miracle but we had started looking at those above us in the table and Swansea had replaced us at the foot of the table with Brighton just below us.

Although the odds were stacked against us we not giving up and travelled up to Sunderland for our next match with a mixture of excitement and fear. We travelled up on the supporter's club coach and parked up by the beach. It was a bit cold but at least it wasn't raining and we soon disembarked and headed away, past the fair and on to Roker Park. I know Roker Park is supposed to be famous for its atmosphere but it seemed to me that the Bluenoses created the atmosphere that day. Even after twenty minutes when we fell behind we still sang our hearts out and kept the faith. After all, we still had the late show to look forward to. In the 82nd minute we were rewarded with a penalty and up stepped Noel Blake to rifle the ball into the net to send the Blues contingent into wild celebrations. 1-1 and we were in with a chance. We could hardly believe our eyes when Mick Hartford scored our winner – once again in the 88th minute! Unbelievable, three matches on the trot all won with goals in the 88th minute! The Blues fans were jumping all over each other. We were all celebrating like lunatics in the hope that perhaps a miracle could in fact happen! The coach was buzzing with atmosphere all the way home and 'staying up, staying up, staying up' rang out loudly on the journey home.

It was another exciting climax to a season for Blues. Brighton came to St. Andrews needing a win and a relegation scrap where we should have been well in front ended as a 1-1 draw but the point was enough to take us above Manchester City and out of the bottom three. It was looking hopeful, especially after taking another three points in a good win over Tottenham at St. Andrews by two goals to nil. And so, with one game left we were fifth from bottom, just one point clear of the drop zone.

Therefore, we set out on our travels to Southampton with hope in our hearts. The girls and I travelled by car to Southampton with some lads that we knew. It was a nice journey, very picturesque and we stopped about half way in a nice village or town and had a quick drink in a nice country pub. We were all really nervous and really excited as we really believed we could win again and stay up. We had a good team with fighting spirit who played with heart, unlike the players we have now. Once we arrived in Southampton, after parking the car, we headed to the pub just across the road from the Dell and stood on the step watching the fans wandering past and heading in and out of the pub.

Just as we were preparing to drink up and head into the ground, the Blues team coach drove past, much to our delight. We waved at the lads with one hand, whilst trying to look girly and hiding our drinks behind our backs with the other hand. Classic! Then we were off towards the ground and were soon settled in the away end behind the goal. The away end, as I have said before, is pretty crap at the Dell, but today they had given us the entire end and it was soon choc a bloc with Blues fans. Some fans were sitting on the walls at the back and there were also Bluenoses sitting on the roof of the refreshments. The view of the pitch was really poor but we were full of hope and excitement and the singing was really loud and we swayed forwards and backwards. It was a lovely sunny day and when the teams ran out onto the pitch we cheered and waved flags and scarves in the air.

The match got underway and a severe case of nervousness set in and I began to ponder the outcome. Half time it was 0-0 and as the second half got under way Blues were now attacking the goal in front of the massed Blue army. As the game drew towards the end there was a bit of a scramble in the Southampton goal mouth in the 87th minute and Mick Harford was on hand to blast the ball into the top on the net and the fans went wild! I jumped on my mates and the wild celebrations began. We were staying up! As the final whistle went the celebrations really began and we headed out amongst mass celebrations. We decided to head out of Southampton and stop at a pub on the way for our celebrations, which we did. Everywhere we looked there were Bluenoses celebrating. It was brilliant! In a final twist Luton had won 1-0 at Maine Road and sent Manchester City down in the third relegation place. We were safe for another year though and I was more than happy.

CHAPTER SEVEN - Relegation

I always enjoy the summer and 1983 was no different. I was young, single and carefree. I was also still playing football for Aston Villa Ladies and was enjoying my football. I was awarded a trophy for most improved player of the season. My brother Neil was still picking me up from training in his red ford escort and would announce his arrival outside with his tuneful horn – I can't remember the name of the tune it played but it was like the dukes of hazard! I never got over the embarrassment of when it was my turn to wash the kit and all those vile shirts were hanging on my mom's washing line though!

Just before the start of the season Blues played Aston Villa in the Senior Cup and it was great to see us begin with a 1-0 win over our local rivals! Perhaps we may have a good season I thought, ever the optimist. The season was to begin with a trip to London and a game against West Ham at Upton Park. The girls and I decided to travel by supporter's club coach and what a good decision that turned out to be. There was a lot of football violence around this time and Blues had a bit of a reputation which is why I think the police decided they were going to make an example of some supporters at the start of the season. When we arrived at Upton Park the Blues fans that were already in the ground told us why our numbers were depleted. As the Blues supporters had disembarked from the football special in Euston the police had met them and hoarded hundreds of them onto coaches telling them they were taking them to the ground. However, the fans were then taken straight to the police station and arrested! Around 200 fans were arrested for no reason at all and in the weeks that followed the club got behind them and hired solicitors to get justice. The match itself was not one to remember and Blues started the season badly with a 4-0 defeat.

Blues lost the next game also away at Nott's County 2-1, but over the next couple of months we won five games and drew one, only losing one more game. One of the memorable games was a 2-0 away win at Wolverhampton Wanderers. There is always an unpleasant rivalry at Wolves, especially away and Blues always take a good away following so it was a very enjoyable win. There were the usual running battles after the game whereby the Wolves fans would confront the Blues and then be chased back up the road. I just headed back to the Station and back to Town for a celebratory drink in Edwards No 7 with the girls.

In October I travelled to Derby for a League Cup 2nd round match and as usual we travelled on the train. It was a great day out, the Blues contingent sang loads and the lads played brilliant and came away with a good 3-0 first leg lead. After 1-0 defeats at the Vile and Spurs, the second leg produced four goals against Derby and Blues were through to the third round with a 7-0 aggregate win. I was beginning to think it may be a good season after all, especially when Blues followed this up with an away win over our other local rivals West Brom! I think this was the day when the villa had been beaten at home by Arsenal 6-2 and Tony Woodcock had scored about 5 goals. I remember because I was on the bus from West Bromwich to Selly Oak and there were some downhearted Villa fan's also on the bus. The Blues fans were getting on and coughing the word 'Woodcock!' as they passed the Villa fans. I had to laugh at that. It was a good day for me as I always enjoy travelling the short distance to West Brom and the atmosphere amongst the thousands of Bluenoses was brilliant as always.

In the 3rd round of the League Cup Blues were drawn against Nott's County and after three draws we were drawn to play the second replay in Nottingham at their place. It was the 5th December when I travelled to Nottingham and as much as I usually enjoy the walk with the escort to the ground it was absolutely freezing and I remember thinking it was the coldest I had ever been. I was convinced my toes had frostbite and were about to drop off! It turned out to be worth it though as Mick Harford scored and Robert Hopkins got two in a good 3-1 win. I may have been cold but I went home happy.

Blues were losing a few games in the league now and were 17th in the league. Blues cup run came to an end after a 1-1 draw at St. Andrews and we lost the replay 3-0 at Anfield. It is at this point that you call it the Mickey Mouse cup and look forward to the real cup – the FA Cup (unless your team gets to the final that is!). The draw for the third round was made on Monday as usual and Blues were drawn to play Sheffield United of the third division at their ground. The cup would make a nice distraction from the league, especially as Blues were currently 19th in the league.

On 6th January I was up early and soon on my way to Sheffield for the cup-tie. Blues had not won a game since early December with the League Cup win over Nott's County but the girls and I were feeling lucky. It was a nice trip on the Shoppers special train this time. It was quite fun really with the shoppers scattered about amongst the Bluenoses on their way to the game and as usual for a cup game there was a carnival atmosphere on the train. Inside the ground it was packed in the Blues end and the terraces were swaying to the tune of 'KA SA RA SA RA' and 'Wembley, Wembley!' Sheffield Utd were also up for the fight and the match itself was the usual exciting stuff that cup-ties are made of. The game ended in a 1-1 draw and I came away fancying our chances at St. Andrews in the replay in a few days time. I was not disappointed either and our lads dispatched Sheffield Utd 2-0 with goals from Mick Harford and Billy Wright in front of a disappointingly low crowd of 10,888. Perhaps it was because Blues were not doing well in the league, but the FA Cup usually inspires larger crowds than this I thought. I guess times were hard. Blues won the next two games including a convincing 3-0 win against West Ham, but we were still in 19th position when we approached the FA Cup fourth round game away at Sunderland.

When the day of the game came round, I was really excited and was really nervous on the coach journey up north. After a long trip we arrived in Sunderland and parked up near the beach and headed off towards the ground for the game. Blues fans were situated on the corner behind the goal and it was packed with Blues fans that were in extremely good voice. The terracing was swaying back and forth and scarves were being waved as 'Wembley! Wembley!' was being sang. Even when Sunderland took the lead the Blues contingent continued to sing, and 'Keep Right On' was belted out loudly. It was the Sunderland supporters who were now singing 'Wembley' and taunting us with 'were going to Wembley, you're not, you're not'.

As the game drew towards the end I began to resign myself to the fact that we were about to go out of the cup and be taunted by the Sunderland fans at the same time. The girls were also feeling the same way, but then in the 89th minute as Blues were throwing everything at Sunderland and attacking the goal in front of the travelling Bluenoses, the ball broke in the box and Martin Khul hammered it home! Unbelievable, the fans went absolutely wild and surged forward like a giant wave. I was swept forward in the mayhem, whilst jumping around madly myself and jumping on everyone around us in celebration. I couldn't believe it; we were going to get a replay at St. Andrews, because surely there was not time for Sunderland to replay. Just as I was back on my feet again I looked up to see the ball being crossed into the area again and Mick Harford got on the end of it and powered it into the back of the net! Yesssss! 2-1 in the 90th minute! The Blues end erupted and once again I was swept off my feet. Within seconds the Sunderland fans that had been taunting us a minute ago were silenced and Blues fans began returning the favour by singing 'we're going to Wembley, you're not, you're not!' It was unbelievable to be thinking, we're out one minute, we have a replay next, then – we have won – we are through! What a feeling, one of the best I have had I think.

It was a fab celebration on the way back, we sang the whole way, including our invasion of the service station at our stop off. Service station stops are always fun due to the fact that you often meet up with various other sets of supporters and there is often some banter to be had. As always I began thinking that this could be our year!

I was so excited as I waiting for the draw on the Monday. Blues were only one game away from the quarter-finals and when we were drawn at home against West Ham I was quite optimistic. Blues had already beaten West Ham 3-0 at St. Andrews this season and at least we had the home advantage. After a win and two draws in the league, including a 2-2 draw against Manchester United, Blues had moved up a place to 18th just prior to the West Ham game.

As I was still selling lottery tickets at the home games, I was able to watch the ground filling up for the cup-tie. The atmosphere was electric, especially as there was a bit of history between Blues and West Ham fans off the pitch. It was a cold day and the pitch looked a little white from the frost, and by the time kick off approached there was 29,570 people inside St. Andrews and most of them were singing their hearts out. I found a good position to watch the game from and began joining the other Bluenoses in the singing. It was a really exciting game and Blues were by the far the better team. With goals from Billy Wright, Tony Rees and Robert Hopkins Blues were cruising 3-0, playing with a bright yellow/green ball because of the weather! However, the West Ham fans were not at all happy by the score line and invaded the pitch in a futile attempt to get the match abandoned. Blues fans came onto the pitch to confront the invading West Ham fans but before long, following announcements that the match would not be abandoned, the police managed to restore order. The West Ham fans were returned to their end, Blues to theirs and the match recommenced for the final few minutes. When the whistle blew the ground erupted and the celebrations began in earnest. Blues were in the quarterfinals of the FA Cup! There had been a lot of cup upsets this year and there were no big teams left in the last four – perhaps it really could be our year? When the draw placed us at home against Watford, all Bluenoses were extremely hopeful.

Following on the heels of the cup win Blues followed it up over the next few weeks with three good wins, 1-0 at Tottenham, 2-1 at home against local rivals West Brom (thereby achieving a double over the yam yams!) and another good away win at Coventry 1-0. Blues were now up to 14th in the league and we were feeling a bit safer.

Two days before the quarter final I was playing in a match for Villa ladies when I received a kick to the back of my head when I was attempting to head a ball. This meant that on the day of the Watford game I was still suffering from concussion but nothing was going to prevent me from being at St. Andrews for the game! I was once again selling tickets before the game but managed to find a good position in which to enjoy the game. The atmosphere was even better than the West Ham game and the Kop looked very impressive indeed. There were blue and white balloons everywhere and the singing almost took the roof of the stadium. There were 40,220 fans in St. Andrews and it looked and sounded fantastic. Unfortunately for Blues an up and coming player called John Barnes was playing and probably had one of the games of his career and his outstanding performance inspired Watford to a 3-1 win over us. In fact our goal was an own goal. I was gutted as was the thousands of other Blues fans in the ground. I felt very let down and I thought the crowd were so brilliant that we deserved better, but alas it was not to be. I was even more gutted when Watford drew Plymouth in the semi-final. I dwelled on just what might have been, as I am sure most other Bluenoses did also.

Three weeks later and it was our local rivals Aston Villa again at St. Andrews and I was really hoping Blues could pull off a victory and cheer up our season a bit. Blues were now up to 13th in the league but the Villa were the clear favourites to win the game. The match turned out to be a game that has stuck in my memory ever since due to the score line and the atmosphere. Because we were the underdogs it was really sweet when our welsh international Byron Stevenson hit a volley on the turn just inside the penalty area and the ball looped over the Villa keeper to put Blues 1-0 up. The ground erupted and chants of 'shit on the villa' rang out time and time again. Unfortunately though, just before half time Villa managed an equaliser, I think it was Peter Withe who scored it. So at half time it was all square and the ground was alive with excitement and tension.

Straight from the second half kick off Villa immediately attacked our penalty area and from the clearance Stevenson hit a long ball into the Villa half for Howard Gayle to run onto. Gayle ran the length of their half before hitting a fabulous shot across the goal mouth and into the far corner of the goal, just ahead of Robert Hopkins who raised his arms in celebration as the ball hit the back of the net. Brilliant goal and Howard Gayle ran straight towards the celebrating Kop where he climbed up onto the top of the railings to celebrate with the ecstatic Blues fans! Excellent, especially as it was shown again and again on match of the day in the evening. What a classic. The match finished 2-1 to Blues and the ground erupted. Celebrations continued late into the night!

On the 4th of April, I again headed to Wembley to see England play Northern Ireland in the home internationals. I love going to Wembley and the old Wembley had so much character and such a fantastic atmosphere. The girls and I were in the upper tier terrace behind the goal for this game and it was packed. It was a very enjoyable game, which was highlighted by a good goal from Tony Woodcock. England won the game 1-0 and we all headed back up Wembley way to get the train to Euston and back home to Birmingham to celebrate.

Unfortunately after the Villa game the season went downhill and Blues lost to Manchester Utd, Queens Park Rangers and an embarrassing loss at Nottingham Forest. I travelled to Nottingham for the game and the Blues contingent were packed into a small area on the corner of the ground with a bloody big floodlight stuck right in the middle. To lose 5-1 was awful, but the Blues fans put on a brave face, refusing to be miserable and when Forest scored their fifth goal, chants of 'we want six' rang out from the Bluenoses in ironic humour. When Mick Harford scored our consolation goal the Blues fans cheered and celebrated like we had just won the league. It was funny in an ironic way. At least the fans did not get on the backs of team like happens today. Blues players were still applauded off at the end of the game.

Despite drawing a game against Arsenal at home, Blues were back down to 18th in the league by the time we took on Liverpool and St. Andrews and it was looking a little worrying as we were once again facing a relegation battle. The boxer Mohammed Ali was due to make an appearance before kickoff and I managed to catch a glimpse of the former hero as he was being led from the changing rooms towards the tunnel. I was really shocked to be honest, at the sight of him being led by his men. He didn't seem very aware of what was going on around him and was just being pointed in various directions to shake hands with people. It was very sad I thought. When he was led out onto the pitch he was treated like a hero and the fans chanted 'champion' really loudly to him as he waved to the crowd. It was a really nice gesture and he smiled as he looked around him. The match finished 0-0 and after an away draw 1-1 at Norwich it was once again down to the last match of the season to decide our fate.

On the last day of the season I was a bundle of nerves as I headed to St. Andrews to see Blues battle for our first division status against Southampton. A draw would be enough against second place Southampton as long as Coventry City did not win their game. I was a bit worried though, especially as we had one of our strikers, Mick Ferguson currently on loan with Coventry. Surely they would not be allowed to play him though. Blues really needed to win.

The atmosphere was electric and after two successive relegation escapes on the last day of the season, there were many that thought we could pull it off again. I hoped we could stay up but I was a little apprehensive, as I had never seen Blues outside of the top division. Despite Blues throwing everything they had at Southampton, they couldn't score and the game finished 0-0. This would be enough so long as Coventry did not win. As the final whistle sounded the news came that broke our hearts. Mick Ferguson had scored for Coventry and secured them a 1-0 win, thereby sending Blues into the second division for the first time I had ever known in my young life. I was shocked and upset. I was angry that Mick Ferguson had been allowed to play for Coventry but I also realised it had been in our own hands but I was devastated! So were all the other Blues fans and as the tears fell the stunned Bluenoses headed out of the ground in utter devastation. There was some trouble outside as Blues fans vented their frustrations on the waiting police vans but nothing very serious. I headed home with a heavy heart. It was one of the many sorrows I have suffered as a Bluenose over the years, but it was my first major heartache and I did not like the sensation. I was down but not out – Blues would be back, of that I was sure!

CHAPTER EIGHT – Hamden Park, Glasgow

As the 1983-84 season drew to an end, Julie and I had managed to get two tickets for the Home International game between Scotland and England at Hamden Park in Glasgow, Scotland. We were both really excited as this would be our first away trip with England. The fact that it was in enemy territory across the border made it even sweeter, if not a bit intimidating, and I for one was really looking forward to it. Although it was in the shadow of relegation I managed to pick myself up and look forward to the trip north.

So, on the 25th May 1984, Julie and I set out to board the train to Glasgow, via Preston, at New Street Station. Because it was such a long trip we had to set out very early, and it was still dark when we set off. For some unknown reason, I thought the train would be full of England supporters travelling up to Scotland as well as us, however, it wasn't and I was soon to discover that not many England fans actually travelled to Scotland for the game.

It was a very long trip despite changing trains and having a little break at Preston station, and Julie and I entertained ourselves with our packed lunches and talk of relegation, the forthcoming season and today's game up in Scotland. The train passed through the Lake District and the view was beautiful, as was the scenery once we entered Scotland. There was lots of green hills, and countryside and it was lovely to see. All in all in was a very nice journey by train and as we arrived in Glasgow's central station I started to become a little apprehensive. The Scots have a reputation for hating the English and I wondered if they felt that way about female England supporters too. Especially as the two of us were travelling alone! Needless to say our scarves were safely tucking away in our bags.

As we disembarked in Glasgow station I immediately noticed that there seemed to be an awful lot of Scotland fans in Scotland football shirts also arriving in the station for the game. Julie and I decided that we should use the toilets before we left the station and as we put our money in the slot and entered the toilets we were followed in by a few 'large' and scary looking women in Scotland shirts. This was a bit worrying, but having kept our mouths closed and scarves hidden, we escaped unscathed. Didn't do much for the nerves though!

After consulting the tourist office and looking at maps and bus timetables, we headed out into Glasgow and caught a bus to Hamden Park. The streets seemed to be filled with Scotland shirt wearing people, including the bus we got on and Julie and I remained silent in the hope that no one would notice that we were in fact the enemy! Getting off the bus and walking up towards the ground I looked around and noticed that every single Scot had at least two flags and a few scarves each. Many of the men wore kilts and had a flag around their shoulders and were waving another one in the air. It looked amazing and I couldn't see another England fan anywhere.

Hamden Park itself looked old but impressive, although nowhere near as impressive as Wembley Stadium. It did have some character though and we made our way inside onto the terracing situated along the side of pitch opposite the seated side. Inside it looked quite big and had terracing around three sides of the ground with seats along one side only. It appeared that the Celtic fans had one end behind the goal while the Rangers fans had the other. I remember thinking that this was a bit bizarre that they didn't all mix together, but Julie and I were to the side just left of the middle. I noticed that we appeared to be in with the Scotland fans and there didn't seem to be any segregation, apart from around a couple of hundred England supporters who were situated behind one of the goals surrounded by Scots. I found that a bit worrying to be honest with the history between the two teams and countries. Julie and I agreed to keep our England scarves in our bags and our comments to ourselves. There were some scary looking characters around us, I can say!

There was massive fencing separating the various sections, but these were being scaled by more that one Scot wearing kilts! This proved to be entertaining if nothing else. Can you imagine, these big burly men, draped in scarves and at least two flags, wearing kilts and scaling a ten-foot fence! Amazing, and for what end? The atmosphere inside the ground was quite good although not as good as Wembley and with not a lot of noise from the couple of hundred England supporters who were being drowned out by the surrounding Scots. At least the English contingent were up for it and were giving as good as they got.

The game got under way and I was finding it extremely hard not to shout my opinions and cheer for my country. Then, when Tony Woodcock scored, I totally forgot where I was and punched the air and cheered in celebration before noticing that everyone had turned towards us. Quickly lowering my hands I attempted to look innocent. 'You English?' some bloke shot at us. We shook our heads and attempted to get away with it. They let it go at that but one guy started talking to us but he was okay really, whereas I don't think the rest of them would have been. There is a really strong hatred toward the English and it was really noticeable that day. The rest of the England fans were celebrating wildly though and I wished we were in there with them. Mind you, if we were I would have been worried about getting back to the station in one piece!

Scotland then got an equaliser and the game finished 1-1. A bit disappointing but at least it increased our chances of getting back to the station alive. The Home Internationals finished with Northern Ireland as champions, Wales second England third and Scotland finished bottom of the group. Oh well, maybe next year!

As all the fans streamed out, Julie and I jumped on one of the buses going to the Station. Just before we got on, someone asked me the way to the station. Shit, too scared to speak and risk getting my head kicked in, I just nodded in the general direction of the station and he said thanks and headed off. The Scots were clearly looking for any England fans to pick off. We reached the station safe and sound and were soon on board the train back to England. There were a few England supporters on the train back and the journey was just as enjoyable as the outward journey. Julie and I reflected on our day and discussed football in general. Despite the intimidating atmosphere up in Glasgow, I had enjoyed the whole experience and could now proudly say that I had followed England away and at one of the most intimidating of venues.

We arrived back in Birmingham worn out but happy and Julie and I had decided we were going to take some holidays and follow Birmingham on the pre season tour. Happy in this knowledge I headed back to my moms and an exhausted sleep!

CHAPTER NINE – Pre season tour of Holland 1984

The summer of 1984 was as enjoyable as ever, I was still working for the same company, playing for Villa ladies and getting out and about with my friends. I was slowly getting over the disappointment of relegation and was looking forward to my brother Neil's forthcoming wedding in September to his long-term girlfriend Sue. But before that, and before the start of the new season, I was really looking forward to the pre season tour with Blues. This pre season tour was going to be in Holland with one game in Belgium, and I couldn't wait! I had just under two weeks holiday and Julie and I were planning to travel to Holland for the entire tour, which would mean we would spend eleven days in Holland and Belgium.

Our accommodation was booked through Birmingham City football club, so it was part of the official tour, and we hoped that we would be located near the team. The hotel that we were booked in was in Arnhem, so that is where our base would be. It was so exciting when the day came that we were due to set off. Our suitcases were packed and we were very soon on the train down to Dover to catch the ferry across to the Hook of Holland and the start of our holiday. The train journey was enjoyable as Julie and I chatted relentlessly about the forth-coming trip and before long we had arrived at the Docks and I was staring up at the massive ferry in front of me. I was really surprised by the size if the ship, it looked like the size of a large hotel and although I do not like being on water, I was looking forward to boarding to see what it was like inside.

I thought the ferry was quite impressive inside too, as Julie and I had a quick look around. However, as the ferry started to leave the docks and I could see water all around me I began to feel a bit queasy. There was only one thing for it, so we headed for the bar, which was just like a real pub, whereby no sea could be seen and I could be fooled into believing I was not in the middle of the ocean! There were several others in the bar and before long 'Keep Right On' was being sang by the many Blues fans on board that were also making the trip. We got talking to some of the Blues lads and had some banter with the other sets of supporters from Newcastle Utd, Nottingham Forest and West Ham Utd. As Blues had the most supporters and West Ham are not exactly popular; the Newcastle and Forest fans sided with Blues against the Londoners. It was quite light hearted at first but after six hours of drinking, as we neared the Hook of Holland, it began to get a little heated. It was when we got off the ferry that it got out of hand and a fight broke out between Blues and West Ham fans in customs and the Newcastle and Forest fans were quick to join up with the Blues fans in the battle against the hammers. The waiting police soon broke it up though and before long we were on our way to the train station to board a train to Arnhem. Another fight broke out at the train station, again between Blues and West Ham, but that was soon diffused by the police.

Julie and I bought a two week rail pass, which involved having our pictures taken and would save us quite a bit over the eleven days as we planned to travel about quite a bit. I quite liked the trains; they were really big and comfortable, not like the old British Rail trains we were used to. They were bright yellow too!

It was lovely weather when we arrived and Holland looked lovely on the train journey. It was really flat and green. The thing I noticed most was how clean it was and that there were no hills, it was completely flat with cycle lanes everywhere. Holland is a beautiful country and very colourful. The houses are quaint and often painted various pastel colours. When we arrived at our hotel I remember thinking it was a bit like the motels I have seen on the television as it was only 3 stories tall. We were shown to our room, which was nice enough and the setting for the hotel was also very nice and situated a short walk from the town so it was nice and quiet. There were a few other Blues fans arriving who had also booked through the football club, but all the lads that we had met on the ferry were making their own plans as they went along!

As soon as we had unpacked, Julie and I set out to explore our surroundings and ventured into the nearby town. Although we were secretly disappointed that the team were not staying in our hotel, we though the location we were in was great and it was also situated pretty much in the middle of all the places we would be visiting for the games.

Blues first game was against De Graafschap and we set out early and joined up with several other Bluenoses that we had met coming over plus several others who had made the trip. We were to find that throughout the tour there was about fifty of us that formed the core of our support plus Julie and I. We all bonded and became good friends and due to the fact that it was fifty blokes and only two girls, we were well looked after by the men. So we had a few drinks before the game with the lads before we headed into the ground a little early for the match. While we were enjoying a drink outside the ground one of the players – Robert Hopkins came over and had a chat with us. Julie knew Hoppy from her childhood and he chatted to us for a while before taking a swig of my drink and heading off to get ready for the game.

Drinks could be easily obtained in the ground and the Blues faithful were already in good humour and enjoying more pre match drinks. As is was early a few Blues fans decided to climb the fencing onto the pitch for a game of football with a few of the Dutch fans who also came onto the pitch to play a game against our fans. The Blues fans had bought their own football and a nice friendly game got under way. This was to be reported later in the British press that there was a lot of trouble inside the ground before the game and fierce fighting broke out on the pitch when rival sets of supporters climbed the fences to confront each other. This was utter bollocks! It was a friendly kick about between the two sets of supporters who then climbed back into their respective ends to carry on drinking before the game. It was quite funny really, because the local police were sitting at the back of the terraces with their rifles propped against the wall, enjoying some of the vodka and beer that the Blues fans were consuming and chatting avidly with the Bluenoses!

I had bought a nice De Graafschap silk scarf as a memento and enjoyed watching proceedings and the game, which ended in a 0-0 draw. It was a lovely sunny day and I enjoyed a really good day of banter with the lads, drinking and football. Fabulous! After the game we headed off to have a few more drinks with the lads before setting off back to the hotel. Next time we met up with the lads though, we were informed that some trouble did occur after the game between Blues and some Dutch supporters who were looking for trouble. According to the lads around ten fans ended up in hospital, although only one of these was a Blues fan, and he was soon out and back amongst the travelling support again.

Next up was a match against Gronigan, which was a bit of a journey, but we set off in good form as usual and had soon arrived at the small ground ready for the game. Once again we met up with the lads inside the ground this time, as there was a nice sort of clubhouse at the top of the terracing where we were situated. The grounds we visited in Holland were small but sort of nice really. Julie and I had a great time inside this small bar in the ground and just before the game we ventured out onto the terraces. We had already had a little look around the ground when we came in earlier and had enjoyed our little tour. All the Bluenoses were in good spirits as always, everyone knows what a good sense of humour us Brummies have! The game got underway and it was extremely entertaining as Blues were in good form also and ran away 4-0 winners. The amazing thing was that drink was available throughout the game and we stood on the terraces, plastic glasses in hand, watching the game fully refreshed. And there was no trouble at all! Everyone was probably too drunk to cause trouble to be honest! It was another fun day out watching the Blues and the weather had stayed sunny, making the occasion extremely enjoyable.

It was not long after this game that we started noticing small posters stuck up on trees, or outside pubs, warning of impending trouble for the last game against FC Breda and threatening violence from the Dutch fans against the Blues fans. Like we were scared! We all just laughed it off to be honest.

Our next match was in Belgium and Jules and I set off from our base for the long trip across the border and into Belgium. We were planning to go to Belgium just for the game, which was a night match, and to travel back afterwards. However, when we arrived we discovered there were no trains back after the game and due to the fact that it was mother's day in Belgium the banks were also closed! We could hardly believe it! We had not bought an awful lot of money with us on the trip to Belgium so we now had to find a really cheap bed and breakfast at the last minute. Luckily we did find somewhere, although it was a bit of a tip to be honest with two single beds and a small sink to wash in! It was not what we were used to! The rest of the travelling Bluenoses were planning to sleep in the local park and we did receive a few offers to share a bench with us should we wish to join them. We politely declined the offer and decided we would rough it in the bed and breakfast for the night.

We met up with the lads it a fab little pub/bar just outside the ground, which was really nice with a sort of veranda/balcony which we could stand outside on and have a bit of banter. It was right outside the ground and we were able to look over at the ground and watch people arrive. Again it was a small ground but perhaps a bit bigger than the previous two we had visited. It was fun chatting to the lads and they had bought a really big Birmingham City/England flag, which was draped across the railings for all to see. We took some photos of quite a few of us standing on the steps of the pub holding the flag up between us all. It was a great day and one of the lads managed to obtain a roll of tickets from the cellar, which enabled us, all to have free drinks the entire time. They were like the old cinema tickets that we used to have and this is what everyone had to buy to get drinks. By the time kick off approached we were all a bit the worse for wear and we wandered into the ground saying we were with the

Birmingham team and somehow we managed to get inside without paying! Once inside a couple of the lads tried to climb the floodlights but were pulled down by the local police and thrown out, but after a short while they appeared inside the ground again. I don't remember a lot about the game itself but Blues won 1-0 and we headed back to the pub for a celebratory drink – or two!

A couple of the players joined up with all the Bluenoses outside the pub for a drink after the game, which was fab. Tony Rees and Robert Hopkins came over for a drink and had a bit of banter with the fans. It was really nice when players joined the fans to celebrate, perhaps this helped towards players playing with passion for there clubs unlike today whereby players are more interested in money and playing for the big clubs. Our players at this time gave their all for Birmingham City and that is why we loved them so much. So, after a very enjoyable day, Julie and I headed back to our grotty little bed sit and passed out in exhaustion. On the way we met some Belgium lads and taught them the 'shit on the villa' song, which they picked up rather quickly to be honest.

Back in Holland again, we decided to have a day trip to Amsterdam, but after disembarking at Amsterdam train station to the sight of hundreds of Manchester Utd fans fighting all over the station, we got back on the train and headed back. Neither of us fancied being in a place full of Man Utd fans!

On the day of the last game we set off early and as it was a Saturday game, we found a nice little pub near the ground which was already full of the Blues lads enjoying pre match drinks. It was another lovely sunny day and everyone was sitting either on or at tables outside the pub and the banter was beginning in earnest as the tour and the final match was being discussed. The lads were also discussing the posters threatening the Blues fans with violence at the game. Apparently there were a gang of Breda fans that were going to 'get us' at the game. Like we were worried!

Julie, the lads and myself enjoyed food and drink outside the pub and in due time we set off for the nearby ground and the game. It was an early evening game and we situated ourselves behind one of the goals. As kick off approached the Blues numbers seemed to increase enormously and before long there were hundreds of Blues fans in our end. I wondered what was going on and I got chatting to some of the newcomers who informed me that they were in fact, international hooligans who had heard that the Dutch fans were threatening violence against the Blues and had decided to join in with the Blues. That amused me somewhat. Before long the game got underway and despite a floodlight failure causing a delay it continued to entertain us. Not long before the end of the game, which finished in a draw, a gang of very young Breda fans made there way towards the Blues end, but after getting the shock of their lives, ended up running their little legs off back to their own end as the Blues lots chased them back. Back on the terraces the rest of the Blues fans laughed at their cheek.

After eleven brilliant days in Holland and Belgium, Julie and I reflected on our great adventure as we packed up and headed back to the Hook of Holland and the ferry trip home. All the lads were also on the same ferry heading back and everyone was absolutely knackered. As we enjoyed our last drinking session together in the ferry bar we exchanged views and some of the lads crashed out in seats to try and catch some sleep. That can be risky when the rest of us are still drinking and a couple of the sleeping lads were covered in newspapers, cigarette butts and one lad had a cigarette placed in his sleeping mouth and his photo was duly taken to show to him when he awoke! And so after a fun packed trip we arrived back on English soil and headed back to Birmingham to tell my mom all about my adventure. It was the sort of thing that memories are made from and a trip of a lifetime for most of us.

CHAPTER TEN – Away wins

The new season was again upon us and I was avidly looking forward to what I hoped would be a promotion battle and not another relegation battle like last season. Blues had what I thought was a good passionate team this season and I was confident that we would be up there fighting it out at the top of the division. I also had my brother Neil's forthcoming wedding to Sue to look forward to. I was a bit gutted that it was on a Saturday in the football season, especially as Blues were at home and I hadn't missed a game at St. Andrews for years. However, my mom informed me that there was no way I was missing it, especially as I was bridesmaid with my sister Annette. My bridesmaid dress was pink and Annette's dress was blue and we both looked nice in our different colours.

The season began with an away trip to Oldham, which was a good day out, and Blues came away with a good away win 1-0 to start the season off well. So many Blues fans travelled to Oldham for this game that hundreds of them charged the gates and got into the game for nothing. I was already inside when this happened! This was followed up with three more wins on the trot, as Blues remained unbeaten, winning 4-2 at St. Andrews against Wimbledon, and away 1-0 at Fulham and 2-0 at Crystal Palace. Then it was the day of my brothers wedding.

So, on the 15th September 1984, I was up early and was soon at the hairdressers getting my hair done ready for the wedding. I don't know whether I was more nervous about being a bridesmaid or stressed over missing a Blues game, but I wouldn't have missed my brothers wedding for anything to be honest. Before long Annette and I were in our dresses and about to walk up the aisle behind Sue, who looked fabulous. My brother looked great too, as well as the rest of my family. There were other Bluenoses at the wedding, which was taking place at St. Gabriel's church in Weoley Castle, and as I walked up the aisle I was informed that Blues were 2-0 ahead, by someone with a radio plugged into his ear! Great news, and with that the wedding went very well and we were soon heading to the reception.

The reception was being held at Calthorpe Old Boys (COB) Club on Bristol Road in the city centre and that is where we headed for after the photos were taken. The reception was being held upstairs in the COB Club and the celebrations soon got underway and my mates that had been at the match then joined me and we ate, drank and danced. As the party continued a buzz of excitement went around with the news that their were, in fact, some Birmingham City players in the bar downstairs enjoying a post match drink. Julie and I went downstairs to invite them up and indeed, Robert Hopkins, Noel Blake and Mick Harford all came and joined the festivities! It was quite funny seeing them signing the paper plate's that the youngsters asked them to sign. One of the player's even gave me his programme when I told him that it was the first match I had missed in years. I can't remember which player it was now though! It certainly made the day even more special for me, and everyone was impressed that the players had joined us. What a great day and night! Tom Ross was the DJ for us that night which was also special as he is such a big part of the local radio station and a big Bluenose.

Three days later Blues lost their unbeaten run at home against Portsmouth 1-0, but soon got back to winning ways again at Wolves in the next game 2-0. Then the League Cup draw paired us with Plymouth with the first leg being at St. Andrews. This was duly won 4-1 and I was really looking forward to the return leg as I had not been to Plymouth before and it would be another new ground for me. Unfortunatly it was a night match and with it being so far away it would be quite a long trek and a late return home. With this in mind we booked on the coach, so with a day booked off work, I boarded the coach and we were on our way.

The coach was quite lively and the lads had a few drinks at the stop over and after a fun, if not long journey down south we arrived at Plymouth's ground. It had been a bit of a dull day really and it looked as though it could rain at any time. Although I was 22 years old, I still looked very young so I decided to try the under 16 turnstile to get in for a pound. Julie laughed and said I had no chance, but undeterred, I pulled my Birmingham cap down a little and headed successfully into the ground for a pound through the under 16 turnstile! Great.

Once inside I took in my surroundings. It looked quite old and the away end was terracing behind the goal with no roof! This did not bode well as it looked liked we were in store for rain and I did not fancy getting soaked and having to travel all that way back home soaking wet. As half time arrived the rain duly started so I went over to a steward and told him that I wanted to go back to my seat as I had just popped over to see some mates on the terraces at half time. He asked for our tickets (Julie had joined me as she didn't fancy getting wet either!), which I told him I must have dropped and he duly let us through the fences and round to a nice dry seat with the other Blues fans in the stands. Excellent! The game was quite good too, Blues played well and Wayne Clarke scored the only goal of the game to give us a 1-0 away win and a 5-1 aggregate win to see us through to the third round.

With the game over we headed back to the coach to join the rather wet looking Blues fans that had remained on the open terrace. Everyone was happy and lively and there was loads of singing on the way back. It was quite late when we stopped at the services and everyone poured off for refreshments and toilet breaks. We got back on the coach before most of the others and it was quite funny watching the lads get back on with their arms loaded with various sandwiches they had just acquired and they happily distributed them amongst us. Just what we needed to see us on our way. We arrived back in Birmingham very late but happy and I arrived home to darkness and slipped quietly into bed and into an exhausted sleep. Funny thing was that the next morning my mom told me she had dreamed that I bought the whole coach load of Bluenoses back to our house to sleep! I think she was relieved to wake up and only find me asleep in the house and not a coach load of Blues fans!

A couple of weeks later I had another nice trip away at Nottingham when Blues beat Notts County 3-1. I quite liked going to Notts County as it wasn't too far and Blues always seemed to win there. By the time the next round of the League Cup came round against West Brom, Blues had lost a couple of games, drew a couple and won a couple, so we were still battling for promotion. Unfortunatly our League Cup exploits came to and end at the Hawthornes, where, after a 0-0 draw at home, we lost at West Brom 3-1. At least the Blues fans gave a good account of ourselves as usual and the Blues end was packed with 'Keep Right On' and 'I do like to be beside the seaside – f*** off West Brom' ringing out loud and clear. And, of course we always do a few renditions of 'Shit on the Villa' for good measure!

In November, we travelled to London to see Blues play at Charlton Athletic. I was looking forward to this match as Blues had just got a player called Tony Morley on loan, and I thought he was quite an exciting player and so was looking forward to seeing him play in Blues colours. We arrived early and ventured round to the player's entrance in time to see the players arrive. This was quite exciting to see our heroes arriving and once they were inside the ground we also headed into the Blues end. This was the old Valley ground before its current refurbishment and although it was old looking I quite liked the large terracing along the side of the pitch, which was very much like our Kop terracing. It was quite sad when we visited again a few years later when that section of terrace was closed and run down with weeds and stuff growing through the concrete. It was quite a big ground I though, for what I thought was not a very big club unlike ourselves who were a big city club. The game got under way and my initial excitement was tempered somewhat by a 2-1 defeat but at least our on loan player Tony Morley scored a goal for Blues and gave us something to cheer.

In our next away game though, Tony Morley scored two goals as we beat Cardiff City in Cardiff. Apart from the fact that the welsh fans can be quite hostile, we had a very enjoyable day out and I got to visit another new ground for me. Again, it was an old looking ground and Blues had a nice terraced end behind the goal giving us a good view of the game. We sang and celebrated quite a lot really and also got to sing 'Eng er land, Eng er land!' quite a bit. The celebrations continued on our march back to the station after the game and on the train back the Birmingham!

Blues followed this win with another home win against Middlesbrough 3-2 and then in was off to Elland Road to take on Leeds Utd on a cold December day. Leeds fans had quite a reputation at this time, not unlike our own supporters so it was always going to be billed as being a bit of a battle between the supporters of both teams. However, we decided to brave the football special, which was extremely lively and a very enjoyable trip to Leeds. We didn't know whether it was safer to stay with the police escort, with the risk of ambush or whether to try and slip away, which was also risky as we had on Blues colours and would be alone. Anyway, we decided to stay with the escort, and after a couple of attempted ambushes with Blues running at the approaching Leeds fans, the police prevailed and we arrived safely at the ground. It was a bit of a misty day though and once inside the ground the view across the pitch was obstructed somewhat by the fog.

It was difficult to see the other goal (we were situated along the side towards one goalmouth) and it was only when I saw the Blues player's running back towards us with their arms in the air that I realised we had scored! Wayne Clarke scored the only goal of the game and we came away with a good 1-0 away win. During the game someone in the Blues end shot a flare right into the middle of the main Leeds end and their fans scattered in panic, much to the amusement of the Blues contingent. The police came into our end in attempt to find the flare gun but to no avail, the Leeds fans, however, where now very annoyed and threatening to get us outside. It didn't help that the Blues fans just laughed and gestured back to them to have a go!

After the game the police kept us locked inside for a while in the hope that the Leeds fans would go home and we could safely be taken back to our train. Or was it for the Leeds fans safety? Anyway, before too long we were led out and back to the station where we were hoarded onto the special to make our trip home. However, various scuffles kept breaking out and the train would start up only to travel for a couple of minutes before the cord was pulled and it would stop again. It took over an hour just to get out of Leeds! I think a couple of windows were broken and everyone was pretty fed up by the time we finally got our journey under way properly! Once we were underway though, the Blues fans continued our celebrations and sang and chatted all the way back to Birmingham.

On the 22nd December, just two days before Christmas Blues had an away fixture, again in London, this time against Wimbledon. The girls and I were really looking forward to this one as it was just before Christmas and we could deck ourselves out in blue and white tinsel – well, I could. It also meant another new ground. At least the rain and snow held off and before long we were standing outside the ground drinking beers and watching people arrive and socialise as we were doing. I had blue and white tinsel round my neck and tied around my wrist and in my hair and was feeling very Christmassy! After consuming our beers we headed into the ground to have a look around and find a good position to watch the game. Blues were situated on the terrace behind the goal with quite a good view, in what was quite a small ground really, although not bad for a small, relatively new club like Wimbledon.

As I looked around for any wombles that may appear, I noticed loads of Blues fans coming in dressed in fancy dress. They had made a great effort and everyone looked brilliant! It was really amusing; I remember seeing a John McEnroe impersonator in complete tennis outfit, with wig, headband and tennis racket – on a cold December day! The outfits really were excellent and even the Blues players were impressed. The players duly rose to the occasion and David Geddis scored two goals to make our Christmas complete with a 2-1 win. The Bluenoses were dancing and singing and promptly sang 'jingle bells, jingle bells, jingle all the way, oh what fun it is to see City win away!'

So Christmas was very good and was made even better with a win over Grimsby Town at St. Andrews on Boxing Day. Then, on New Years day, complete with hangovers after our New Years Eve celebrations, I headed off to catch the football special to Sheffield for a match with Sheffield Utd. There were hundreds on the special and the police escort to the ground seemed to stretch for miles. Once inside there were thousands of Blues fans on the terrace behind the goal and it took ages in the queues outside to get in! I think this was the game when, by the time we got inside and onto the packed terrace Blues were already 2-0 down. However, as we took up our spot amongst the heaving mass of blue and white, Blues began the fightback and the goals started to fly in. It was so tightly packed that every time Blues scored the whole stand seemed to shake and we would be carried forward in the surge of celebrating Bluenoses and then carried back again to end up round about where we started. The match finished 4-3 to Blues and was an absolute thriller. Even with my New Year hangover, I was very happy on the march back to the station with the celebrating Blues fans. It is brilliant to win on opposing turf and Blues were doing that a lot this season and I was enjoying it immensely!

The FA Cup had again come round again and with it our hopes of a trip to the twin towers. Blues had been draw at home against Norwich City and I, personally was quite hopeful. Well, as hopeful as you can be, being a Bluenose. The tie proved to be a relay and after a 0-0 draw at St. Andrews I was planning my long trip to Norwich on the eve of my birthday. I had booked the day off work and we had arranged to go with Alan, Julie's uncle, and some of the lads. It was a long trip but quite nice as it was through the countryside and we chatted avidly amongst ourselves as Alan drove. We arrived in Norwich early and headed to a pub, not too far from the ground where Alan had been before and suggested as a good place for pre match beers.

Once again the game ended in a draw, this time 1-1 which meant that there would now be another replay at St. Andrews in a few days time. Anyway, as it was my birthday the next day, we headed back to the pub after the game for a few more drinks before heading back. This proved to be a big mistake for me, as I drank way too much, due to the fact that it was my birthday in a couple of hours. It was a very very long journey back, and Alan had to stop the car a couple of time for me to be sick! Never again. Alan had a bit of a joke with the barmaid before the game, telling her that if we drew and came back he would bring chocolates! When I got up the next day I was so ill I had to ring in sick for work! My mom was handing me birthday presents and I was way too sick to open them! Not one of my better birthdays I can tell you! My brother popped round to bring my birthday presents and said I looked green!

And so it was that three days later we again played Norwich and surprise surprise drew again! 1-1 and Blues lost the toss, which meant another bloody trip to Norwich for a fourth game against them! Alan again drove us and we went back to the same pub, where Alan presented the barmaid with a large bag of maltessers as promised! I was soon off the wagon and having a few pre match beers with the girls and the lads before heading into the ground. We had seat tickets this time but soon climbed the railings and onto the terrace to join the real fans singing and chanting in the away end.

The game was really frustrating as most of the decisions were going against us and we were beginning to feel victimised by the referee, to which we aimed our verbal opinion. I was chatting to one lad who said he was getting sick of the bad decisions by the man in black and if it continued then he was going to get on the pitch and tell him himself! I told him I would happily come on with him and contribute my opinion if needed! Then, unbelievably, the tosser gave a penalty to Norwich! The Blues fans were up in arms and the lad I had been talking to earlier was now scaling the fence and onto the pitch. In my drunken state of mind I decided I was going on too, but luckily for me I only got half way up the fence before Alan pulled me back. By this time the lad was now in the centre circle, finger pointed, giving the referee a piece of his mind. He was at it for ages before the police came on and escorted him from the pitch. I thought it was hilarious, as did the rest of the Bluenoses! However, it proved to be the turning point in the match and we were robbed 1-0 and our Wembley dreams were over for another year. We also had a very long trip home to look forward to as well! Time for more beers.

Blues soon got over it though, with a 1-0 away win at Huddersfield Town four days later before the cold weather really took hold, causing the postponement of the next two games. Then, following a surprise defeat at Shrewsbury town by 1-0, Blues were off to Oxford Utd for a top of the table clash. I was so looking forward to this and had heard other Bluenoses planning this trip for weeks beforehand. So, on the 2nd March the girls and I boarded the football special and were soon on our way to Oxford. The atmosphere on the train was brilliant with loads of singing, and after consuming our packed lunch and beers we were soon arriving in Oxford.

There seemed to be Blues fans everywhere and we sang all the way to Oxford Utd's small ground. Once inside the Blues fans were in carnival atmosphere, with chants of 'were gonna win the league' etc. Blues fans were situated on the open terraced end behind the goal, and had completely filled our end. I thought that Oxford's ground was small but quite quaint. I though one of the ends along the side with a small stand on its own in the middle was strange and different. There were quite a few Oxford fans present as well as they were on a good run and favourites for promotion. There were 11,584 inside the small ground but the atmosphere was great, just apt for the top of the table clash that it was.

It was a brilliant game and when Blues scored the away end erupted and I was swept off my feet and carried a few yards further on. Our end was swaying like an ocean and 'Keep Right On' was sung loud and proud. There was a gang of Blues lads dressed a bit like the blues brothers in our end. Before long Blues were 2-0 up and I was lifted off my feet again on a massive wave as we again celebrated. I was in heaven when the third goal went in and we came away 3-0 winners in such an important game. Once again it was great fun following the Blues and life was again enjoyable as a Bluenose. Blues goals were scored by David Geddis and Wayne Clarke, who got two of them. There was loads of trouble as we headed out of the ground and towards the train station as the Blues fans fought with the police and I saw a couple of police vans turned onto their sides. I don't know who was coming off worse to be honest but the Oxford fans were nowhere to be seen. I headed back towards the relative safety of the train home!

The next two games were at home and we were brought back down to earth by a 1-0 defeat against Oldham but picked ourselves up afterwards to beat Notes County by a 2-1 scoreline. Then it was a long trip in store for us up north to Carlisle as we prepared to take on Carlisle Utd. This would be another new ground for Julie and me and I was again travelling in Alan's car for the long trip. As was usual we sent off early and after a short refreshment break we arrive in Carlisle, parked the car and headed for a pub near to the ground. As it happened the pub we chose was right across the road from the ground and a nice little pub to have a few pre match beers.

I was in my usual excited pre match mood and chatted avidly, sang a few songs enjoyed a few beers and then we were off to join the other Bluenoses inside the ground. Due to the fact that it was such a long way and it was a night game there was not the usual massive Blues away following, but there was still quite a few, never the less, and they were in good voice. Carlisle's ground was really small and there were only 4,099 inside to watch the game. Probably good job really as Blues reminded us what it can be like being a Bluenose as we lost 2-1 with Clarke again scoring for us. It didn't give us much to cheer about on the trip home so we stopped off at local Chinese just before we left Carlisle for a takeaway for the journey. I must admit it was quite a memorable takeaway too, as it was the first time I had had a curry and rice in the same takeaway carton – neatly separated side by side! It was really tasty too, but that could have had something to do with the beers I had consumed earlier!

Just under four weeks later I had another long trip and another new ground to look forward to. This time we were off to Grimsby and we were taking the train. As Julie, Pam, Debbie and I boarded the train we were joined by more Bluenoses including Lee Pitman who sat with us and chatted avidly about 'Blues stuff'. It was a long journey and quite a few refreshments were downed as we all got to know each other and began having quite a laugh. As we arrived in Grimsby we all stayed together and before long we were all inside the ground cheering on the lads. The Blues fans sang their hearts out for the lads but once again we were disappointed and the game ended in 1-0 defeat. However, we were still in the mood to enjoy ourselves, so as we headed back to the station we continued to sing and celebrated our victory of outsinging the home supporters.

Once back on the train we were still in party mood, but as our train got under way out of Grimsby at a slow speed, we were ambushed by Grimsby fans who had decided to see us off by throwing bricks at the train. Big mistake picking on a train full of Bluenoses and the train was brought to an immediate standstill by the pulling of the emergency chain by a few of the Bluenoses. The Blues fans streamed off and chased the, by now petrified Grimsby Town fans across a field and over a fence. It was quite funny to see really as the Grimsby fans had quite clearly not been expecting this and had got the fright of their lives! Before long, the Blues fans returned the train and we got away again, only to be ambushed again a few minutes along the track. Of course, the Blues fans carried out a repeat of earlier and again chased the remaining few Grimsby fans across more fields and this time they well and truly got the message. However, the train driver was by now fed up and was seen sitting on the embankment with his head in his hands. He told Blues fans that this happened regularly after the games but the Blues fans were the first ones to stop the train and give chase! After much persuasion and promises not to pull the cord again, the driver returned to his cab and the train got underway again. That had been fun. Best part of the trip really!

As boredom set in on the long journey back, we began thinking of ways to enjoy ourselves. With this in mind we decided to see how many people we could get in the tiny British rail train toilet. I think we managed about nine but we were really squeezed in with people standing on the toilet etc. After laughing amongst ourselves as we ran out of air, we decided to wait until someone outside went passed and then file out one after the other. It was really funny to see their shocked face when nine of us calmly filed out of the small toilet. I did say we were bored at this point! We were in very good spirits when we got back so we headed into Boogies in the town centre for a couple of drinks before heading home after a very entertaining day. Who said following Blues wasn't fun eh!

Blues soon got over our disappointment at Grimsby and the promotion wagon was underway again with a good win over Sheffield Utd 4-1 at home, and then we were off down south to take on Portsmouth at Fratton Park. Once again we decided to travel by train and it was the same group of us that embarked on the three-hour train journey south. It was another entertaining trip as we all chatted and laughed together, clad in our Blues colours. I personally was full of optimism this season and was enjoying the promotion battle. I don't know which is more nerve wracking to be honest, a relegation battle or a promotion battle! Although I know which I prefer and it's not the former!

Once we arrived at the ground we were let into the away end which at this time was open terracing behind the goal. As everyone who has ever been to Fratton Park will know, there is no roof on the away end and most times the away fans end up getting soaking wet and it always seems to pour with rain when Blues visit. On this occasion however, it was a nice day and there were quite a few Bluenoses that had made the long trip. It was certainly made worthwhile when David Geddis, our new blonde striker put us ahead. Brilliant! As the second goal by Geddis went in to make it 2-0, I turned around to celebrate with the girls only to be caught in a surge forward – or for me –backwards! I was pinned against a crash barrier and I was very fortunate not to break my bloody back! I will never be doing that again I can tell you! Our day was complete when Geddis got his hat trick – scoring the third goal right in front of us celebrating Bluenoses! The Blues fans went wild and we celebrated for ages, singing the jingle bells song again – 'oh what fun it is to see City win away!' We have been singing it a lot this season. So, after a fantastic 3-0 away win at Portsmouth we headed back to Birmingham very happy indeed.

April was a brilliant month, Blues won the next three games against Crystal Palace 3-0 at home, Charlton 2-1 also at home and then Barnsley 1-0 away to set up a potential promotion clincher at home against Cardiff City. And so on a lovely sunny day in May, St Andrews was buzzing with excitement and tension as Blues prepared to do battle with Cardiff. I was really excited taking my place on the Kop and I could feel the atmosphere around me, adding to my excitement. I had butterflies in stomach and although I am always optimistic, I couldn't help worry that Blues may somehow drag it out to the last day of the season against Leeds Utd. But, when Blues ran out onto pitch to a crescendo of noise and Blue and White scarves being waved in the air, my thoughts were only positive and I was sure we could do it. The game got underway and the Kop swayed like an ocean and the singing made my hairs stand on end at times, it was so loud. The Blues team rose to the occasion and played their hearts out and once we had taken the lead we were unbeatable. When the second goal went it the fans went wild and Keep Right On rang out around all four sides of the ground. When the whistle sounded and we were promoted the ground erupted and fans from all sides ran onto the pitch to celebrate with the lads. I was unbelievably happy – Blues were back where we belonged, back in the First Division again! I don't think I was the only Bluenose who celebrated late into the evening and for most of the next week.

A few days later we travelled the long distance to Middlesborough and although it was only a 0-0 draw, we Bluenoses continued our celebrations, singing 'going up, going up, going up!' to the tune of 'here we go'. It was brilliant!

On the last day of the season Blues were playing Leeds Utd at St Andrews and although we were already promoted, it was Leeds last chance to sneak in for the third promotion place and was therefore a massive match for them. As we were out to celebrate our promotion and the Leeds fans were hoping for promotion also, St. Andrews was packed and the atmosphere was electric. There was a lot of hostility between the Blues fans and the Leeds fans and this had already been billed as a potential battle of the fans. The game got underway but as it proceeded the tension between the fans was rising and once Blues took the lead the Leeds fans became extremely agitated and began tearing apart the refreshment stall at the back of their terraced end on the Tilton. If the result stayed the same Leeds would miss out and their fans clearly did not like this. Some Leeds fans began scaling the fencing and came onto the pitch and the game had to be held up as police with riot gear and horses came onto the pitch to force the fans off the pitch to enable the game to restart.

The game got underway again and when the final whistle blew, Blues had beaten Leeds by 1-0 thereby ending any hope they had of promotion, and of course we were promoted back to the First Division. It was complete mayhem as the Leeds fans invaded the pitch and came running across towards the Blues fans. The Blues fans were anticipating this and were annoyed about the vandalism to our refreshment stand and they had also scaled all the fences and were now running at the Leeds fans in great numbers with the police caught in the middle. It was a hell of a battle between Blues fans and the police as they tried to get at the now retreating Leeds fans. Some fans had ripped out seats and these were being used as weapons or thrown across the police line at the Leeds fans. It was a really terrible sight and as the Leeds fans retreated and were penned back in their end a wall collapsed onto the fans outside the ground and a young boy was killed. No one knew of the horror at the time but everyone was in shock afterwards once the battle was bought under control. There was more devastating news on the way home when we learned of the other disaster in Bradford. This was far worse than our disaster as we heard how one of the wooden stands at Bradford's ground had caught fire during their game and had claimed the lives of many people. It was a very very sad day for football, and one I will never forget.

Birmingham City finished in second place and gained promotion, whilst Manchester City gained the third and last promotion place and Oxford Utd were crowned champions. We were back.

CHAPTER ELEVEN – Arrested at Chelsea

Following the Bradford disaster Aston Villa had organised a charity match against varies all stars with the proceedings going towards the Bradford disaster fund. Villa ladies were invited to play a five a side game against a ladies team from the newspaper, the Express and Star, before the game. I was quite looking forward to playing in this match, as it would be my first game in front of a crowd and at a big ground – even if it was the vile! There would be some big stars there too, including George Best, so I was quite hopeful of meeting them. I was also quite keen to be picked to play, as I always liked playing and hated being sub. Anyway, it was a nice sunny day and 5,000 people turned up at Villa Park to watch the game – the main game of course!

I was picked to play and the five a side nets were set up on the pitch for our game. Of course the Express and Star Ladies were more like models and not very good at football to be honest, but at least it was a game. Whilst our game got under way the stars of the game were having a kick about on the rest of the pitch that wasn't being used for our game. It was really exciting playing in front of so many people and it felt really weird when I slid in for a cross and put the ball just wide of the post to gasps of 'ooooh' from the crowd supporting us. It sounded really loud and until then I had forgotten that there was a crowd watching us.

It was great when we scored too, as the crowd cheered and we easily beat the Express and Star Ladies and although I cant remember the score that day it was by quite a few goals with none conceded. I had thought the lads would have supported the 'models' but they supported us as we were representing the Villa.

At one point the ball went out of play for a throw in and flew across the pitch towards the all star team that was having a kick about. I was over the moon when George Best passed the ball back to me for me to take the throw in! Not many people can claim that George Best passed the ball to them!

I had a nice summer and I was still working in the same job, which was not exactly exciting but provided a living. As the new season approached I went to St. Andrews for the pre season friendly against Derby County and I was surprised to see myself looking back at me from the front cover of the programme. The photo was of the crowd waiting outside of the town hall when the team made an appearance on the balcony for the civic reception to celebrate promotion back to the first division. And right at the front leaning over the crash barrier were Julie and I, with me proudly waving a Blues flag! It is funny looking back at that programme now as I looked so young, but I guess I was really! It was brilliant!

The new season got under way with a home game against West Ham which Blues won 1-0 with a goal by Robert Hopkins in front of a crowd of 11,164. Attendances were becoming a disappointment at Blues around this time, especially as we were back in the first division. And after an away defeat at Watford 3-0, the girls and I were planning a trip to Chelsea for the next match. Debbie had told her mom that she was going shopping in town as her mom would not have let her go to a match that was so high profile due to the reputation of Chelsea and Blues fans off the pitch. Both had a reputation of violence and it was expected that there would indeed be trouble before and after this game in the capital.

Julie, Debbie and I met at New Street Station in order to get a train to London for the game. However, we discovered that we were unable to get a train that would get us there in time for the match. As you can imagine we were becoming extremely stressed! There were some other guys that we knew including Lee and they were also trying to get to the game and as we chatted to them, one of them said he would go and hire a van and come back, pick us up and drive to London. This was considered a good idea and we waited patiently for him to come back. We knew most, but not all of the lads, and before long he was back with a van and eleven of us got in and we headed off to London.

We were in good spirits and had a couple of beers on the way but we were in for a shock when we arrived in London. As we made our way across London towards Chelsea, police cars and vans arrived from everywhere and we were pulled aside like something out of the Sweeney! We were all dragged out of the back of the van, searched and put into police vans with no explanation as to what we were supposed to have done! They took us to Fulham Broadway police station where we were again searched. I asked one policeman what we were supposed to have done and what we were being held for and was quite shocked when he told me it was suspicion of carrying explosives! What did they think we were going to do? Blow up Stamford Bridge? It was ridiculous and probably just a ploy to keep us from the match.

All eleven of us were then put into tiny cells in a large police lorry in the grounds of the police station where we were then kept for the duration of the game. To this day I have never been inside Stamford Bridge, this was the closest that I got. Inside the cells the lads were still having a laugh and singing, the favourite being the laurel and hardy theme tune that was always sang to take the piss out of the police, and also several 'pig noises'. We were talking to each other through the bars of the cells and the lad opposite me was taking the mickey and telling me to stand up when I already was! I'm not that small but I guess it was funny. Julie was really upset because it was the first match she had have missed in years and Debbie was upset about her mom finding out that she was in London, as the police had taken our addresses and told us they were sending someone around our houses!

One of the policemen informed us that we were losing 2-0 and sounded quite pleased about it. We just gave him some stick back and carried on singing and chatting and taking the piss out of the police. After the game we were released and ordered to get into our van and drive out of London. We were told that if we so much as stopped we would all spend the night behind bars. Nice! So, after such friendly hospitality we headed off down the road and stopped at the chip shop. After acquiring chips, loaf of bread and a tub of butter we got back in the van and headed off out of London. As we approached a bus stop full of people, the passenger window was rolled down and the now redundant tub of butter was lobbed out towards the bus stop. It was quite funny seeing everyone duck. It didn't hit anyone so no harm was done but it did give us a few giggles.

We stopped at some shops and I took the opportunity to call home to assess the damage. I thought that maybe the police had just been winding us up and hadn't sent anyone round to our homes. When I spoke to my mom I calmly said 'everything okay?' my mom answered 'yes, you've been arrested haven't you?' At least my mom was very calm about it, although I dreaded facing my dad. Apparently they had turned up on the doorstep when my mom and dad were at work and my brother Neil had answered the door. When they asked if I lived there and that I was being held in Fulham, Neil had said 'what's she done now?' I said afterwards 'what did you think I would have done?' and he said probably invaded the pitch or something.

When I told my dad, he was quite supportive, as he understood that we had just been victimised and said I should get a lawyer onto it. I explained that if I did, the London police would just pick on me on every time I returned there to watch a game, so he relented in the end. Debbie had to go home and face her mom though, who thought that she was in town shopping! Julie went with her for support as they lived on the same side of town. Lee wrote several letters and tried in vain get something done about the injustice for months afterwards but to no avail. I just put it down to experience.

It turned out that one of the lads that got into the van with us had previously been in trouble with the police for assaulting a police office. One of the police officers at New Street Station had recognised him and had radioed ahead to London giving them the plate numbers of our van. None of us in the van had known this guy either! What a day.

Blues did quite well over the next couple of months winning four games, losing once – away to Everton and a home draw against our rivals Aston Villa at St. Andrews 0-0. Then it was time for the League cup again and Blues had been drawn against Bristol Rovers with the first leg away in Bristol. I had never been to Bristol Rovers ground but it didn't look like I would be able to go as it was a night match and there was no way we could get back after the game if we took the train.

To cheer us up and take our mind of the game that day, Julie and I decided to go to Northfield and have a wander around the shops. As we were about to wander into Woolworth's for a browse we saw a minibus full of Blues fans pull up outside. One of the lads headed for the nearby cashpoint and another headed into Woolworth's. I was gutted that we were going to miss the match so I decided to ask the lads if they were going to the game and if there was room for two more! To Julie's delight and mine they said yes and told us to jump in. This was brilliant and Julie and I jumped in the back of the minibus and after introductions all round we were soon chatting away with the lads. The driver was a lad called Steve Woolley, who is now going out with my sister and it was only during one of our chats about Blues years later, when I was talking about going to Bristol in the minibus that I found out Steve was the driver!

One of the lads had a massive ghetto Blaster and he had just been to Woolworth's in order to obtain batteries for it as he intended to take it onto the terraces at Bristol. We drank beers and chatted and before long we were in Bristol and headed towards the ground. The lads had decided that they were going to stay overnight after the game so that left us stuck in Bristol with no lift home but I wasn't too worried at this point as I was already looking forward to the game. There were quite a few Bluenoses on the away terrace and Julie and I soon got chatting to them and joined the singing. I saw one of the lads I had come to know at the away games called Brendan Anderson and as luck would have it he had driven down on his own and lived in Bartley Green, which is near where I live. He said he would be happy to take us back after the game, so with that cleared up I joined in the singing with the background music of the massive ghetto Blaster and looked forward to the game.

Bristol Rovers were only in the old third division at the time therefore there were only 4,332 inside the ground but we were treated to a good game of football. Goals from Robert Hopkins, Andy Kennedy and an own goal gave Blues a 3-2 away leg win and we celebrated all the way home in Brendan's car. It had been a surprise trip for Julie and I as we had thought we wouldn't be able to get to the game so both of us were thrilled that we had been to the match and come away with a win. A week later when the return leg came around Blues again beat Bristol Rovers, this time 2-1 and we were through to the next round and we were rewarded with draw against Southampton.

However, that was our last win for some time as Blues went on a four month run without a win including being knocked out of the cup away at Southampton 3-0 after a home draw. In December Blues were playing Watford at St. Andrews and were 1-0 ahead with twenty-five minutes remaining when there was a bomb scare. Everyone had to leave the ground immediately and when we returned and the players returned to the pitch we went on to lose 2-1! Everyone was convinced this bad run was due to the gypsy curse and loads of 'remedies' were attempted including the players wearing red soles on their boots when they played Arsenal – which finished 0-0. Nothing seemed to be working though and Blues hit rock bottom when we were knocked out of the FA Cup at home to a non-league team called Altrincham. To add injury to insult it was our player Robert Hopkins who scored the winning goal – an own goal for them. I was so disgusted that when I got home from drowning my sorrows I took off my scarf and my Blues gloves, dropped them on the floor in the middle of the living room, looked at them in disgust and stomped off to bed, much to my mom's amazement! How much worse could things get?

There was a really exciting game away at Coventry City though, which resulted in a 4-4 draw! And then our season was brightened with a trip to Vile Park and a fantastic 3-0 away win. The Blue half of town were in heaven again and we danced and sang for hours afterwards.

That was to be the last win of an awful season for Blues as we then drew with Manchester Utd before losing the last seven games! It was a shocking end to the season, which began with so much hope, and Blues were relegated back to the second division in 21s place along with Ipswich Town and neighbours West Brom. Liverpool won the championship and Everton finished runners up. Not a good season and with life in the second tier to look forward to next season. Oh well, ever the optimist I was hopeful of another promotion winning season to come.

CHAPTER TWELVE – Birmingham City Ladies

It was in 1986 that I left Aston Villa Ladies and moved up in the world by signing for Birmingham City Ladies. I was over the moon to be joining Blues ladies as they shared their name and colours with the team I loved. It was a great honour for me to wear the Blue shirt of Birmingham City Ladies. Blues ladies were in a different league than the one I had been playing in with Villa and it was by far a better and harder league. As Blues ladies were a top team, they had two teams playing in both first and second tiers. The first team was fantastic and it was always between Birmingham City Ladies and Solihull Ladies that the championship trophy went to at the end of each season.

In my last season at Villa I had won the 'most improved player of the season' trophy, but at Blues it was always going to be much harder to get into the team. The first team was full of fantastic players and they won many trophies together. So it was the second team that I played in when I started and they were a great bunch of girls. I became good friends with many of the first team as well, and the spirit at the club was brilliant. I loved my time at Blues and I loved my time on the pitch and partying with the girls off the pitch. Like our counter parts at Blues, we played hard and partied hard and had a great team spirit.

When I started at Blues there were two other girls called Debbie and so I was to get a nickname like a lot of the other girls in the team. Mine was to be 'Hoppy' due to the fact that the rest of the team thought I played a lot like Robert Hopkins at the Blues. I guess I was a lot like him as I was often to be seen running down the wing or as an out and out centre forward and was always diving in to score goals. My number was usually number 11 also, just like our Blues hero. This nickname was to stick with my throughout my time at Blues and in fact it was still used when I went out drinking with the girls. There are probably a lot of people from this time who only know me as 'Hoppy'. I think of my time at Blues ladies as being my wild days due to the fact that we partied a lot and had a really wild time.

I remember my first goal for Blues, which was a bit of a tap in really, and I don't remember who it was against but I remember celebrating like it was the greatest goal ever! It was a fantastic feeling, scoring for the Blues and I still miss playing football even now. The Blues girls were great and we would mob each other when we scored and run around like lunatics – it was great. I remember a lot of my goals, especially a couple that I curled into the top corner!

One game that stands out in my memory was when the first team was drawn against the second team in the FA Cup. This was an extremely unusual event as there are many teams drawn in the early rounds of the Cup. As you can imagine the FA Cup was the biggest prize of them all as it involved all the English teams and only the top teams ever got to the finals. Our first team usually did very well though and would get quite far in the competition so you could imagine our shock at drawing each other. I was playing in the second team at the time and due to the fact that the first team was so good we knew we would get a thrashing. Anyway, I was looking forward the game and didn't intend to give in easily.

I was playing centre forward for this game as usual and I kicked off to a team mate who then lofted it up the wing to one of our players who was now running up the wing. As she crossed the ball into the penalty area our left winger met the ball on the volley and it crashed against the post and rebounded towards me as I was running across goal. I tried a cheeky flick with the side of my right boot and the ball flew into net! 1-0 to the second team and I was mobbed by our girls and the first team looked on shocked! Some of them laughed, as they couldn't believe it and our manager shouted at them – 'its not bloody funny!' This made the rest of us laugh then. It was a fantastic moment, even if we did go on to lose about 8-1. At least we had scored and had the satisfaction of being 1-0 up in the first minute against the odds. I can still remember the feeling as everyone dived on me in fits of laughter. It was brilliant!

At the end of the season at the awards ceremony I came away with the top goalscorer trophy for the second team. I was quite proud of that really. Top goalscorer for Blues – what more could I want. We were due to play in a big tournament in Clacton that year against some of the countries top teams, which included all the international players too. It was a great trip away and I enjoyed it immensely, even if most of it was a drunken blur. One of our games was against Millwall ladies who had 9 England internationals playing. Needless to say I did not get much service to me up front against them but we were quite proud that we only lost 2-0 to them. All the girls raised their game and we played really well. I was disappointed not to score though, but then I was always disappointed if I didn't score.

It was good fun meeting up with the other teams off the pitch also and there were lots of parties. It was a really memorable trip and I had a lot of fun. My best friend was a girl nicknamed 'Ballie' and she was loads of fun and together we pulled many tricks on unsuspecting teammates. The whole event was a ball and we all returned much the worse for wear, knackered and without a trophy.

They were fabulous times at Blues ladies though and the only thing I would have changed is that I would have stayed much longer than I did. In fact the only reason that I left was that I moved to Liverpool to live. I really loved my football, although I hated the training. I would always enjoy the practice match after the training itself but I always found the training a chore. I loved pulling on the Blue shirt of Birmingham and wore it with pride. Unfortunatly I picked up a nasty injury whilst playing against my old team Aston Villa that I never really recovered from which happened when I was tackled from behind by an old Villa team mate that twisted my near and tore my cartilage. I remember the pain as I lay on the ground, I thought my knee was broken in some way as the pain was that severe. Anyone who saw me play knows that I always get up from a tackle and the watching first team girls knew it was bad and were calling for someone to put the ball out. When they did put the ball out of play my best mate Ballie came running on to see what I had done and the referee was the first to my aide and began rubbing my knee vigorously. This hurt even more to be honest but I guess he knew what he was doing as it began to ease a bit. I was carried off and tried to get up again as I wanted to get back on but my knee kept collapsing. I didn't want to go to hospital and I kept saying it was okay, but over the following weeks my knee kept collapsing and I often couldn't put any weight on it. It was only later when I had to have a MRI that I learned of the extent of the damage and that I had torn the cartilage. I didn't want surgery so I just rested it. Even now I have trouble with it and get severe pain or the knee just collapses again. No doubt I will have to have surgery at some point but I'm avoiding it as long as I can!

CHAPTER THIRTEEN – Hillsborough

The 1986 to 1987 season passed rather unremarkably to be honest. My hope of promotion at the first attempt was dashed and Birmingham finished in nineteenth position in division two. There were some good results and some bad results but for me the year seemed to be one of playing football for Birmingham City Ladies and partying with the girls quite a lot. I remember going out after the FA Cup final of 1987 whereby Coventry City had beaten Tottenham Hotspur 3-2 at Wembley and I had had several bets with my friends that Coventry would win. Everyone else had gone for the favourites Tottenham and when I arrived in the pub there were several drinks lined up on the table waiting for me! In the second division Derby County were champions and were promoted with Portsmouth. Sunderland, Grimsby Town and Brighton were relegated. Blues escaped by one place finishing in 19th position and lost our last game of the season at St. Andrews 2-0 against Shrewsbury Town. I sincerely hoped that next season would be better and that this was not the start of a decline.

Blues started the 1987 –1988 season well with a 2-0 home win against Stoke City and a 2-2 away draw in the first leg of the first round on the league cup against Mansfield Town. Then it was off to Villa Park for the local derby against Aston Villa. I was really looking forward to this game as always and I now had a couple of mates who were Villa fans so we planned to go to the game together although to separate ends of the ground! We all met up in town and decided to head to Villa's main pub, the Holte, just outside the home end of the ground. Most of us were Bluenoses and only two were Villa fans so we zipped up our jackets to cover our colours following pleading from our Villa mates and headed into the pub.

Once a few drinks were consumed I suggested to my Villa mates that I undo my jacket as I was getting hot, much to their horror. This edged my· mate Deb on, and she said that she would chalk her nose blue from the pool table nearby if I would unzip my jacket. Despite the now growing panic from my mates, I agreed and Deb chalked her nose and I unzipped my jacket. It didn't take long for us to be noticed but just as a few newspapers were being thrown at us as we stood proudly on the seats arms aloft, a load of Blues fans arrived and all hell seemed to break loose. Most fans spilled outside and it wasn't long before the police arrived and we had lost sight of some of our mates in the mayhem. Two of my Bluenose mates and I headed towards the Witton terraces and the Blues end.

It was buzzing inside on the terraces amongst the away support and having consumed quite a few drinks beforehand, my friends and I were in a great mood. Blues were massive underdogs for this game but the Blues end was packed solid. Scarves were being waved and 'shit on the villa' rang out loudly as well as our anthem 'Keep Right On'. It was a brilliant atmosphere and it was a fantastic shock when Ian Handysides belted the ball into the net right in front of us to put Blues in the lead. Our end erupted and I was quite literally swept off my feet and I ended up on the floor, as did my mate. I felt a strong pair of hands on my waist and I was swept back to my feet in an instant and carried on my celebrations. I got some lads to help me onto the crash barrier and for a little while I balanced there holding onto someone's hand for support and proudly waving my Blues colours. It was brilliant, and the Blues fans were in heaven.

Then, unbelievably right in front of us, Tony Rees smashed the ball into net for Blues second goal – 2-0! Once again the Blues end erupted and I found myself on the floor once again before the same pair of hands found my waist and lifted my to my feet again. I was so happy and we celebrated like mad things, everyone hugging everyone else, including people we didn't even know. It was at times like these when being on the terracing felt fantastic and to this day I wish they would bring back a terraced area as it would bring back the atmosphere that is sadly missing these days. And so it was 2-0 at half time and we sang our hearts out. The score remained the same and when the final whistle went the Blues end went wild before heading back into town for a night of wild celebration. The town was Blue and White!

The remainder of the season seemed to pass by and once again there were good games and bad games and Blues finished once again in 19th place, this time escaping relegation by two places as it was now 21st, 22nd and 23rd that were relegated due to the restructuring of the leagues. Millwall were crowned champions and were promoted with Aston Villa and Middlesbrough with Sheffield Utd, Reading and Huddersfield Town being relegated to the third division. Wimbledon won the FA Cup beating Liverpool 1-0 in the final and causing an upset.

It was in 1988 that I decided to leave my job that I had being doing for almost ten years as I wanted to move on and do something else, although I wasn't sure what I wanted to do at this point. As I had friends from Liverpool I took the decision to move to Liverpool for a change. I moved in with a friend and went about looking for work. I had never been out of work before and haven't since and so after a couple of months I was bored to death and desperate to get back to work. Also, I would need the money to enable me to get to the Blues games and get home to see my family. My sister Annette used to love coming up to Liverpool to stay with me and I would take her out and about around Liverpool. After three months I got a job in an office in the city centre where I would remain for six months before I got another job in the general office at Mill Road Maternity Hospital. I loved working in the hospital and I was feeling much happier in myself.

Hence I couldn't get to as many games as I would have liked in the 1988-1989 season but I was still in Birmingham for the league cup-tie against archrivals Villa at St. Andrews. I had been telling my mate Angela from Liverpool about how different our local derbies were and I took her to this game to prove my point. I don't think she could believe how hostile it was and when a Blues fan climbed the fence and ran towards the villa goalkeeper before being tackled by a steward, she was amazed. The atmosphere was amazing as always and at the end of the game which Blues lost 2-0, riot police surrounded the pitch and helicopters hovered over head. When we came out of the match the villa fans were trying to make themselves invisible but here and there they would be spotted and fights would break out. It was incredibly tense and my mate definately spotted the difference between Birmingham and Liverpool Derbies.

The following season 1988 to 1989 was soon upon me and I again took my mate from Liverpool to a match with me (even though she was a Liverpool supporter) only this time it was away at Oldham which is really easy to get to from Liverpool. We headed to Oldham on the train and my mate got to experience how fantastic Blues away support is. Unfortunately Blues lost 4-0 but I bumped into my mate Julie who I hadn't seen for a while and also my friend Alan. After the match Alan took us to a nearby sports club for a drink afterwards. One thing about Alan is that he always knows a good boozer to go to both before and after matches wherever Blues are playing. The club that we went to this time was a member's only club but somehow Alan managed to get us all in and we had a few drinks and some banter with the locals for a little while after the game. It was really good fun despite the result.

In April 1989 one of my friends Paula had managed to get three tickets for the semi final at Hillsborough for the FA Cup semi final between Liverpool and Nottingham Forest. The tickets were for the Liverpool end on the Leppins Lane terraces. I had told my mom I was going but then the night before the game Paula, Angela and I went out for a couple of drinks and Paula said she had a funny feeling about the game and now didn't want to go. Angela said that if she had a bad feeling then she wasn't going either. I still quite fancied a semi final trip so said that I would go on my own then. However, the next morning with my hangover in full force and both of my mates not going to the game I decided that I wouldn't bother either. So you can imagine the horror with which I witnessed the events that unfolded at Hillsborough that fateful day when I turned on the TV to watch the game.

I was devastated watching people being pulled from the Liverpool terraces onto the pitch to escape the crush and watching people dying in front of us. I tried to call my mom to tell her that I had not gone in case she had remembered that I was supposed to be going but couldn't get through as the line was engaged. My mom and dad both worked in neighbouring shops and my dad had seen the events on the TV but not being a football fan he had not thought it was Liverpool. When he went in to tell my mom that fans had died at the semi final my mom knew I was there and was shocked. My dad said it wasn't Liverpool, that it was Nottingham Forest and Sheffield but my mom knew that it was and sent him back to find out what was happening and if there was an emergency number. My dad soon returned with the emergency number and the news that it was in fact Liverpool and that it was the Liverpool end where the disaster was taking place. Therefore my mom was upset and was busy trying to get through to the emergency line while I was trying to get through to her. It took quite a while for me to be able to reassure her that I was safe having eventually managed to get hold of my brother and ask him to go round and let mom know I was safe. All of my family were affected by this, thinking that I was there, even my Nan had sat crying while she watched in on her TV thinking I was there. Blues were playing at nearby Barnsley that day and a request for any doctors or nurses that may have been at the match was made over the tannoy.

A few days later all my family came up to visit me and they were all overcome by the sadness in Liverpool and the closeness of the community. Everyone I knew had lost someone at Hillsborough and I still find in difficult to think about that day or see it on TV, as I am sure is anyone at all connected to events on that awful day.

The season turned out to be awful with quite a few bad results and Blues finished in 23rd place and we were relegated to the third division for the first time in our history. It was absolutely devastating and probably our lowest point ever. I was heartbroken once again and could not imagine life in the third tier. Chelsea were crowned champions of the second division and were promoted with Manchester City and Crystal Palace. Shrewsbury Town and neighbours Walsall were relegated along with Birmingham City. Liverpool won the FA Cup beating Everton in the final 3-2 and Nottingham Forest beat Luton Town 3-1 to win the League Cup. It was definitely a season I wanted to forget. Because of the violence at some of the Blues games a ban on was put on our travelling support for the season 1989 – 1990. Also a terrace membership scheme was introduced at St. Andrews. Things were not good. The ban was lifted for the away trip to Bolton on 24th February and Blues were on probation for the rest of the season.

Of course when the 1989 to 1990 season began I was full of hope and thought that we would easily win promotion back to the second division at the first attempt. By the end of September Blues were third and I was still full of hope following a 2-0 home win over neighbours Walsall.

In December things began to get better with a 2-0 home win against Colchester Utd in the FA Cup, a 1-0 win against Hereford Utd in the Leyland Daf Cup and a home win in the league against Preston 3-1 and Blues were up to seventh in the league.

Then on the 14th December 1989 my nephew Stephen was born in Birmingham to my sister in law Sue and my brother Neil. I was so happy and so looked forward to seeing him. Stephen was a gorgeous baby, blonde and a Bluenose in the making, although as it turns out Stephen was born a Bluenose like myself. Neil and Sue bought him up to Liverpool to visit me when he was a few months old and he was such a happy baby, he would sit in his baby seat and dance to the music.

In January 1990 Blues drew Oldham Athletic in the third round of the FA Cup and following a 1-1 draw at St. Andrews, the replay was due to take place at Oldham's ground on the 10th of January.

It was an evening game and I asked Angela if she fancied coming too. Angela has some relatives in Oldham, so we decided to head over there early to visit her family. They were really nice people and one of the lads was an Oldham fan and he was also going to the game. So, after being fed we headed to the pub with him for a few beers before the game. It was a really cold night and I remember thinking what a really cold place Oldham is once we were inside the ground. The game resulted in a disappointing 1-0 defeat for Blues but the Bluenoses had been in good numbers and good voice and 'Keep Right On' was heard loud and proud as usual. Once the game was over Angela and I headed for the local train station and I remember thinking I would die of the cold while we were waiting for the train to take us back to Liverpool.

After our cup dream was over for another year Blues stayed mid-table for the rest of the season which ended with a 1-0 home defeat by Reading and we finished the season in seventh position – not the immediate return to division two that I had hoped for. Bristol Rovers were crowned champions of the third division and their neighbours Bristol City along with Nott's County were promoted with them to the second division. Cardiff City, Northampton Town, Blackpool and our neighbours Walsall were all relegated to the fourth division. Manchester Utd won the FA Cup 3-2 against Crystal Palace following a replay and Nottingham Forest again won the League Cup beating Oldham 1-0 in the final.

It was in April of 1990 that I was again given tickets for a FA Cup semi final, this time it was to see Liverpool take on Crystal Palace at Villa Park in Birmingham. I decided to take my sister with me this time and as two of our tickets were for the Liverpool section on the Holte End and one was for the Liverpool section on the Witton End, Annette and myself took the tickets for the Holte End and Angela would be in the Witton End. The atmosphere was quite good, but of course not as good as at a Blues game. The game went into extra time, which was a bit of a blow, as this would mean the pubs would be closing once we got out after the game. It was a really good game but it ended with Crystal Palace winning 4-3 and progressing to the final against Manchester Utd. However, as we headed out it seemed that not much had been learned from Hillsborough the previous year, as the gates remained locked thereby resulting in those at the front being crushed as the people at the back were not aware that the gates remained closed. I tried to take the weight off my sister by putting my arms either side of her against a crash barrier and taking the weight on my back. It was awful and someone shouted 'for fucks sake open the gates, haven't you learned anything from Hillsborough!' I was petrified that we would die in the crush and felt awfully guilty for having bought Annette to the game. All I could think was that my mom would kill me, but then someone opened the gate and we managed to get out, all be it a bit the worse for wear. At last we were safe and we soon met up with Angela and told her what had happened before heading home to my moms. What a day!

CHAPTER FOURTEEN – Leyland Daf Trophy Winners

I was once again filled with optimism at the beginning of the 1990 to 1991 season as I always am at the start of any new season. I hoped against hope that we would win promotion back to the second division at the end of this season.

Blues started the season well with four wins in the first four league games. However, Bournemouth knocked Blues out of the League Cup in the early rounds. Then Blues went on a run of drawn games.

In September I travelled the few miles from Liverpool to Wigan for the match. I remember thinking what a strange place Wigan was as I noticed bouncers in suits outside all the bars early in the day and it was impossible to get in to any of them for a pre match drink. Angela and I headed for Wigan's ground (their old ground) and noticed that a social club was attached to the ground. So, I put on my best scouse accent to get inside only to find, when we did get in that it was full of Bluenoses in full voice singing 'Keep Right On'. This was brilliant and I immediately recognised several people I knew, including Alan and Lee Pitman. It was great to catch up with everyone again and Lee was amazed to hear the scouse accent that I seemed to have picked up during my time in Liverpool. Then it was inside the stadium and into the seats to watch the game. The ground was really small with terraces behind both goals, which resembled grass banks to be honest, and a small stand at each side. There were only 3,904 people inside and the game ended in a 1-1 draw with Paul Tait scoring the Birmingham goal.

When we were due to play Crewe away Blues were on their seventh successive draw. I headed down to Crewe from Liverpool and was delighted to meet up with Julie again. Julie informed me that she had bumped into our old friend Debbie with whom we had travelled to away games with in the 1980's and that she was now living in Crewe and was seeing a Crewe fan. It was a tiny ground but it had character and there were many Blues fans squeezed into the tiny away end. The Bluenoses sang throughout the game but were unable to inspire our heroes and the game finished in another draw, this time 1-1. We were convinced that someone had told the Blues team that if they drew eight games in a row then they would win the pools!

In November Blues began our adventure in the Leyland Daf Cup, which is a fairly new competition for the lower two leagues only and the final is held at Wembley Stadium. The journey began at the home of our near neighbours Walsall and Blues began with a 1-0 away win. This was followed with a win over Cheltenham Town at St. Andrews 1-0 in the FA Cup and then it was a good home win over Lincoln City 2-0 in the Leyland Daf Cup. Unfortunately Brentford then knocked Blues out of the FA Cup and so our last hope of a Cup would be the Leyland Daf Trophy.

In February Blues had been drawn at home in the quarter final of the Leyland Daf Cup against Swansea City and they were soon dispatched 4-2 after extra time. I had travelled down to Birmingham for this game and was proud to be amongst the 3,555 people inside St. Andrews that night. I would dearly love Blues to get to Wembley.

At the beginning of the year I had decided that I wanted to train to become a midwife as I really enjoyed working in the hospital but felt I would be better suited away from office work and the role of the midwife appealed to me. I applied for a place on the training programme and although there were many applicants I was chosen as one of the fifteen lucky people for this years course that was due to start in March 1991. I was so happy about this and the course was to take three years and then I would be a qualified midwife. Hopefully, some of my training would take place in Mill Road Maternity Hospital in which I already worked in the general office with Roy and Anne. Because I was already working in the NHS I would continue on my salary rather than having to train on a bursary like most of the other girls on the course with the exception of one other girl who was also working in the NHS as a dental nurse when she applied. I was indeed very lucky and was very much looking forward to starting my training.

My colleagues Ann and Roy in the general office were very pleased for me and bought me a lovely silver nurse's fob watch on a chain with my name inscribed on it. I was really touched by their generosity and they gave me a great leaving party. I had some fabulous times while I was at Mill Road including a few parties in the nurse's home opposite with the Doctors and Nurses. Many a party I have seen doctors leaping from cupboards and landing on sofa's in that small room after consuming too much punch! I have also been sitting on that sofa when a doctor has thrown himself through the air and landed next to me on it! Like I said, many fun times were had there.

My friend Ann was also great fun. She was a great friend and we had many sessions in the local pub whereby she would down 'Red Witch's' and I would drink 'Black Russians'. Ann had a lovely home and a lovely family and was a truly great friend.

Mill Road was an old hospital that had the old nightingale wards with around twenty beds on each ward. One of the wings was missing as it was bombed in the war killing many women and babies at the time. There were old underground passages that reputedly led to the nurse's home on the same grounds just opposite. I have to say, I would never have been brave enough to venture down there and many a ghost story was told by the staff. I began my training in March 1991.

On the 5th March 1991 Blues played Cambridge Utd in the Leyland Daf Cup area semi final at St. Andrews and won 3-1 thereby booking a place in the area final against Brentford. Four days later and Blues were away at Rotherham and I arranged to go with my sister and Julie from Birmingham.

Annette, Julie and I set out armed with sandwiches and goodies put together by my mom. Julie was driving and it wasn't long before we were parking up not far from the ground in Rotherham. On our way to park the car we had spotted a nice looking pub just down the road by a large island so this is where we headed for a pre match drink. It was nice inside and was full of Bluenoses who had also travelled to the game. I noticed a lad called Tom who I knew from when I lived at home with my mom and hadn't seen for ages. I had a bit of a chat with him and the others as we watched Blues fans playing pool on the nearby pool table. Before long the Bluenoses began to sing Blues songs and then it was time to head up to the ground. I had dreamt that I was being chased by Rotherham fans under a subway the night before so I insisted on negotiating the traffic across this very busy island to avoid my dream coming true, much to Annette's dismay! We just about made it across the island alive and happily headed to the ground. I had never been to Rotherham before and once again I was faced with a small ground that did have a bit of character. The away section was situated behind the goal and there was already a lot of Bluenoses inside in full voice once we got through the turnstiles. Once again it was a small crowd of 5,028 and a lot of them were Blues. The game finished in a 1-1 draw for which we had to settle and then it was off to the car and back to Birmingham. Annette and I both agreed that we had quite enjoyed the outing.

I started my midwifery training on the 18th March 1991 and was quite excited about it. My first day was great; it was in the Liverpool Maternity Hospital and was spent going over what the course would include and trying on our uniforms. My student midwife uniform was a lilac dress with a white belt for the first year and then a purple belt for the last two years. My mom and dad had a beautiful solid silver buckle made for my belt that was specially designed with two stalks holding babies in the shape of a heart. I was over the moon to receive this and it is one of my most prized possessions, even though belts are no longer worn.

At the end of March Blues played Brentford at St Andrews in the first leg of the Leyland Daf area final and won 2-1 in front of 16,219 which was a record attendance for the competition. Then four days later it was the away leg in Brentford and Julie and I set off from Birmingham in her car to watch the game. We parked up not too far from the ground and headed to a really nice little pub not too far away and joined the many Blues fans that were already drinking outside the pub. Then it was off to the ground, another new ground for me, and the Blues were in jubilant form. It was a really good game which finished 2-2 meaning that Blues won 4-3 on aggregate and were now going to Wembley for the first time in our history. We were ecstatic and celebrated for hours afterwards. Fantastic!

It was back to the nitty gritty of the league afterwards but before long the season finished with Blues finishing in 12th place with a cup final at Wembley on the 26th May to look forward to and make up for a poor league finish. Cambridge Utd were champions of the third division and were promoted along with Southend Utd, Grimsby Town and Tranmere Rovers. Crewe, Rotherham Utd and Mansfield Town were relegated to the fourth division. Tottenham won the FA Cup beating Nottingham Forest 2-1 in the final and the League Cup final finished Sheffield Wednesday 1 Manchester Utd 0.

Disappointingly I was unable to go to Wembley for Blues first ever visit and had to make do with watching it on the TV back in Liverpool. Even on the TV the atmosphere appeared fantastic and it could be clearly seen that there where many thousands of Bluenoses and they greatly outnumbered the travelling Tranmere Rovers fans. The game was really exciting with Blues going 2-0 ahead before Tranmere managed to drag it back to 2-2 in the second half. The game was won for Blues with a fantastic 'Pele like' overhead kick from brummie John Gayle in the 86th minute, which flew in the net to make it 3-2 to Blues. Wembley stadium erupted and as much as I celebrated, I was heartbroken that I wasn't at Wembley to enjoy the moment. It was fantastic to watch the Blues team walk up those famous steps and hold aloft the trophy. What a brilliant finish to the season – Leyland Daf Cup Winners 1991 – Birmingham City!

The first year of my training was quite intense and I couldn't get to as many Blues games as I would have liked but I went to as many as I could the next season – 1991 to 1992. It was a really good season for Blues who won the first six games to take us to the top of the table. Exeter City and Luton Town were dispatched in the League Cup before Blues went out to Crystal Palace by the odd goal after a replay and extra time. The only cloud on the horizon was losing at Torquay in the first round of the FA Cup, which was a bit of a shock. In fact Blues went on to beat Torquay there in the league.

The best event of 1992 happened on 12th March when my niece Nicola came into the world, the second child for my brother Neil and sister in law Sue. Nicola was also a beautiful baby with lovely coppery colour hair. I was over the moon to have a niece and I was so looking forward to seeing her.

By the end of the season Blues were promoted in second place and only missed out on the championship on the last day of the season losing 2-0 away at Stockport County. Blues were top on the table right up until that last game and were promoted as runners up. This was fantastic for us Bluenoses and along with Brentford who won the championship, and Peterborough Utd, who won in the play off's, we were the first teams to be promoted from the third division to the first division. This was due to the restructuring of the leagues as the first division became the premiership, the second division became the first division, the third division became the second division and the fourth division became the third division. Confusing yes, but Blues were now going to play in the first division next season. Manchester Utd won the League Cup beating Nottingham Forest 1-0 in the final and I was off to Wembley to see the FA Cup final in which Liverpool were to take on Sunderland.

Angela had been to a few Blues games with me and so I was off to watch Liverpool in the final with her. It was a really nice day but all I could think off really was that I would love to see my Birmingham City team run out at Wembley in the FA Cup final. Yes, it is still my dream! Our tickets were so high up that I expected the queen to take the seat next to me ready to present the cup to the winners. The tickets had cost a fortune as well, and Liverpool ran out easy winners by two goals to nil. Overall it was a nice day out and a trip to Wembley. I told myself that next time it will be with Blues. The other good news of the season was that Blues were rid of the Kumar Brothers at last and David Sullivan and the Gold brothers became our new owners.

I was now into my second year of my midwifery training and was now wearing a purple belt in place of the first years-white belt. I was really enjoying my training and it was giving me a new lease of life. I got on well with the small group of girls on my course and began going out and about with some of them. I got on really well with a girl called Jeanette who was really lovely. Jeanette lived across the Mersey on the Wirral and was married, but this didn't stop her from becoming my drinking partner. Quite often if a day finished early then we would head across the road to the local pub for a drink which would then become two, three, four etc. We would always say it would be just the one, then it would be 'you got the last one so I have to get one!' and on it would go, usually until we fell out of there. Many a happy time I had with Jeanette and the girls in my group.

The 1992 to 1993 season began with four league wins, which took Blues to third in the table, but unfortunately Exeter City extracted revenge on us in the League Cup by knocking us out 4-1 on aggregate. Perhaps Blues were concentrating on the league a bit too much. I was optimistic with our new chairman and the wind of change and would be happy with a top half finish for this season. I went to as many games as I could but of course it was difficult at times because of my training and all the hard work I was putting into my assignments which were Diploma level. Not easy when I had done no form of studying since I left school at 16 years old. Much had changed!

Blues were struggling at the bottom of the table and as April 1993 began Blues were in 20th position and a relegation place. On the 12th April I travelled down to Birmingham for the home game against Swindon Town and one of the most memorable and shocking games I have seen. I was standing on the Kop near the old score board and Blues were cruising at 4-1 with about twenty minutes go and the fans were singing 'easy, easy' Blues had beaten Sunderland 2-1 at Rover Park the previous week, so we thought things were on the up. How mistaken I was, Glen Hoddle came on for Swindon and every attack they then made resulted in the ball being in the back of the net. I was stunned when Swindon equalised at 4-4 but the whole of St. Andrews were in shock as the final whistle blew with a 6-4 result in favour of Swindon. What had gone wrong? The Bluenoses left the stadium in total silence, no one could understand how we could let a 4-1 advantage with twenty minutes to go, end in 6-4 defeat. Only Blues could manage that one!

Blues followed this with a 1-0 win at Watford, and draws at home against Tranmere Rovers 0-0, and away at Bristol Rovers 3-3. This left us in big trouble in 23rd place and we would be relegated straight back down if we failed to win against Charlton in the last match of the season at St. Andrews.

On the 8th May 1993 with my bag packed for an overnight stay with my mom, I boarded the train at Liverpool Lime Street for Blues most important game for a long time. Once the train arrived in Birmingham, I disembarked and headed straight towards the ground and the Watering Hole Pub, which was just across the road from the ground. Although it was early the pub was packed but I immediately spotted my mate 'Ballie' who I used to play football with at Birmingham City Ladies. The pub was too packed to get into comfortably but Ballie took me through to the back bar where her brothers were drinking. As soon as I got there her brothers got me a pint and I joined the banter. Due to the lack of glasses as there were now so many people inside, every time one of my mates brothers went to the bar he had to take the empty glasses. This meant that Ballie and I had to match the lad's pint for pint and I have to admit that I struggled. It was after a few pints that I pointed out to Ballie that I didn't have a terrace membership so I had no way of getting in. Ballie informed me that none of them had memberships either and not to worry as we would just go in the away end. That sounded like a good plan after all the beer I had consumed so ten minutes before kick off we headed off towards the away section in the Tilton terrace. Because we were late we had to cut through a fenced off area which meant climbing a rather large fence and sprinting across to the next fence and climbing that also. The fence proved no problem but while we were sprinting across to the other side, one of Ballie's brothers stepped on the end of a plank of wood which shot up in front of me, catching me right in the knee and sending me sprawling. I picked myself up, looked down at my white jeans that were now muddy around the knees, and continued to the other side where I climbed the fence and headed towards the Tilton with the others who looked at me in awe.

When we arrived at the away section we had hidden most of our colours, except our Blues pendants. The guys on the turnstiles looked at us suspiciously but let us in anyway, and we were soon inside with the Charlton fans. It took the police all of about 30 seconds to spot the fact that we were in fact, Blues fans in the Charlton end and they immediately surrounded us and marched us into the opposite end of the Tilton to join the Blues fans. This was great and had been the general idea anyway. Once amongst the Blues fans we joined in the singing and I began to feel quite nervous. If Blues fail to win then we are relegated and I could just not bear the thought of going back to the third division again.

It was a really tense game and nothing seemed to go for us, the ball just would not go into the net. Just when I was thinking it was not to be our day and we would get relegated Blues scored! St. Andrews erupted and Ballie and I celebrated wildly along with thousands of other jubilant Bluenoses. 'Staying up, staying up, staying up' rang out around the stadium followed loudly by our anthem 'Keep Right On'. When the final whistle went there were jubilant scenes and Ballie and I joined the thousands of others who had invaded the pitch and were now celebrating and calling for the players to come back out.

It was fantastic and before long we were back in the city centre and headed into one of the pubs for a celebratory drink. I was supposed to be going for a meal with my mom and dad and two of their friends that evening, so I called and asked if Annette would pick me up in town. Annette said she was on her way and I amazed people in the pub by heading into the toilets looking like someone in a war zone and returned looking lovely in a dress. The barman said 'wow, that was pretty amazing!' which Ballie found highly amusing. Before long Annette had picked me up and also laughed at me in my dress with my battered knees.

I joined my mom, dad, Terry and Beattie and spent the whole night singing 'the Blues are staying up!' in a nice quiet (before I got there) country pub! Blues finished the season in 19th place and escaped relegation by one place. Newcastle were champions of the first division and were promoted with West Ham and Swindon Town, who won in the play off final. Brentford, Cambridge Utd and Bristol Rovers were relegated to the second division. Both of the cup finals were competed by Arsenal and Sheffield Wednesday with Arsenal winning both the FA Cup and the League Cup.

BLUES NEWS

DIVISION ONE HERE WE COME!

City fans celebrate promotion to Division One during the civic reception at the Council House at the end of last season. More pictures from this event and some of the goals that gained our promotion can be seen in a booklet to be published shortly to mark the return of Blues to the Big Time!

SAVE OUR SOCIETY... RON SAUNDERS SAYS Stand up and be counted!

15p

A programme from 1985 – I am at the front waving a flag, 4th person to right of policeman with Julie on my right.

143

City Commercial

Several fans have asked if the start of the new Daily Draw scheme shortly will mean the end of the ever-popular rub-off lottery ticket.

The answer is an emphatic: "NO"

Sales of this type of fund-raising ticket will remain as vigorous as ever — as this picture shows.

Development Association Manager Alf Wood is seen with three of the attractive girls who circulate among supporters in the stands at matches — two Debbies with Morag in the centre.

The new scheme is designed to run alongside the rub-off lottery ticket NOT to replace it so the message is simple: Why not partake in both?

Xmas is just around the corner . . . and we can solve your "gift" problem.

Simply purchase the vouchers reproduced here (prices 50p., £1, £2 and £5) and between now and the Xmas rush you can satisfy every Blues fan in the family.

They can be exchanged at any time for any item from our superb line of souvenirs. Pop into Cattell Road and see for yourself.

My time working as a Blues lottery seller – I am on the left and Debbie is to my far right.

Stephen, Myself and Nicola.

ATARI SIX SHOOTERS!

2. Hero Tony Coton with the Cup.

1. The triumphant team after beating Ipswich in the final.

3. How the fans enjoyed it.   (Pictures: Evening Mail & LAT Photographic)   4. Skipper Alan Curbishley shows his style.

I am next to Tony Cotton in the middle picture with Pam and Julie to my right at the soccer six championship.

Millenium Stadium, Play off Final 2002

Back row: Stephen, Mom, Jake, Me, Annette, Jason. Front row: Eddie, James and Steve at Play off Final – Cardiff 2002

Setting off for Cardiff for Play off Final – Stephen, Annette, Mom and Me.

Millenium Stadium – Cardiff 2002. Play Off Final

Promoted 2002 – Stephen and I celebrate at the teams home coming.

Annette, Myself and Stephen continue to celebrate being back in the top flight for the first time in 16 years.

Carolyn, Myself, Janine and Roxy in Germany 2006

'Enjoying the World Cup finals in Germany' 2006

Janine, Snowy, Fiddler, Carolyn, Myself and Roxy in Germany

Myself, Roxy, the England lads and Superman!

Me, Mark, his mate and son Josh in Dusseldorf.

Paul Hockey, Steve, Annette and I at Soccer Six in 2008

Stephen, Steve and the lads before a home Blues match

Back in Abu Dhabi, UAE.

Brendan, Graham, Steve, Craig and Ron at Doncaster away.

Also Doncaster away -2009

Abu Dhabi – Trish, Jean, Wilf and Me at the back.

Me, Trish and Tracey celebrating a Blues win back in Abu Dhabi

CHAPTER FIFTEEN – The Double

It was in 1993 that Birmingham City was taken over by our current owners, David Sullivan and David and Ralph Gold. So, with the new owners, reputed to be very rich, I was full of optimism for the 1993 to 1994 season. Karen Brady became our Chairwoman, the first woman to do so in football, and Barry Fry was appointed manager of the team. However, it was not to be a good season and Blues were in the bottom half of the table for most of the season and were knocked out of the FA cup at St. Andrews by non-league Kidderminster Harriers. Blues did win some games but lost many more.

Our new owners declared that they would be improving St. Andrews and turning it into an all seated stadium. The Kop and Tilton terraces were to be torn up to make way for new all-seated stands and this would start after Blues last home game against Bristol City on 16th April 1994. Blues last four games of the season would then be away from home. It was a sad day for me because I have always loved standing on the old Kop terracing and would welcome it back with open arms should it have been possible. The last game in front of the Kop terracing ended in a 2-2 draw against Bristol City, which did not help our current position of 23rd in the table.

Blues did go on a bit of a run though, with away wins at Portsmouth 2-0, West Brom 4-2 and a 1-1 draw at Bolton. This meant that Blues had to win their last game away at Tranmere and rely on West Brom not winning at Portsmouth. I met Julie at the Rocket Pub just at the end of the M62 in Liverpool and we set off early through the Mersey tunnel and were soon parked up at

Prenton Park, the home of Tranmere Rovers. We headed for the pub just across the road from the ground, which was already packed full of Bluenoses in good voice. It was Tranmere's main pub but there was not a Tranmere fan in sight. It wasn't too long before one Tranmere fan did come in though and he was carried around the pub shoulder high, in good spirits. He loved it, and told me afterwards that he though the Blues fans were the best supporters he has ever known and that we were great fun. I must admit it was fun inside and everyone was in good voice and we were ever the optimists and hoped we could pull off the great escape. As is always the case at the last away game of the season, many Blues fans had come in fancy dress and there were many amusing costumes to be seen.

Once inside the ground the atmosphere in the Blues end was amazing. Blues had the whole of the terraced end behind the goal and it was absolutely packed with Bluenoses in full voice. It was as though we were playing for the championship not relegation. It was a really good game and as soon as Blues took the lead the atmosphere seemed to go up yet another notch. One of the policemen at the front told the Blues fans that West Brom were losing, so the news soon went around and the whole of the Blues contingent began celebrating. The players looked over and seemed to wonder what was going on. You can imagine our devastation when we were informed that this was not true and West Brom were in fact not losing but winning which would relegate Blues no matter what our score was. It was really awful, Blues won the game 2-1 but it soon dawned on us that we were now down.

When the final whistle went we were stunned. The Tranmere fans came streaming on the pitch from the other end and came running over to us. I don't think anyone in the Blues end had the heart for a fight but to my amazement, the Tranmere fans stopped in front of us and stood and applauded our support. Blues fans applauded them back and despite our disappointment we headed out of the ground to drown our sorrows. In the car going back through the Mersey Tunnel, it was an amazing sight. Every single car had Blues flags and scarves hanging from the windows and they were all blasting their car horns as they drove through the Tunnel. It sounded absolutely amazing and I was completely over awed. I was (and still am) immensely proud to Be a Birmingham City fan. Despite our relegation I, like all Bluenoses, never give up and was optimistic we would be back again as champions the next season.

Blues final position was 22nd and Oxford Utd and Peterborough Utd were relegated with us. Crystal Palace were champions of division one, Nottingham Forest were promoted with them as runners up with Leicester City winning in the Play off finals. Manchester Utd won the FA cup beating Chelsea 4-0 but I won't mention the League Cup!

In March of 1994 I completed my training with a Diploma in Higher Education in Midwifery and was now a qualified Midwife. Jobs were scarce in the region but I was lucky and was the first in my group to get a job. We did not know whether there would be any vacancies in the Hospital were I trained and if there was they would be scare and probably on a temporary contract. Mill Road Hospital had closed down and Liverpool Maternity Hospital was also due to close down when the new Liverpool Women's Hospital opened up nearby. I had enjoyed some good times there, especially in the local pub, the Cambridge across the road. I had also had some good times in the Irish Centre also just across the road from the Hospital. It was in the Irish Centre that I arranged to have our leaving party and went about getting nice invitation cards printed and inviting many of the Doctors, Nurses and friends we had made along the way. It was a fantastic turnout with over two hundred people turning up for what turned out to be an incredible party. My family also attended, which made it even more special.

I had got an interview at a hospital just outside of Liverpool near to St. Helens called Whiston Hospital. It was my first interview and I got the job ahead of many others and I was over the moon. It was also a permanent contract, which was like gold dust. Whiston usually took on their own students, therefore it was rare to employ an 'outsider' which I was. It took a while for everyone to accept me but once they did I made some great friends there. It was a really nice hospital with the maternity wing being attached to the big general hospital. It was the regional burns unit also, in fact the only black spot was the fact that the local pub across the road was named the Holt!

Now that I had a job whereby I had to travel quite a way to, I decided the time was right for me to recommence my driving and take my test. As I had not driven for many years, despite having had two cars when I was younger, I decided to embark on some proper lessons. I also found a nice second hand car that was not too old and in very good condition. It was a lovely red ford escort and would do very nicely once I passed my test.

I was really looking forward to the 1994 to 1995 season and decided to get a season ticket in the new Tilton Road Stand. By the start of the new season the Tilton Road Stand had been completed and work was underway on the new Kop Stand. My season ticket was in the one of the lower blocks just behind the goal and was next to my friend Julie and her niece. I felt that with the ground improvements and new owners that things could really start to look up for Birmingham City.

The first game of the season was away in London as Blues prepared to take on Leyton Orient to start their campaign. I made sure I was not working and I set off for Birmingham from Liverpool to meet up with Julie who would be driving us to Leyton Orient. It was another new ground for me and I was please to be able to stand on the terraces behind the goal with the away support. There were quite a few Bluenoses there and as usual were optimistic and in good voice. The ground was an old ground with the majority of the home support taunting us from behind the opposite goal but being out sung by the Blues fans. Unfortunately the game did not go as plan and despite a Steve Claridge goal, Blues lost the game 2-1 and I headed home somewhat downhearted as I had expected an easy win. I guess I should know better really, being a Bluenose!

Next up was an away trip to Shrewsbury Town in the first leg of the League cup and again Blues lost 2-1. Not to worry though, as we won the home leg 2-0, therefore going through to the next round 3-2 on aggregate. Blues first home game was against Chester City and it was an amazing sight I was faced with when I entered St. Andrews. The new Tilton Road Stand was fabulous and the atmosphere inside was great. It was really strange looking across at the empty space where the old Kop terrace once was and to see the metal framework and the beginning of the concrete base for the new stand. It was also strange only having three sides to the ground at this time. There were 12,188 inside St. Andrews as, of course the capacity was reduced due to the building work. Blues won the game 1-0 and were in eighth place in the league table.

A week later and I was again on my way back to Birmingham to meet Julie and this time we were heading into Wales to play Swansea City at the Vetch Field. Once again Julie drove and mom had packed us a bit of a picnic for the journey. Once in Swansea we parked up and headed to the ground, only to discover that we had parked right by their main end and had to walk to the other end of the ground to join the Blues fans in the away end. Inside I was once again standing on a terraced end behind the goal where Blues fans had half of the end with Swansea fans occupying the other end with fencing separating us from them. It was a nice day and Julie and I sat on the terrace while we waited for the teams to come out and tucked into our packed lunch. Mom had put a couple of peaches inside, so once I had consumed them I lobbed the peach stones over the fence into the Swansea end, much to my delight. The game soon got underway amid much noise from the Blues fans. It was a really good game and Steve Claridge scored twice to give Blues a well-deserved 2-0 away win.

It was after the game that the trouble began, and it was really tricky getting back to our car safely. We were subjected to some vile abuse from the home fans as we headed back and considering we were just two girls it made it even worse. There is a sort of code amongst football fans considering women and children and I found the Swansea fans to be complete wankers. Once we got away, Julie and I decided to stop at the services for a bite to eat and we met up with a few other people who had had their car windows smashed by the Swansea fans as they left the ground. They still had to travel to St. Andrews yet and I knew that the Blues fans would be eagerly awaiting them with revenge on their minds. Blues were now sixth in the table.

I was really enjoying travelling to St. Andrews and watching the new Kop stand grow each time. I was managing to get to all the home games but could not make all of the away games because of work. I did get to quite a few though. Unfortunately I couldn't get to the away League cup game against premiership Blackburn Rovers, but I was able to get to the return home leg. As the new Kop stand was growing then so was the capacity as they put some seats in the corner section joining the Tilton and there were 16,275 inside the ground. Blues put on a good show and came away with a very creditable 1-1 draw despite going out of the cup 3-1 on aggregate. Blues had held our own against premiership opposition and I was proud of my team.

Blues were also doing very well in the Auto Windscreens Trophy, having beaten Peterborough and now Walsall and because of the special offers for the fans Blues were getting record attendances for these games. In October, I again travelled to Brentford for a league match and Julie and I headed once again to the nice small pub not far from the ground. It was another nice day out, especially as Blues won the game 2-1. Blues were now in ninth place but I was sure we could climb the table.

Blues drew non-league Slough Town in the first round of the FA cup away but Slough decided to switch the game to St. Andrews for the extra revenue they would get. It was a good game though and Blues won 4-0 to progress to the second round and a home draw against Scunthorpe Utd. Then, in November Blues had arranged a friendly to mark the opening of the new Kop stand and neighbours Aston Villa were to be our opponents. Blues had not played Villa for a long time and 19,766 were inside St. Andrews to see Blues get a very creditable 1-1 draw once again against premiership opponents. When McGavin scored against the Villa the whole of St. Andrews went wild and the atmosphere was brilliant. Blues were now third in the second division table. Life was good.

On 29th November Blues were again playing in the Auto Windscreens Trophy, this time against Gillingham and the prices were cut and it was really cheap for children. My nephew Stephen was now nearly five years old and I asked him if he would like to come. Of course he said yes, but I was a little worried he may be frightened by the noise and not want to go again. Because I had a season ticket in the Tilton, I would not be able to sit with him, therefore I got three tickets for the old railway stand and my mom and Annette also came and took Stephen with them. There were 17,086 inside St. Andrews and it was definitely a good first game for Stephen as Blues won easily 3-0 and the atmosphere was electric. I needn't have worried about the noise as Stephen loved it and was a true Bluenose like his aunt! This was to be the first of many many more Blues games that we have been to together.

A few days later I again travelled down to Birmingham for the second round FA Cup tie against Scunthorpe United at St. Andrews which was being shown live on TV. Once again I took Stephen and despite Blues having a few chances the game finished 0-0 and so going to a reply up in Scunthorpe two weeks later.

Just over a week later I was headed to what would be a more local match for me, just across the water in the city of Chester where Blues were to take on Chester City at their home ground. I headed to Chester form Liverpool by local train and before long I was disembarking in the really nice city of Chester. It has a nice little station and just outside, opposite the hotel facing the station is a nice pub to which we headed for our first pre match drink of the day. Soon it was off to the ground, which was another new ground for me. The ground was really small compared to what I was used to, but it was kind of quaint and I was astonished to find that the travelling Bluenoses had in fact three ends of the ground. The home support were situated in just one stand behind the goal. The other three stands were jam packed with Birmingham supporters; in fact it was more like a home game for Blues! It was brilliant and the atmosphere was fabulous. The Bluenoses sang throughout the game as Blues coasted to a good 4-0 away win. Each goal was celebrated wildly. When Liam Daish scored his goal he ran towards the celebrating Bluenoses at one side of the ground where a rather long trumpet was passed to him, which he then proceeded to blow into as part of his celebration! It was brilliant and we all loved it, unfortunately though, the referee was not quite as keen and he proceeded to book Liam Daish for his celebrations to loud boos from three ends of the ground. It was a great result and moved Blues up to second in the table and I headed back to Liverpool in jubilant mood.

Four days later I headed down to Birmingham to meet up with Julie for our journey to Scunthorpe for the FA Cup second round replay. Julie was driving there in her car so I left mine at my moms and once Julie picked me up, we headed off to Scunthorpe on a very cold frosty night. When we arrived in Scunthorpe the ground was easy to find from the motorway as it could be seen clearly, so we parked up and headed towards the pub that could also be seen just up the road. The pavements were white with ice as we made our way to the pub. Once inside though, it was a bit warmer and the pub was full of travelling Bluenoses in their blue shirts. Despite the cold, everyone was in good spirits and looking forward to the cup-tie ahead. It was also a new ground for most of us, so that was something to look forward to also. As we headed back down the road towards the ground we were a bit like Bambi on ice as I for one, slipped and slid down the road to the ground. Once inside I looked around and although it was another smallish ground, it was quite nice. The away end behind the goal was full of Bluenoses despite the fact that it was on a cold winter's night. The atmosphere was great amongst the Blues fans and when Blues took the lead right in front of our travelling support our end erupted. Barry Fry, our manager, jumped in the air and sprinted maniacally down the wing towards the Blues support and we all enjoyed the sight of his celebrations immensely, joining him in his celebrations.

When Blues scored a second the celebrations began in earnest as we sang our 'Wembley, Wembley' loudly. Much had been made of the fact that our keeper had not conceded a goal for quite a while, and it was a shame the way in which Scunthorpe's consolation goal was conceded. As the Blues defence was preparing for a Scunthorpe free kick, the Scunthorpe player took it early into the unguarded goal as the keeper was lining up his wall. The Blues players protested that the whistle had not been blown and they were still getting ready but the referee ignored their pleas. I personally was disgusted, as were the rest of the Bluenoses who felt that the goal should not have been allowed to stand and was in fact – cheating. However, it did not make a difference to the outcome and Blues won the match 2-1 and we headed back to Birmingham celebrating our passage to the next round of the FA Cup. The draw had already been made prior to the replay and Blues had been drawn at home against the mighty Liverpool. I was looking forward to this immensely!

I was enjoying my trips to Birmingham this season and the next three games produced another two wins and a draw. On 31st December I again travelled to Birmingham for the home match against Blackpool. Once again I was taking Stephen with me and he was looking forward to the game as much as I was. As we were heading into the stadium I decided to make it a little more fun and put a bet on the match at the bookies inside. After asking Stephen what he though, I decided on a Blues win by 6-1. It was just a bit of a mad bet really to give us a bit of a laugh. Anyway, it wasn't long into the game when Blackpool scored. Stephen and I could not believe it. Neither could anyone else inside St. Andrews. Luckily though, it was just a blip and Blues soon got on top again scored. Before long Blues were in front and as the game progressed a few more goals went in and before I knew it Blues were 6-1 in front. I turned to Stephen and we both had a bit of a laugh. Stephen decided we should have halve the winnings but before we could decide how to spent them (they were long odds!), Blues scored again! 7-1. Unbelievable, I celebrated with Stephen once again and as I lifted him into the air, neither of us was bothered about losing the bet. It had been a great game and a great result and we both went home happy, which is more than can be said for the orange clad Blackpool fans that had made the trip. Birmingham City were now sitting proudly on top of the table.

Two days later on 2nd January, Julie and I headed off to Bradford for a league game. Once again Julie drove there and once we had parked up we headed to a nearby bar in town not too far from the ground. It was a nice bar and I had a couple of beers before we headed to the ground. Bradford City's ground was okay but the little terraced stand that housed the away fans was tiny. It ran along the side of the pitch and the Blues fans were situated to the left goal side. I was amazed at how small the terrace was; it felt like it was only about ten people deep! The view of the pitch was okay though, if I stood on tiptoe, and the atmosphere amongst the Blues faithful was great. The game got under way and Julie and I began to think that Blues would never score. Bradford scored and I was beginning to think that it was not going to be our day when Cooper hit a great shot from just outside the area and it flew into the top corner. I must admit that I had been giving Cooper some stick during the match and due to our close proximity I am sure he heard me because when he scored he came running over to where I was standing for his goal celebrations. Point made and great goal! So the game ended in a draw and Blues remained top of the table.

It was a busy January and in total I attended all six of the matches played including the Bradford City game. A week after the Bradford game Blues returned to FA Cup action with a home tie against Liverpool. Once again it was televised live and an entertaining match ended in a 0-0 draw with the replay scheduled for two weeks time at Anfield. Alan Hanson on match of the day commented that it should just be a formality for Liverpool at Anfield and they would win easily. He would come to regret his comments on a cold night in Liverpool at the replay!

Following the FA Cup game, Blues were again in cup action three days later, but this time it was the Auto Windscreens Trophy. This time it was against Hereford United and resulted in a 3-1 win for Blues with goals from Ward, Claridge and Ricky Otto. I was amongst the 22,351 inside St. Andrews to watch the game and like all the other Bluenoses I was quietly hoping for a trip to Wembley.

Four days later Julie and I headed off to the picturesque town of York for an away match against York City. This would be another new ground for me; in fact I had never even been to York. When we arrived and parked up, Julie and I set out to explore a bit of the town before heading for a pre match drink. York is a lovely place and I really enjoyed what I saw. It was really picturesque and we found a lovely little pub, which we stopped at, for a drink. There were a few nice little pubs around and most of them seemed to be filled with Bluenoses enjoying a sing song and a pre match pint.

The ground appeared old inside and the away fans were situated behind the goal and on the corner on a standing terraced area. There were loads of Blues who had made the journey and as league leaders, we were really looking forward to the game. Blues were unbeaten for 26 games, which I think was a record, and were expecting to make it 27. We were brought down to earth with a bang though. I think the player's minds were already at Anfield and Blues played awful. We never looked liked coming back once Blues went a goal down and when the second went in it was all over. The York fans celebrated like they had won the league as us Bluenoses headed out of the ground disappointed in the performance of our lads. If we play like that at Anfield we would have no chance. Despite losing our unbeaten run Blues remainded at the top of the table and ever the optimist I was looking forward to the Liverpool game.

I had arranged to meet Julie before the game as she was travelling up for the match amongst the 9,000 other Bluenoses that had tickets. I didn't live far from Anfield, so we walked from mine to the Arkles pub by the away end. There were Blues fans everywhere and the atmosphere was brilliant. Once inside Anfield the atmosphere was electric and Blues had the whole of the Anfield Road Stand behind the goal and half of the Kemlyn Road Stand along the side of the pitch. It was an amazing sight with so much of Anfield being a sea of Blue and White. All the singing was coming from the Bluenoses and I must admit feeling a lump in my throat. I was so proud to be a Birmingham City fan that day inside Liverpool's ground, listening to Blues out-singing their Premiership opposition.

There were 9,000 Blues fans amongst the 36,275 inside the ground and when the teams ran out onto the pitch there was an almighty roar to meet them. Once the match got underway Blues gave a good account of themselves and were not about to become pushovers as Alan Hanson had suggested. It was really quite amusing as the 9,000 Bluenoses gave many loud renditions of 'Alan Hanson – what a wanker, what a wanker!' I remember he said after the game that he would never make comments like that again! It was sung really really loud and must have been heard on live TV!

Blues went behind somewhat unfortunately to a deflected shot before half time and I must admit we felt a bit hard done by. Mind you, we were two divisions below our mighty opponents! The second half got under way and the Bluenoses continued to sing our hearts out for our lads. Then an amazing thing happened right in front of us. Ricky Otto got the ball and from just outside the penalty area he curled a wonderful shot into the top corner of the Liverpool goal! The Blues end of the ground erupted. It was a brilliant goal and we were in heaven! As the stunned Liverpool fans looked on Blues fans took the roof of the stadium with our wild celebrations. All those Bluenoses that were there that day will remember that feeling as the ball hit the back of the net - forever. What a night. The game went to extra time and then finished 1-1 meaning penalties. It also meant that Alan Hanson would have to eat his words!

Blues, however, have a terrible record when it comes to penalty shoot out's having lost many important games in the dreaded penalty shoot out. This run continued as all of our players missed their penalties and although a couple of the Liverpool players also missed, Blues went out of the FA Cup losing 2-0 on penalties. I was determined not to be disheartened though, especially as Blues had given a good account of themselves against Premiership opposition two divisions above them. After all, Liverpool had failed to beat us home and away during both games.

The following match saw Blues progress in the Auto Windscreens Trophy by beating Swansea City 3-2 at St. Andrews in front of 20,320 fans as Claridge, Francis and Tait scored the goals. This was followed by a 1-0 win over Stockport County and then a 2-1 defeat at Crewe that meant that Blues dropped down to third place. This was a little worrying because only first place would gain automatic promotion this year, anything less meant the dreaded play offs. However, in the next match Blues gained revenge over York City, beating them 4-2 at St. Andrews.

Blues were now in the area final of the Auto Windscreens Trophy, which was just one step away from a Wembley appearance. The area final would be played over two legs and Blues had drawn Leyton Orient with the first leg being at St. Andrews on 28th February. I was so excited when I travelled down for this match. I had decided that nothing would stop me getting to the final this time if Blues progressed. It had always been my dream to see Blues play at Wembley and although it was not the FA Cup final, it would still do nicely. I think the 24,002 fans packed into St. Andrews also felt the same and the atmosphere was fantastic. 'Keep Right On' echoed round the new Stadium loud and proud. When Shearer scored what turned out to be the winning goal, the stadium erupted with celebrations. It was only a slender lead to take into the away leg but I was as ever, hopeful that it would be enough to take us to Wembley.

After a draw at Hull City and a 1-0 home defeat against Swansea City, Blues were fourth in the table when I met up with Julie to head to London for the second leg of the area final. As usual Julie was driving to London and it wasn't too long before we were parked up and wandering around Leyton Orient's ground looking for a pub for a pre match drink. There were loads of Blues that had also arrived early and were milling around outside. As we were standing outside a local pub enjoying a beer I bumped into one of my old teammates from my days at Birmingham City. It was great to see 'Ballie' again and we had a great laugh catching up together. Ballie had tickets in the seats amongst the Leyton Orient fans and I had a ticket for the away terrace behind the goal but I said I would look for her when we were inside for the match. Many Blues fans had also had to get tickets in the Leyton Orient end; such was the demand by the Bluenoses for tickets. Every Bluenose was desperate to see our heroes play at Wembley Stadium.

Once inside Julie and I took up standing positions just behind the goal and the game got under way. It wasn't long before Blues scored, and our end erupted wildly, I jumped on Julie and the entire terrace seemed to come alive like an ocean of waves. I looked across to the side of the pitch where some Blues in the home section were also celebrating, and there in the middle was 'Ballie' also celebrating wildly. The police moved in and they were all herded into our section and 'Ballie' came over to join us. Blues scored two more goals to much celebration and although Orient pulled two back, the match finished 3-2 meaning that Blues were in the final at Wembley with a 4-2 aggregate win. We all celebrated for much of the night, including the journey back to Birmingham. It was a brilliant feeling, looking forward to seeing Blues run out at Wembley. I was so looking forward to seeing Wembley way as a mass of Blue and White.

Carlisle United won the other area final and so were due to meet Blues in the final at Wembley on 23rd April 1995. When the tickets went on sale at St. Andrews, people queued all night in the hope of getting a ticket and it wasn't long before they sold out completely. I queued for about 6 hours and was over the moon when I got our tickets. There would be 55,000 Blues fans heading for Wembley and I would be one of them!

Next up for Julie and I was a nice little trip to Wycombe to see Blues take on Wycombe Wanderers. This would be another new ground for me and I was looking forward to the experience. Blues had dropped to fourth in the table and I for one was getting a bit nervous. It would be disaster to miss out on the one automatic promotion spot after doing so well so far. We arrived in Wycombe and after finding a chip shop we had a look around.

Wycombe was a really nice place and as we headed for the ground I admired the country feel to it. Once at the ground we headed to the club shop to see what was on offer and I bought a small vintage van with the Wycombe Wanderers crest on the back for my Dad's collection.

The ground itself was really small but nice. It was situated on the edge of a really large hill where people could stand and see into the ground. During the match I could see a few people on the hill attempting to watch the game. Don't know what sort of a view they had though. The Blues fans were situated on terracing behind one of the goals and once again the turnout was superb for Blues. We sang and cheered and thoroughly enjoyed Birmingham's 3-0 demolition of Wycombe. The third goal was superb as a lovely long distance chip over the keeper nestled in the back of the net right in front of the travelling Blues contingent. Although we remained in fourth place we all headed home happy.

A week later and I was again taking Stephen to St. Andrews as Blues prepared to take on Oxford United. As had become habit of late, I had a pound bet on Blues to win 3-0. Amazingly this was the score as the game went on, but just before the end Oxford were awarded a penalty right in front of where Stephen, Julie, Emma and I were sitting in the Tilton. I can't believe it, I said to Stephen, I never win any bets. Just as I spoke the penalty was taken and our keeper dived and saved it! Fantastic, I won the bet and gave Stephen some extra pocket money, which added to the smile already on his face from another good Blues win.

On the 28th March, Julie and I once again set off on our travels this time to Bristol to see Blues play Bristol Rovers. It was a cold day and once in Bristol we headed to a pub close to the ground for a warm and a pre match pint. There were a few Bristol Rovers fans inside and we got talking to a couple of them. I was quite surprised how bitter they were towards us. They called us the big spenders of the league and seemed really jealous, seeming to think that Blues could buy whomever they wanted and would get promotion because of this. Of course Julie and I put them right but there seemed a bit of a hostile atmosphere both in the pub and in the ground afterwards. The ground itself was old and small and the terraced end we were in seemed cold and open. The match wasn't much to write home about either as Blues conceded a really soft own goal from a back pass that seemed to trickle past our keeper into the net. Luckily Steve Claridge saved our blushes by scoring the equaliser and the match finished 1-1. Blues were now up to third place in the table and closing in on the leaders.

Following four wins, a draw and a defeat Birmingham were back at the top of the table and it was time to head to Wembley for the final of the Auto Windscreens Trophy. Julie had organised a double decker Birmingham bus to take us all to Wembley. It was going to be great, even my mom and my sister Annette were coming, as well as my friend Angela from Liverpool. I was really excited as we boarded the bus in the city centre, with our packed lunches and beers. The journey along the motorway was brilliant as car after car with blues scarves and flags draped from the windows passed us. Yes, that's right – PASSED us. As it was a double decker bus it was extremely slow. None of us minded though as we downed beers and discussed our chances of winning the Trophy.

We also saw a few limousines with Blues fans standing up through the sunroof waving flags as they passed us. It was brilliant. I haven't seen anything like it before or since, the whole of the motorway was a sea of blue and white. I don't think there could have been anyone left back in Birmingham. One of the girls was doing some face painting and I had 'BCFC' in blue across my face, as did Annette.

It took us ages to get to London, and just on the outskirts the bus pulled off the motorway and stopped at a local pub for everyone to get a pre match drink before we got to Wembley. It was quite funny really seeing a Birmingham bus draped in blue and white flags and scarves pulling up at a bus stop outside a pub on the outskirts of London. People just looked in amazement, as did the bar staff when a busload of Bluenoses burst through the doors into what had been an empty pub minutes before our arrival.

The bar staff had to rapidly call in more staff to help and the Bluenoses embarked on a drinking spree.

Following a nice session in the pub we boarded the bus again and headed into London towards Wembley Stadium. The traffic as we neared the Stadium was terrible and I became desperate to get off and get to the toilets by the ground, which was now in sight. Eventually I could stand it no more and jumped off and hurried to the toilets by the entrances closely followed by Annette. I must admit I jumped the queue claiming to be pregnant, much to Annette's distress and only afterwards did I wonder how we would all meet up now that I had lost the bus! Luckily we were just outside the entrance that we were supposed to use and before long the rest of the crew arrived including my mom and Julie.

Once inside Wembley the atmosphere was absolutely brilliant! Wembley was a sea of blue and white, I had never seen or heard anything like it before. Three quarters of the ground were blue and white of Birmingham with about 20,000 Carlisle Utd fans at one end. It was awesome seeing 55,000 Bluenoses inside Wembley waving flags, banners and scarves. 'Keep Right On' was sang like I had never heard before, in was fantastic. It wasn't long before Barry Fry led the team out and onto the pitch amongst a crescendo of noise from the Blues fans. Blues were top of the league and in the final at Wembley, life was very good. There were 76,663 people in Wembley, a record attendance for the competition. In fact there were more for the Birmingham City v Carlisle game that there had been at the League cup final between Liverpool and Bolton a few weeks before.

The game was full of chances but neither team seemed able to score and it finished 0-0. This meant extra time and for the first time in a final a golden goal could decide the match. This meant that the first team to score a goal in extra time would win the game. It was nerve wracking now. And so into extra time it went and before long the ball was crossed in as Blues attacked the end in front of their supports and there was Paul Tait to head the ball home. Wembley Stadium erupted as 55,000 Bluenoses celebrated wildly. Paul Tait, a Bluenose himself, ran towards the Blues fans and lifted his shirt to reveal a T-shirt, which read 'BIRMINGHAM CITY SHIT ON THE VILLA!' Brilliant! The camera's got a lovely shot of it and it was plastered across the back pages of all the papers the next day. Yes, Paul Tait got fined but he became a real Blues hero that day and it must have been worth every penny of his fine! In fact when he ran out for the next home game at St. Andrews he received a standing ovation!

I was on my seat celebrating and couldn't believe I had just seen Birmingham City win at Wembley! I was so overcome. As the Birmingham City team made their way up the Wembley steps and then lifted the Trophy I was so proud. This moment was what being a Birmingham City fan was all about. The likes of Manchester Utd and Liverpool will never know what it feels like as they win things so easy and they take it for granted. It was a fantastic experience and one I wouldn't have missed for anything. Blues still had the second division championship in their sights too; all in all it was a great time to be a Bluenose.

We were all so excited as we boarded the bus to take us back to Birmingham and we continued to celebrate as we headed home. However, with so many Bluenoses having travelled from Birmingham, the traffic heading away from Wembley towards Birmingham was more or less at a standstill. At one point we were stuck in traffic so long that loads of the lads got off, crossed the road into the local off licence and stocked up on beers for the long journey back. It took us six hours to get home! We were so happy though that none of us complained. It was a fantastic day out and one that will live in my memory forever. Personally I think Paul Tait should have got a knighthood.

Three days later it was back to league action and the most important last four games of the season that would decide the championship and whether or not we would return to the first division. A home game against Brentford, who were currently second and challenging us for the championship, resulted in a brilliant 2-0 win that saw Blues keep our place at the top of the table. This meant that if we won our next home game against Brighton Blues would be champions. However, as we all know, things never go as planned with Blues and Brighton fought hard for a 3-3 draw which meant a nerve wracking last two games. Then our last home game of the season against Bradford City again meant we could win the championship at St. Andrews if Blues win. And again Blues drew 0-0 meaning it would go to the last match of the season away a Huddersfield. There was a cocktail of scenarios that would see us win the championship involving other teams but basically it was in our own hands and if we beat Huddersfield Town then Birmingham City would be crowned champions.

Saturday 6th May 1995, Julie and I set out early for the last match of the season. I was nervous and excited at the same time. Knowing Blues as well as I did I was expecting them to fall at the last hurdle as we so often do. But there again we had won the cup at Wembley so perhaps we could also achieve promotion on the last day of the season. As we headed towards Huddersfield in Julie's car, on a nice day, there were Bluenoses everywhere I looked. Getting closer to Huddersfield on the country roads, we passed several country pubs with beer gardens and all of them were packed with Bluenoses enjoying a pre match pint whilst soaking up the sun. Julie, her brother and myself headed into Huddersfield and made our way to the ground before parking up and heading for a pre match drink. It would take more than a pre match drink to calm the nerves today.

Once inside Huddersfield Town's McAlpine stadium the atmosphere amongst the Bluenoses was fantastic. Huddersfield's ground is a new one and at this time only had three sides to the ground with one end behind the goal being completely open with nothing behind it. Blues had been given the entire stand behind the other goal and it was completely full with noisy singing Blues fans. There must have been about 7,000 Blues fans present, with many in fancy dress, as is traditional for Blues last away game of the season. Blues fans never stopped singing for the entire time. 'We're gonna win the league' was ringing out loudly as well as our anthem – 'Keep Right On' and flags and scarves were being waved in earnest. Even the home supporters seemed quite impressed by our support. There were many fans carrying small radio's to keep up to date with other relevant games should our plight require it.

The match got underway and Blues were up for it from the start, especially with the vociferous support from the Blues contingent. As time went on I began to get more and more nervous, but then Blues scored. Our end erupted and there really were wild celebrations amongst the Bluenoses. I was so excited but worried at the same time that we would let it slip. Blues second goal settled my fears and I celebrated like someone possessed, jumping all over everyone around me. Mind you, everyone was jumping and hugging each other, including complete strangers, such was the delight. 'We're gonna win the league' was belted out loud and proud and 'the Blues are going up, the Blues are going up!'

It did get a bit stressful when Huddersfield pulled one back but I really felt we could hold on and win. Then the final whistle blew Blues had won 2-1 and were champions! The Blues end erupted into wild celebrations that were unbelievable. 'Champions! Champions!' rang out loudly as the players left the pitch. The home supporters were applauding us and we continued to sing calling for our players to come back onto the pitch to celebrate with us. 'Bring on the Champions!' was being sang really loudly by the Blues fans but after about twenty minutes a tannoy announcement asked for the Blues fans to leave the stadium as the players would not be coming back out onto the pitch. Blues fans started singing 'we're not going anywhere, we're not going, we're not going, we're not going anywhere!' and the home supporters themselves remained in the ground watching the proceedings with amazement. Forty five minutes later with the tannoy still asking us to leave, Blues fans were belting out 'Bring on the Champions!' to the applause of the Huddersfield support. There was no way, any of the 7,000 Blues fans were going home without seeing our heroes back out on the pitch taking our applause.

About an hour after the final whistle the tannoy again pleaded with Blues fans to leave the stadium as the players would not return to the pitch. At this point all 7,000 Blues fans sat down and started singing 'all night, we're gonna stay all night, we're gonna stay all night, we're gonna stay all night!' I think this was when those in power realised that the Blues fans really would stay all night and the Champions came out onto the pitch. They were still in their Blues kit and had bottles of Champagne in their hands and the celebrations really began. A large union jack with Champions was passed to the players and they happily waved it back at us from the pitch. Ricky Otto was seen hugging a blonde female fan and all the players were celebrating with the Bluenoses —it was brilliant. It was another precious memory that will live on in my heart forever.

Once the players had left the pitch we were also happy to head home. Julie and I headed out of Huddersfield and stopped at a nice country pub just outside Huddersfield with a beer garden full of celebrating Bluenoses. I ordered a pint of cider and called my sister, who was due to meet up with me when I got back to celebrate. 'Don't be late back!' she said to me, 'just one and I will head back and meet you in the Castle Pub' I stated. So after reassuring her and finishing my pint's, I headed back to Birmingham and the Castle Pub in Weoley Castle.

Annette was standing outside the pub drinking when she saw Julie's car rounding the island and approaching the pub with me hanging out of the window celebrating. She said she couldn't believe her eyes as she spotted the car. She said that half my body was out of the window and I was waving wildly at her. She was in stitches when I fell out of the car singing when we pulled up. The atmosphere in the pub was brilliant, as it was full of Blues. Although it was the last day of the season for Blues, there was one more game left for all the premiership teams and Villa were in serious danger of getting relegated the following weekend. That was cause for double celebration and the Bluenoses were singing 'ho oh, scum's in trouble, villa's going down and the Blues have done the double!'

It was a fantastic day amid great celebration, a day that I will cherish and as always I was proud to be a Birmingham City fan!

Birmingham City finished the season as Second Division Champions and Auto Windscreens Trophy winners. Huddersfield Town were promoted with us via the play off's even though they finished the season in fifth place. Brentford who had competed with us for most of the season and finished second missed out on promotion.

I was half way through my Degree in Midwifery, which I was doing part time whilst I was working as a midwife at Whiston Hospital in Merseyside. Life was good and I was looking forward to watching Blues play first division football next season.

CHAPTER SIXTEEN – League Cup Semi Final

I was looking forward to the new season – 1995 –1996 back in the first division and I was as optimistic as ever. I would be happy for Blues to avoid relegation to be honest and then build towards a Premiership challenge in a couple of seasons. I had enjoyed a good summer and was still in my current employment as a Midwife at Whitson Hospital. I had passed my driving test and I still had my lovely red ford escort car. For the new season Stephen now had a season ticket in the seat next to mine on the Tilton Road along with Julie and Emma. I was sure Stephen was looking forward to the new season as much as I was. He was six and a half now, and a real Bluenose.

The season began well and by 8th November Blues were second in the first division, had knocked Plymouth and Grimsby out of the League Cup and following a home draw against Tranmere Rovers, were due to meet them again in a replay. This was great for me as it was a local game and I only had to travel across the water from Liverpool to Prenton Park. It was a lovely day and I enjoyed a good game that saw Blues progress to the fourth round of the League Cup following a good 3-1 away win.

The fourth round draw was made and Blues were drawn away at Premier league team Middlesborough. This would be a very hard tie for Blues as Middlesborough were a strong team and were doing really well in the Premiership. Blues had slipped down to 5th in the table by the time Julie and I headed to Middlesborough for the cup-tie.

We arrived in plenty of time in Middlesborough and Julie and I managed to park not too far from the ground and near to the centre of town to which we headed for a pre match drink. Once we had found a nice pub full of Bluenoses we obtained drinks and got down to chatting about our chances. Most people didn't hold out a hope really and Middlesborough were hot favourites to progress through to the next round. I just hoped for a draw and to take them back to our place to be honest. After a while we headed out towards the ground. Although it didn't look too far away, it was a good walk, which included going through a concrete tunnel/subway beneath the overpass that looked a bit daunting with so many red clad supporters around. We survived though and I must admit, with only one way in and out I did wonder about the safety of the ground. What if ambulances needed access? The only road into the stadium was packed with cars and fans. Seemed a bit dangerous to me, and the ground was on the river edge thereby blocking off access to one side of the ground.

Once inside, Middlesborough's new ground was much the same as most new grounds these days and I thought it lacked character although it was a nice stadium. The Blues end was packed and everyone in the away end was in good voice. The ground appeared full and the Middlesborough fans sang a couple of times too. The Bluenoses were singing 'where were you when you were shit?' loudly – referring to their (up until recently) time in the lower leagues when their support had been much less. It was quite funny really. There were 28,031 inside the ground and Blues did brilliantly to hold on for a 0-0 draw to enable us to take them to a replay at St. Andrews just before Christmas.

By the time the replay came around on 20th December, Blues had slipped down to 8th in the first division but we were all really looking forward to the Middlesborough game. Stephen and I enjoyed it immensely as I got to lift him in the air a couple of times as Blues won the game 2-0 against our Premiership opponents with two goals from Kevin Francis. It was brilliant and definitely brightened up the season for us. The draw was made for the fifth round and Blues were drawn away to Norwich City. I was hoping for a home draw but hopefully Blues could at least manage a draw and bring them back to our place for a replay that would see us in the semi finals for the first time in a long, long time.

The tie at Carrow Road ended in a 1-1 draw with a Kevin Francis goal bringing the tractor boys back to St. Andrews for a replay that would take place on my birthday on the 24th January. It turned out to be a great Birthday as Liam Daish and Jason Bowen scored for Blues in a 2-1 win that saw Blues through to the semi finals of the League Cup. I for one was over the moon and so were Stephen, Julie and Emma!

By the time the first leg of the League Cup semi-final against Leeds United of the Premiership came around, Blues had slipped to 11th place in the first division table. Nobody gave us a chance against highflying Leeds Utd but I knew our lads would give a good account of themselves and I headed down to Birmingham with hope in my heart. This would be Stephens's first semi-final and hopefully not the last! We were all so excited and the atmosphere amongst the 24,781 inside the ground was fantastic. Blues played really well and I thought we were really unlucky to lose the first leg 2-1 with Chris Whyte scoring our goal. There was an incident during the game when a Leeds Player about to take a corner in front of Kop/Tilton corner was hit on the head by a snooker ball. When I returned to work the next day, one of the senior doctors asked me if I had been to the match and when I said yes he asked had it been me that threw the snooker ball! I jokingly replied 'yes, good shot wasn't it!' which bought a smile to his face as he replied 'not bad'. The culprit was caught though and received a ban from St. Andrews. Personally I thought they should have signed him up – it was probably the best shot of the match!

Two weeks later when we set off to Leeds for the second leg Blues were in 13th position and there seemed to be a bit of unrest at the club. Personally I think this affected the team in the second leg and could not have come at a worse time. Thousands of Bluenoses made the trip to Leeds and the away end was packed. I must admit the new stand at Leeds is very impressive and so big.

There were 35,435 inside Elland Road and the atmosphere amongst both sets of supporters was fantastic. The Bluenoses never stopped singing throughout the game despite going down 3-0. Our players did put up a fight and I think the scoreline somewhat flattered Leeds. We already knew that the other finalists would be Villa and we had been desperate to meet the old enemy at Wembley. However, once we knew this dream has slipped away the Blues fans belted out 'we hope you the beat the villa!' to the Leeds fans who in turn applauded us loudly all round the ground. Bluenoses then broke into a rendition of 'shit on the villa' which the Leeds fans also joined in and soon the entire stadium were singing 'shit on the villa'. I must admit it sounded brilliant with both Blues and Leeds fans singing it at full blast. It gave me a right laugh and almost made up for the disappointment of defeat at the last hurdle. It was not to be though and even worse was that Leeds then went on to lose to Villa in the final. Shocking!

Blues had also been knocked out of the FA Cup by this time by Wolves in a replay at their ground 2-1.

And by the time we came to play Wolves at their ground in the league on 23rd March Blues were 13[th in] the table. Whilst at work I had delivered a baby of someone connected with Wolverhampton Wanderers and they had given me their number to call when we played at their stadium telling me that they would get me tickets. True to their word I was surprised to discover that they had got me two tickets in one of the executive boxes which was really kind of them. So Julie and I headed to the match and took our place in the executive box amongst others also in the box. It was a really nice change with nice food available and an outdoor balcony where we could sit and watch the match whilst also enjoying the atmosphere. We were situated just behind the Wolves fans and we got some funny looks as we celebrated each of Blues two goals. Unfortunately Blues lost the game 3-2 but it had been a nice day out and the Blues fans had sang their hearts out. I must admit I did miss being amongst the Blue army even though Julie and I created our own atmosphere, much to the disgust of the Wolves fans!

Just before the end of the season I decided to take Stephen to his first away game. It would be a somewhat local derby with Derby County who were flying high at the top of the table. So on the 20th April 1996 at the age of six Stephen experienced his first away match. We went in Julie's car and this time I chatted away about the game to Stephen during the journey. I bought him comic's etc for the journey as it is hard to keep a six-year-old entertained for long periods! Once in Derby though we parked up and with his hand in mine I led him towards Derby County's old baseball ground. It was quite funny as we approached the ground and I asked Stephen what he thought of the ground, as it was his first away ground and he looked up at me and replied 'it's a shed!' Julie and I laughed; he had been spoiled having St. Andrew's as his home ground!

The away end was packed with Bluenoses and Stephen loved it. Blues fans sang throughout the game and as Derby had been promoted to the Premiership they were singing 'going up, going up going up' to which the Blues fans were replying 'you're going straight back down, you're going straight back down!' There was a coloured player playing for Derby who had a hairstyle whereby all his hair was in sort of dreadlocks sticking up and throughout the game the Blues fans were singing 'he's got a pineapple on his head, he's got a pineapple on his head' etc, which I though was really funny. They sang the same song over and over throughout the game and I read in a newspaper years later that this had really affected him and ruined his career! I think it took off a little bit really and all other sets of fans sang it to him wherever he played at. I still think it was really funny and so did Stephen. Derby went 1-0 ahead and when Gary Breen scored our equaliser the Blues contingent went wild and I lifted a celebrating Stephen high into the air as we went mad. It was a great day and Stephen really enjoyed his first away game.

Blues went on to lose the final two games of the season away at Leicester City 3-0 and at home against Reading 2-1 and finished the season in 15th place. At least we had avoided relegation back to the second division as I had hoped and had managed to achieve a League Cup semi-final appearance before losing to Leeds Utd over two legs. Sunderland won the first division championship and were promoted to the Premiership, whilst Manchester Utd won the FA Cup beating Liverpool 1-0 in the final.

I finished my Degree with honours in Midwifery and had a fabulous graduation ceremony at the Liverpool Cathedral. Life was good and I was looking forward to next season, once again with hope in my heart.

When the 1996 to 1997 season kicked off I was hopeful that Blues would achieve a higher position that last season and whilst establish ourselves in the first division also begin to look towards challenging for a promotion spot. The season began with a home win against Crystal Palace 1-0 and a cracking 4-4 draw away at Sheffield United sandwiched by two games that saw Blues progress into the next round of the League Cup by beading Brighton 3-0 on aggregate. Unfortunately Blues were then knocked out over two legs by Coventry City 2-1 on aggregate, thereby ending our participation in the League Cup for another season. Oh well, we could concentrate on the league from now on. Things weren't going too well in the league either though and by the time Blues lost at Huddersfield we were in 23rd place and facing the fear of relegation again. There was still a long way to go though and by the time we took on Stevenage in the 3rd round of the FA Cup Blues were up to 9th and 15,363 saw Blues progress to the next round following a 3-0 win at St. Andrews.

The 4th round of the FA Cup saw Blues draw Stockport County at St. Andrews and a crowd of 18,487 saw a good 3-1 win that meant a 5th round draw against Wrexham at St. Andrews. By the time the Wrexham game came around Blues had slipped down to 19th position and in the danger area once again. Hence it was a truly miserable day to see Blues beaten by our lower league opposition 3-1 with a player by the name of Bryan Hughes scoring for Wrexham. This inspired Blues to go out and buy him and he went on to play for Blues for quite a while. However, our cup dream was over for another season and we were struggling at the foot of the table.

By 29th March 1997 when Julie and I were heading to London for the away game at Crystal Palace, Blues were still in 19th position. There were loads of Bluenoses at Palace for the game and when the teams came running out for the match we all stood and looked on in amazement. There were two teams both wearing Crystal Palace kits! Crystal Palace were in their home kit and Birmingham City were in the Crystal Palace third kit! Apparently the referee had decided that our away and third kit clashed with the Crystal Palace kit so Blues had to play in Palace's third kit in which Palace had never won! Blues then proceeded to show their opponents exactly how to win in that kit and won the game 1-0! Quite a good night really and Blues were up to 18th place.

This was the start of Blues recovery and by the last match of the season, which would be away at Ipswich; Blues were up as high at 10th place. Even though it was quite a long way to Ipswich I had decided to take Stephen with Julie, Emma and I. I patiently explained to him that there might not be many Blues fans at Ipswich like he was used to seeing because of how far away we were going. However, after a 4 hour journey involving a few comic's and a bit of entertaining for Stephen including a stop off, we arrived in Ipswich and parked up in a car park jam packed with Bluenoses! Stephen looked on in amazement and as we headed into a pub just opposite the train station packed with Blues fans, he turned to me and said 'I though you said there wouldn't be many Blues fans?' I had to laugh, especially as we looked out of the pub window and hundreds of Bluenoses were streaming out of the station having obviously just got off a train from Birmingham.

I saw Alan in the pub and we all had a couple of pints and caught up on Blues news. As I came out of the toilet I found Stephen standing outside the men's. 'What are you doing?' I asked and he held his hand open revealing a pound coin saying 'I'm the lookout!!' I had to laugh as I led him back to our friends. He was made up with his pound and off we headed to the ground. I blamed Stephen for our constant trips to the toilet during the game but really it was the few pints of cider I had consumed in the pub! It was a good atmosphere amongst the travelling Bluenoses and I got to swing Stephen about again when we scored as the match finished 1-1.

Blues finished the season in a creditable 10th place, Bolton were first division champions and were promoted with Barnsley as runners up and Crystal Palace in the playoff's. The FA Cup was won by Chelsea who beat Middlesborough 2- 0 and Middlesborough were again losing finalists in the League Cup when they were beaten by Leicester City in a replay 1-0. This was to be my last full season in England as I was about to set my sights on moving abroad.

CHAPTER SEVENTEEN – United Arab Emirates

I had been thinking of changing my life and moving abroad for a couple of months and following the end of the season in 1997 I decided to do something about it. I had been thinking of moving to New Zealand and had started the application process only to discover that I would have to pay for my own flight or commit to at least two years in New Zealand if the hospital were to pay for my flight. I was not prepared to commit for so long at this point so I began to consider a move to the Middle East in order to save the money for my New Zealand flight, which as you can imagine was quite expensive at this time. With this in mind, I applied to an agency and soon had a reply regarding a hospital in a small place called Ruwais, which is situated, on the coast in the United Arab Emirates. The matron was quite keen to employ me and won me over after she personally called me from Ruwais and convinced me to at least travel out and see what it was like for the three month trial period. If I found it too small I was told I could always move to the larger 'Corniche Hospital' in Abu Dhabi which was also run by the same British company. Abu Dhabi was a big city and the Corniche hospital was really big, much more like what I was used to but the salary was not good which was why I opted for Ruwais Hospital. The salary package was much better because of the fact that the hospital was much smaller and had no on site medical cover out of hours, meaning that Doctors had to been called in from the nearby complex.

I had to give one months notice at Whiston Hospital and as I already had two weeks holiday booked it meant that I only had to work two weeks before jetting off. Therefore I handed in my notice, much to the shock of my friends who never thought I was serious, and a couple of days later I boarded a flight with my sister Annette for our holiday in Cyprus. I had been to Cyprus with Annette for the last three years as we both really loved the resort of Aya Napa and always had a fab time. We were going for two weeks and my mom was joining us for the second week. Annette and I had a fabulous time and at the end of the first week we sat in the bar of our accommodation waiting patiently for mom to arrive. She was not booked into our apartment but we were going to bunk her in with us. However, we waited and we waited and she never arrived so we then waited outside in the courtyard and still no sign of her. As time went on we got a bit worried and we couldn't ask the apartment staff, as she was not officially booked in. So we approached one of the local taxi drivers in case he might have any news of the incoming flights. The taxi driver informed us that Larnaca Airport was closed due to fog.

As it was getting late we heading to our apartment for a bit of a sleep after phoning my brother Neil who informed us that mom had in fact boarded the flight okay. We didn't really know what to do and kept taking it in turns to get up and check if mom had arrived. At around six am I opened our door in my pyjamas and looked over the balcony only to see my mom happily sitting on her suitcase in the middle of the courtyard! It really was a hilarious sight! I dashed back into the apartment shouting to Annette, 'quick get dressed mom's sitting on her cases in the courtyard!' It was like something from the movie 'Shirley Valentine'

It turned out that her flight had been diverted to the other airport on the other side of the island and mom had been bought back to Larnaca by coach. At least she had found us okay and we all really enjoyed the rest of the holiday together. As it was quite hot, I mistakenly thought that I would now have adapted to the heat for my impending move to the United Arab Emirates two weeks later.

I worked the rest of my notice and had a great leaving party with the girls from Whiston Hospital, which included a stripper, dressed as an Arab with sunglasses etc. I had told them not to get a stripper as I wouldn't be impressed but it was quite amusing in the end and I had quite a laugh. I was sad to leave my mates behind though when it came time to leave. I had made some wonderful friends during my time in Liverpool and at Whiston Hospital. I had also had the pleasure of working with some lovely people during my time at work in Liverpool and during my midwifery training. I considered myself a better person for having known them all. And so on 18th July 1997 I boarded a flight to Abu Dhabi where I would be met and transferred to Ruwais to begin my new life.

It was a long flight and very traumatic as I thought of my family that I would miss very much and the uncertainty of what awaited me. When I got off the plane and stepped into Abu Dhabi airport I was over-whelmed by the cultural difference around me and I headed to passport control somewhat stunned, despite the fact that I was being chatted up by a British diver, who was trying to get me to meet him in Finnegans if I came to Abu Dhabi on my days off! Once I got to passport control I saw someone holding up a board with my name on and I went across and was handed my temporary visa that would enable me to enter the county. It was such a shock when I came out of the airport as I was faced with such fierce heat even at that time in the evening. It was just like having a hairdryer in your face – there was not much air about, which I know is down to the humidity which is at its highest in the summer. I then faced a three-hour car journey through the desert with the hospital driver that had been sent to collect me.

Once I settled in though I began to find my feet. I was sharing a big four-bedroom villa with two other British girls who were nice and friendly. Lisa became a good friend during our time together in Ruwais and that helped a lot as the complex we were living on was extremely quiet. In fact there was only one bank, two supermarkets, one Arabic restaurant and a few small shops. There was just one bar and that was situated in the only hotel that was a bus ride away. The hotel was called the 'Dhafra Beach Hotel' and the bar inside was called the 'Falcon Bar'. I was to have many fun times in this bar I can tell you. The hotel had its own beach too and it was so quiet. The pool wasn't cooled though and was really hot in the summer, although there was often nobody there so it was nice and relaxing. When Annette and my mom visited me they really loved it.

The hospital was really small and was a general hospital with a maternity wing attached, which was where I worked. It could be really quiet but I enjoyed working there. Quite often when the ward was empty I could be found just outside the door at the end of the ward getting some sunshine as I sat on a chair outside. It was like being on holiday. There were not many westerners in Ruwais but those of us that were there became good friends and would often be found at each other's villas sharing drinks and throwing the odd barbecue or party.

So when the new season 1997 to 1998 got underway I could only call home on the Saturday nights to get the Blues results from my mom or Annette. I must admit I really missed the Blues matches even if I was enjoying being bathed in constant sunshine. Blues began the season well and were in the top half of the table most of the time moving between third and thirteenth place by November.

It was at the end of November that I met a guy who was to become the love of my life for quite a few years. During my first few months in Ruwais I had partied hard with my mates, Gillian, Irene and Lisa and it was at a barbecue at my villa that I met Steve. Steve was a deep-sea diver who had just been moved to Ruwais and had already spotted me a few days earlier at a darts evening. He had been cheeky enough to send a message with my mate Lisa asking me to call him if I wanted to go out with him and leaving his number on the boat where he was stationed. I just laughed when Lisa told me but when I woke up a few days later after my night duty and Lisa told me we were having a barbecue at our villa, I was to meet him again. Lisa was going out with a Dutch guy called Erwin and it was Erwin who had arranged the barbecue. It turned out to be really good fun and I found Steve's charm too good to resist and we began dating.

The following day I was in the Ruwais team for the raft race in Abu Dhabi at the Corniche hospital and I must admit I was feeling pretty hungover. I didn't let that stop me though and proceeded to row our raft and lead from the front as we progressed to the final and finished runners up. It was great fun even if I did feel a bit rough.

The next couple of months were great and I really loved being with Steve. Both Gillian and Irene were now also going out with divers and this period turned into one of the best I have known. It was just like the TV series 'Friends' and we were often all together having fun. Steve was a Manchester United fan unfortunately, but I let him off as he was in fact from Manchester originally. At the time though he lived in a small village called Ashton near to Liverpool. Steve and I had some great times and spent a great Christmas day together with the others after the girls and I had cooked a turkey diner for the lads.

By Christmas Blues were in 11th place and had been knocked out of the League Cup in the third round by Arsenal at Highbury 4-1 in extra time. However, in January Blues progressed to the fourth round of the FA Cup after beating Crewe Alexandra away 2-1. The next match on 10th January was away at Stoke City and I would be home for it! I had planned my first trip home to see my family and after nearly six months away I was really looking forward to seeing everyone again and to see the Blues play once again.

I was so excited being back in Birmingham and was really looking forward to the trip to Stoke City's new Britannia stadium for the match. Stephen was now eight years old and was also really looking forward to the trip, and so we headed to Stoke once again with Julie driving us. The new Britannia stadium was very nice but once again just like all the other new stadiums being built up and down the country. Blues fans were situated behind the goal and there were already quite a few Bluenoses inside the ground when we arrived. The atmosphere was great and Stephen loved it, as did I. Blues were playing in our away kit of yellow shirts and black shorts and it wasn't too long before the Bluenoses were singing 'it's just like watching Brazil, it's just like watching Brazil' as Blues raced into a three goal lead. It was brilliant and before long Blues were winning 6-0 and taunting the Stoke fans by singing their 'Delilah' anthem back at them. They were fuming! We however, were enjoying ourselves immensely and at one point I turned to look at Stephen who was gazing at the scoreboard, which read Stoke City 0 Birmingham City 6. I asked him what he was doing and he replied he was looking at the scoreboard because he couldn't believe it. He was over the moon and once again the Bluenoses broke into a chorus of 'it's just like watching Brazil, it's just like watching Brazil'. There were thousands of Blues fans there and they all began singing 'stand up it your 6-0 up' and all the Bluenoses stood up. All the seated Stoke fans looked on in despair and the Blues fans then sang 'sit down if your 6-0 down' to the already seated Stoke fans. Quite amusing really.

To add insult to injury Blues scored a seventh and completed a 7-0 rout as 'oh what fun it is to see City win away' rang out to the tune of jingle bells, followed by chants of 'easy, easy!' It was a brilliant day out and Stephen and I had a fantastic day. A week later I again took Stephen to St. Andrews to watch Blues take on Huddersfield. Blues were now in eight place and a 0-0 draw saw Blues finish the day remaining in eight place in the league.

The following week saw Blues take on Stockport County in the fourth round of the FA Cup at St. Andrews on my birthday. Stephen and I were amongst the 18,882 inside St. Andrews to watch Blues win 2-1 and book a place in the fifth round. What a great birthday present I thought as we celebrated together and I swung Stephen around and around. Brilliant. Three days later Blues again met Stockport County only this time in the league and a great performance at St. Andrews ensured that Blues again came away winners, this time by 4 goals to 1 and I was once again inside the ground to enjoy the celebrations.

On 31st January, with Blues in 7th place we set off for Reading. This was Reading's old ground and it was Stephen's first experience of the old terraces. Blues fans had been given the terraced end behind the goal and Stephen looked on in amazement as he had only ever sat in the seats at games and up to now had never stood on the terraces. Today he would experience it for the first time and only time as terracing was now almost completely phased out in the top divisions of English football. While Julie and I stood against a crash barrier, Stephen moved down to the front by the fencing at the edge of the pitch whilst I watched him and the game. He seemed to enjoy the atmosphere and the standing and would run up and down to me, then back to the front. Blues were up against it from the start and when we had a player sent off it began to go down hill. However, Blues held out until we had another player sent off and with only nine men on the pitch, went 2-0 down. The Bluenoses remained upbeat though and even at 2-0 we all sang 'we've only got 9 men, we've only got 9 men', back at the Reading fans. It was not to be our day and we headed back home with yet another new experience under Stephen's belt.

Then it came time for me to return to life in the sunshine in Ruwais and long distance phone calls to get the Blues results on a Saturday evening. I would once again miss the atmosphere of a live game for a while longer. Blues had drawn Leeds United in the fifth round of the FA Cup and on 14th February our participation in the tournament ended with a 3-2 defeat at Elland Road.

Meanwhile, Steve's job had been moved and he would now be based off shore and would no longer be at Ruwais. His trips on shore would now be to Abu Dhabi, which was a three hours bus journey that I would now have to make in order to see him. Sometimes it would be at short notice and I would have to catch the seven am bus from Ruwais Hospital, which only travelled once a day. I would arrive in Abu Dhabi just after ten am and I would book into the Sands Hotel and await Steve's arrival, which was usually in the afternoon. Then, after just the one night together every couple of weeks, I would say bye to Steve in the morning and then get the afternoon bus at 3pm from the Corniche Hospital Social Club back to Ruwais feeling very sad. These were hard times for me as I missed Steve so much when he was away.

He would write loads of letters to me and I would call him on his boat but I missed him.

By March Blues were in 7th place and that was where they stayed until the last match of the season when 25,877 turned up at St. Andrews to see Blues take on Charlton Athletic and a last chance to make the play offs. However, a 0-0 draw kept Blues in 7th place and we just missed out on a play off place. Nottingham Forest were first division champions and Middlesborough were promoted as runners up and Charlton also went up winning the play off final. Manchester City, Stoke City and Reading were relegated to the second division. The FA Cup was won by Arsenal who beat Newcastle United 2-0 and Chelsea won the League cup after extra time beating Middlesborough 2-0.

In July I decided to leave Ruwais and move to the Corniche Hospital in Abu Dhabi to be nearer Steve and to make it easier to see him on his trips on shore. I was also getting bored at Ruwais hospital, as it was so quiet although I must admit it was lovely and peaceful and probably the longest holiday I have ever had. I really enjoyed my fourteen months at Ruwais and met some lovely people and had some fabulous experiences. I gave my notice in, which would be three months and I planned my starting date at the Corniche Hospital, which would be 2nd November 1998. This meant that Ruwais hospital would fly me home and after one month at home, the Corniche Hospital would fly me back to Abu Dhabi.

CHAPTER EIGHTEEN – Penalty shoot out

Whilst I was working my notice at Ruwais Hospital the 1998 to 1999 season began with Blues starting the season in winning style at Port Vale 2-0. In fact Blues won four games in August and drew two games before their first defeat on 31st August at Bradford City. In the League Cup Blues beat Millwall over two legs 3-1 on aggregate and drew Macclesfield in the second round.

My last three months seemed to drag, probably because I was working lots of night duties, which I hate, and because I was missing Steve. By the time I was due to leave Ruwais I had already been allocate a flat in Abu Dhabi which I would be sharing with a South African girl and I had moved my things in ready for when I would come back at the end of October. My flight home was on the 25th September 1998 and by this time Blues were 3rd in the first division and had beaten Macclesfield 9-0 on aggregate in the League Cup to set up a 3rd round tie at home against Wimbledon.

It was really great to be home and see all my family and friends and my first match was away at Portsmouth on 29th September. Stephen was once again by my side as we headed to Portsmouth with Julie and we enjoyed a good day out as we cheered Blues on to a good 1-0 away win which we watched from the open away end. Luckily it didn't rain and we went home happy and Blues were up to 5th in the table.

Next up was a home game against Tranmere Rovers on the 3rd October which turned into a very enjoyable day out as we were treated to a good performance which resulted in a 2-2 draw which took Blues up to 4th in the table. I was really enjoying my trip home. It was lovely not having to work for about 6 weeks as well, as I was not starting at my new hospital until the 2nd November.

A week later Julie, Stephen and I were off on another away trip, this time to Watford. It's not too far to travel to Watford and I usually quite enjoy the trip. The away end is quite big as well and it was another new ground for Stephen to visit. The atmosphere amongst the Bluenoses was as great as always and it was another good away day as Blues moved further up the league to 3rd place after Dele Adebola scored our goal in a 1-1 draw.

The following Saturday Stephen and I were back on the Tilton as Blues swept aside Crewe at St. Andrews 3-1 in front of 20,087 to move into second place in the first division table. It was proving to be a great trip home and wonderful to be able to get to live games yet again. I miss the live matches so much when I am away from England and it is always so much sweeter when I am home and get to enjoy that marvellous atmosphere amongst the Bluenose at both home and away games.

My final game before I returned to Abu Dhabi was at St. Andrews against Swindon Town and I soaked up the atmosphere amongst the Blues faithful as Marsden scored for Blues in a 1-1 draw that meant that we stayed in second place in the league. I left the ground thinking that this could be the season when we regained our place in the top flight, although Blues being Blues never do anything the easy way and I was also slightly nervous that we were also capable of messing it up.

A few days later I boarded a plane back to Abu Dhabi so that I would have a week to settle into my new flat before I started work at the Corniche Hospital. Once I arrived back I got a call from Steve who told me that his ship would be going to Ruwais for a few days so I hastily arranged to hire a car and drove to Ruwais to meet up with him. It was my first time driving in the UAE and was all the more daunting because they drive on the right and cars are left hand drive, and it was a 3 hour drive! I made it okay though and had a lovely few days with Steve staying at one of my mates villa's. Then it was back to Abu Dhabi and to a new job.

I soon settled into my job at the Corniche Hospital but I was not happy in my flat. My flat mate and her husband made it a little uncomfortable for me, especially on the odd occasion when Steve came to stay. I couldn't stand it for very long to be honest, so when another girl was leaving I moved into her room in a really massive 3 bedroom flat with 2 British girls and I was much happier. Each bedroom was really big with a large en-suite bathroom, so I hung my Blues calendar on the wall and settled in.

During my period of settling into life in Abu Dhabi, Blues were knocked out of the League Cup at Home by Wimbledon 2-1, won away games at Queens Park Rangers 1-0 and West Brom 3-1 but dropped to 3rd place because of a home draw against Huddersfield Town 1-1. By the time Blues lost away at Wolves they had dropped to 8th in the league and I was getting worried. Blues then had a good 4-2 home win against Bristol City and then, following a 1-0 defeat at Ipswich, had a brilliant 7-1 away win at Oxford United and were back up to 4th in December.

The FA Cup draw threw up an away tie against Premier League opposition in the form of Leicester City and despite a brave performance by the Blues of Birmingham we were knocked out of the competition 4-2. It was, however, a very brave performance against Premiership opposition.

By March I had booked some holidays and flew back to Birmingham on the 23rd for a two week break with my family. It was really nice and the first game came a week later away at Crewe. Once again Julie, Stephen and I travelled to Crewe and had a good day out even though the game finished in a goalless draw. Two days later I went to St. Andrews for my last game of my current trip as Blues lost against Watford 2-1 and remained in 4th spot. Another two days later on 7th April I again boarded a plane and headed back to Abu Dhabi having had a nice holiday despite the results.

The final six games of the season saw Blues achieve four wins and two defeats which meant that we finished the season in 4th spot and a place in the playoffs. I was really excited about the play offs due to the fact that we were so close to getting into the elite premier league after so many years outside the top flight. It was also our first time in the play offs. There was just a small matter of Watford to get past in the semi-final before we could even think of the finals and a place in the premiership. The first leg was away and Blues lost 1-0, which although not ideal, it was not impossible to get back into it in the second leg at a packed St. Andrews. As I was still in Abu Dhabi I had to listen in as Blues won 1-0 on the night meaning an aggregate of 1-1 and the dreaded penalties. I should have known there and then that our blue hearts would be broken once again as we always seem to have such an awful record when it comes to penalty deciders. Sure enough Blues lost on penalties and our hearts were broken.

Sunderland were crowned champions of the First Division, Bradford City were runners up and Watford won the Play Off final and were also promoted. Bury, Oxford Utd and Bristol City were relegated to the Second Division. Manchester Utd won the FA Cup, beating Newcastle Utd 2-0 in the final and Tottenham won the League cup defeating Leicester City 1-0.

I was beginning to enjoy my life in Abu Dhabi, which was a big city after living in tiny Ruwais for just over a year. I had made some good friends including my mate Gillian who had also moved from Ruwais to Abu Dhabi not long after I had. We also shared the same flat, which could be challenging at times because Gillian was a real party animal! I also became good friends with a girl called Alex and we had many great nights out together. We are still really good friends to this day, even though she now lives back in England and I am still in Abu Dhabi. I even introduced her to the man she was later to marry and they are still very happy together. Craig was a mate of Steve's and was also a deep sea diver. I introduced them to each other one day in Finnegan's bar. Craig is probably the best male friend I have ever had and he has always been a good friend to me throughout all my ups and downs and I will forever be grateful to him for that. He is, however, a

Newcastle Utd fan, but I must say, his love of Newcastle is as true and unconditional as my love of Birmingham City. Alex and I had some great times when the boys were in shore and it was a great time to be in Abu Dhabi. When the boys were away we would go out and party and would often stagger home in the early hours, go back to Alex's flat (which was in the same apartment block) and blast 'sugar baby love' as we poured another vodka and danced around. Alex has also been a great mate and was always worrying about me and looking out for me.

The 1999 to 2000 season began on 7th august with a home game against Fulham which resulted in a 2-2 draw. I decided I would go back to Birmingham in September and by then Blues had beaten Exeter City and Bristol Rovers in the League cup and were in 2nd place in Division One when I arrived home on the 23rd September. My first game was two days later at St. Andrews and the atmosphere was great as Blues beat Queens Park Rangers 2-0 to go top of the table. I was over the moon to be top of the First Division and also it was great to be back in Birmingham.

A week later I was off to London to watch Blues take on Charlton at The Valley. Once again Julie was the driver with Emma, Stephen and I travelling with her. It was a nice day and before long we were parking up not too far from Charlton's end of the ground. It was a bit intimidating when I got out the car in my Blues shirt and found myself surrounded by red shirts! It didn't help that Julie and Emma had Blues red away shirts on! Thanks girls. We joined the red mass heading towards the ground with me standing out like a sore thumb in my Blue shirt. Just before the ground we stopped at a chippie, where I once again found myself surrounded by red shirts and getting some very funny looks indeed. I decided not to hang about trying to retrieve the vinegar from the Charlton fans and headed off towards the ground with chips in hand.

As we arrived at the turnstiles, chips still in hand, the policeman informed me I couldn't take my own food inside. I informed him that it wasn't mine and was in fact Julies! Ah a smart one! He replied – 'go on then' he said as he gestured with his thumb towards the entrance. So inside we went and the minute we got inside Julie managed to drop her tray of chips on the floor. Nice. We should have known at that point that it wasn't going to be our day. We had really good seats and the atmosphere was great amongst the Bluenoses who had come in great number. Unfortunately Blues lost 1-0 and it was off back to the car amongst that bloody sea of red again! A few days later Julies face was circled in a photo in the newspaper from that very match with me sitting next to her! It was a name the fan competition in which the person in the circle contacted the magazine and won a year's supply. Brilliant!

A week later and just before I was due to fly back to Abu Dhabi, I took Stephen to Walsall for an away trip that unfortunately ended in a 1-0 defeat. Blues were now in 4th place but there was still a long time to go before the end of the season so I headed back to the sun with hope in my heart still. In fact, I flew back on the very day that Blues were to take on Newcastle Utd in the third round of the League Cup and I was gutted that I was going to miss it, especially as it was against premier opposition. I was even more gutted when I realised I had missed a fantastic 2-0 cup win which put us into the fourth round where Blues again drew premiership opposition in the form of West Ham Utd at St. Andrews.

The West Ham game took place at the end of November with Blues now in 7th place in the league and despite a very spirited performance Blues lost 3-2 with goals from Grainger and Hyde. However, two days later Blues were again in cup action, this time the FA Cup which threw up an away tie at Watford. I really fancied our chances in the FA Cup – as I always do – and Blues repaid my optimism with a 1-0 win, courtesy of a Gary Rowett goal.

This year I had decided that I wanted to be home for Christmas and the New Year celebrations as it was the new millennium. I was lucky and was one of the few that managed to get holidays from work over this period and so once again I set foot back in Birmingham just prior to the home game against Sheffield Utd.

The previous week Blues had lost at Wolves 2-1 and we were down to 8th in table and having a bit of a crisis. Annette, Stephen, Dave Brueton and I had tickets in the new railway stand for the Sheffield Utd game on Boxing Day. We all met up in the Greenways Pub and enjoyed a few drinks with Dave and his mates before heading to our seats. It was difficult to leave the pub because Dave and his mates kept buying 'one more quick vodka before we go', which seemed to go on for quite a while. Stephen was getting a bit worried about missing kick off so we headed to the ground with a few minutes to spare. It is quite a walk from the Greenways to the railway end as you have to go all the way round the school (the bloody gates were locked so we couldn't cut through as we had been hoping!) and as we neared the turnstiles we heard a roar that was not loud enough to be a Blues goal and probably meant Blues had fell behind in the first minute or so. Sure enough, when we got inside Blues were 1-0 down and it wasn't just Stephen that was pissed off now – I was as well! Needless to say we played crap and were soon 2-0 behind and that is how it stayed.

When Paul Devlin (an ex Blues player now at Sheffield Utd) was subbed and had to walk past our end, I was on my feet letting him know in no uncertain manner, exactly what I thought of him. I know he heard me as he looked up and some bloke shouted 'well said love!' Meanwhile Dave was dancing around in front of me waving his arms about saying 'no Deb, you can't go on to the pitch!' It was really funny as Annette had tipped him off before the game that I occasionally lose the plot and try to invade the pitch. Dave is really tall and was a gentle giant and the incident looked really funny. With five minutes of the game left I said 'still time for two yet!' to which Dave replied 'what? Vodka's' and I had to laugh. The game finished 2-0 and Blues were down to 11th in the table and things were looking grim.

A few days later Stephen, Julie and I headed off to Nottingham for a game against Forest. Once we arrived at the ground it started to rain so we headed to the Chippie near the ground, obtained chips and curry sauce and headed to a covered area just across the road to eat them and discuss the forthcoming match. I bought a badge and a programme for Stephen before heading into the ground where a large and vocal Blues following witnessed another defeat, this time 1-0. I was starting to get worried.

I had been invited to a party on New Year's Eve, along with the rest of my family and of course it would herald the new millennium. Unfortunately the party was being held by a villa fan who was quite put out when I turned up wearing a Birmingham City Crest necklace. 'You had better take that off 'he said, 'you just try and make me!' I replied and the necklace stayed put! It was quite funny really because I had been put in charge of the lighting the fireworks but that was soon put a stop to when I was asked if I knew what to do and I replied 'yes, point them at the any villa fans and light them!' I don't know what their problem was?

By the end of the night I had discovered that most people at the party where, in fact, Bluenoses and I had them all singing "Keep Right On!' in the garden as we saw in the new millennium.

By the time the next Blues game came along on the 3rd of January, we had all just about recovered from the New Year celebrations and I was looking forward to the next game which was against Huddersfield Town at St. Andrews. Once again it was off to the Greenways pub to meet Dave and his mates and have another session before the game. Stephen was again worried that we would miss the kick off but this time our seats were on the Kop which was considerably closer than last match when we had been in the railway end. So, with five minutes to go to kick off we dashed across the road and would have made the kick off if we hadn't stopped for a programme on the way in! As we headed up the steps there was a big roar and we were just in time to see Blues celebrating the first goal of the millennium scored by Bryan Hughes. Stephen glared at me but was still happy because we were 1-0 in front. Because the match was an early kick off, the goal was also the first goal of the millennium for any team! The game ended with a 1-0 win which I was extremely happy with as we headed home. Blues were now in 12th place and the next game, which would be the day before I go back, would be FA Cup action up in Liverpool as Blues were to take on Everton at Goodison Park.

It was going to be difficult for me to get to Liverpool as I couldn't hire a car because I wouldn't be around to return it so my brother Neil kindly offered to drive us up. Sue and Nicola also came and they dropped us at the ground while they went shopping in the city centre. This was going to be an exciting match as once again it was against premiership opposition. It was Stephens first time inside Everton's ground and I think like me, he wasn't too impressed with the old stand that the Blues fans were situated in just to the side of the goal. It had another stand which came overhead of us and the seats were wooden and old. The Blues faithful were in good voice though and we had travelled in large numbers. A lot of fun was had and lots of songs were sung, especially aimed at the scousers. 'Stand up if you robbed your car' got a laugh from the scousers as did 'hey scouser, I wanna know where's my DVD?' Blues also sang 'my garden shed is bigger that this' in recognition of their ground.

Blues gave a great account of themselves and were robbed by two very dubious penalties losing 2-0. I still had heart though because I felt we were much better than our premiership opposition on the day and were extremely unlucky to lose with the score somewhat flattering them. It was quiet as we headed out and I don't think the Everton fans realised just how many Blues fans were amongst them in the streets outside as every time they taunted the odd Blues fan many more Blues would appear and skirmishes kept breaking out and the Everton fans would run off down the road where another skirmish would break out. The police soon arrived in force but they couldn't quite fathom out what was happening as once they arrived at a fight it would stop suddenly and then break out further up the road. Once they arrived at that skirmish it would stop and again start in another place! It was like a comedy sketch, and I don't think they knew what hit them.

As we arrived back at the car, Neil and sue could see all the flashing blue lights down the road and asked Stephen if he was okay as he was still only young and he bravely answered 'yes, we always fight when we lose!' I must admit I had to laugh. Then it was off back to Birmingham and for me to prepare to fly back to Abu Dhabi again.

Blues were in 12th place when I left but went on quite a run with good wins which included good derby wins against West Brom 3-0 and Wolves 1-0 and finished the season with a 0-0 draw at St Andrews against Grimsby Town which meant Blues finished in 5th place and a place in the play offs once again. Any hopes that this time it could be our lucky year were dashed in the home leg of the playoff semi final when Blues were soundly beaten 4-0 by Barnsley. I was gutted. I never gave up hope though and Blues went on to win the away leg at Barnsley 2-1 but unfortunately this was not enough and Blues lost on aggregate 5-2 and were to stay in Division One.

Charlton Athletic were Champions of Division One, with Manchester City runners up and 3rd placed Ipswich Town winning the play off final and also gaining promotion. Our neighbours Walsall were relegated along with Port Vale and Swindon Town to Division Two. The best end to the season came when our near neighbours Villa were beaten in the FA Cup final by Chelsea 1-0. Another team in Blue won the League Cup final as Leicester City beat Tottenham 2-1 in the final.

CHAPTER NINETEEN – League Cup Final!

I was optimistic at the start of the 2000 to 2001 season following our achievement of a place in the play-off semi finals two seasons running. I was still living and working in Abu Dhabi and I was hoping to get to see a few live games in the forthcoming season.

My first trip home would be in August and I was already looking forward to it. The season began with an away tie in London at Queens Park Rangers and a 0-0 draw saw Blues begin the season in 10th place. The following week saw the first game of the new season at St. Andrews and 21,659 saw Blues lose their first game 3-1 to another London side, Fulham. This was not what I was hoping for. However, four days later Blues got our first win of the season in the first leg of the League Cup away at Southend 5-0.

I was back in Birmingham for the next game which was away at Nottingham Forest. Stephen and I were really looking forward to this trip and we met up with Julie and headed to Nottingham by car with Julie driving. It was a great day out with loads of Blues fans making the trip. The atmosphere in the Blues end was fantastic and it was made even better each time Blues scored in a great 2-1 win with goals from Eaden and our Brazilian Marcelo. Although Blues were only in 14th place, things were looking good and I had hope in my heart. I was convinced that this could be our year (as always).

The following week and my last game before I headed back to sunny climates was a home tie against Barnsley. I really wanted revenge against Barnsley for knocking us out of the play offs last season and this was duly gained with goals from Grainger,Holdsworth, Hughes and Ndlovu in a great 4-1 win which took us up to 5th in the table. It had been a great day, with a great atmosphere inside St. Andrews and I had enjoyed a lovely trip but it was time to head back.

Three days after I returned back to Abu Dhabi, Blues played the second leg in the 1st round league cup tie against Southend with a 0-0 draw seeing Blues through to the next round 5-0 on aggregate. Blues followed this up with a 1-0 home win against Sheffield Utd, another home win against Preston 3-1 and an away draw at local rivals West Brom 1-1 which moved Blues up to 4th in the league table.

Then it was back to League Cup action and an away tie at Wycombe Wanderers in the second round first leg. This was a really exciting game with lots of goals and finished in a good 4-3 win for Blues with two goals from Andy Johnson and two goals from Geoff Horsefield. Sandwiched in between the cup ties was a home game against Tranmere Rovers which finished in a 2-0 win for Blues keeping us in 4th place. The return leg of the League Cup tie against Wycombe at St. Andrews resulted in a 1-0 win with Blues going into the third round draw after a 5-3 aggregate win.

Blues slipped up in the next game losing 2-0 away at Watford and slipped to 5th but a good 2-0 away win at Crewe the following week saw us move back up the 4th spot. This was followed by a home win over Crystal Palace 2-1, another home win over Stockport County 4-0, which took us to 3rd, but then another slip against Sheffield Wednesday losing 1-0 away from home. Blues soon recovered though and won the next game at St. Andrews against Gillingham 1-0 and then drew away at Portsmouth 1-1 and remained in 3rd place. Things were looking good and Blues were drawn to play Premier League team Tottenham at White Hart Lane in the 3rd Round of the League Cup which was now at the knock out stages.

It was an amazing night as 27,096 saw Blues beat Tottenham 3-1 on their own ground with goals from Burchill and two from Dele Adebola. What a brilliant result! I couldn't believe it and was beginning to fancy our chances in the cup as well as the league now. The fourth round draw paired us with another Premier League club Newcastle Utd at St. Andrews and I was really optimistic despite again drawing a Premier club.

Back to league action and a home game against Bolton Wanderers which ended 1-1, followed by a rare defeat away at Norwich City 1-0. Then followed three wins on the trot, 3-2 at home over Burnley, 2-1 at home over Huddersfield Town and a another fantastic result in the League Cup – 2-1 over Premier League Newcastle Utd with goals from Michael Johnson and Dele Adebola. Birmingham were now in the Quarter Final of the League Cup and were rewarded with a home tie against Sheffield Wednesday. Could this be our year I wondered? I thought so.

By the time we came to play in the Quarter Final, Blues were now in 2nd place in the league following a good 2-1 away win at Gillingham and 22,911 were inside St. Andrews to See Blues beat Sheffield Wednesday 2-1 to book a place in the League Cup Semi Final. I was so excited; I would so love to see Birmingham City win a major trophy. The Semi Final draw was made and Blues were to play Premier League Ipswich Town who were currently flying high. It would again be two legged with the first leg being at Ipswich in January.

Five days later Blues travelled to Wolves for a local derby and came away with all three points following a 1-0 win and were then held 0-0 at St. Andrews by Queens Park Rangers and Blues remained in 3rd place in the table. Unfortunately Blues finished the year on a losing note, being beaten at Blackburn 2-0 and began the New Year also on a losing note, going down 2-0 at St. Andrews to a Nottingham Forest side and we were now 5th in the table.

Next up was FA Cup action away at Maine Road as we lost 3-2 to Premier League Manchester City despite a spirited performance and goals by Granger and Adebola. However, we still had the League Cup Semi Final to look forward to and I was really excited about this.

The first leg of the Semi Final took place at Portman Road in Ipswich on 9th January and 21,684 saw Blues lose 1-0, which despite being a defeat, I thought that we could turn it around at St. Andrews in three weeks time. Blues bounced back from this by winning at Barnsley 3-2, completing a comprehensive double over the team that ruined our hopes of promotion last season. A week later and a stunning away win over table toppers Fulham who were on a high, but Blues came away with all three points and a 1-0 win.

And so on the 31st January 28,624 packed into St. Andrews for the second leg of the Semi Final. The atmosphere was fantastic as I watched it live on the television. I could feel the atmosphere from 3, 500 miles away! Could we be in our first major final since back in 1963 when Blues beat rivals Villa in the final 3-1? Ipswich were stiff opposition and began the match well. A good appeal for a penalty for Blues was turned down when an Ipswich player clearly handled inside the box but it was not given. Then Lazaridis crossed in a great ball for Adebola to head goalwards but his effort was saved by the Ipswich keeper. Then came the breakthrough as Martin Grainger headed home and the place erupted. It was now 1-1 on aggregate and 1-0 to Blues on the night.

Into the second half and when the ball fell to Geoff Horsefield just inside the penalty area he smashed it into the back of the net and the roar was unbelievable. Blues fans poured onto the pitch and mobbed Horsefield as the tanoy asked the supporters to return to their seats. It was now 2-1 and hope was in our hearts, but almost immediately from the kick off Ipswich raced into our half and scored, it was now 2-2 on aggregate. What a game it was becoming and just afterwards Horsefield hit the crossbar and then had another shot saved by the keeper and the game finished all square and would head into extra time.

So it was into extra time and before long the ball was played to Horsefield and his shot nestled into the bottom corner as the ground once more erupted – 3-1 on the night and 3-2 on aggregate, the final in Cardiff was beckoning! Andy Johnson wrapped it up in the second period of extra time as he latched onto a back pass that the keeper miskicked and scored the fourth goal on the night and I was in heaven along with thousands of other Bluenoses who were once again invading the pitch to mob Johnson in celebration! Once again we had shown Premier League opposition what we could do and blues were in the Cup final at Cardiff where we would meet the mighty reds of Liverpool. I was so happy, but unfortunately because of work I would not be able to get home and would have to be content to watch it live on television in one of the pubs.

Following our great semi final victory it was back to the bread and butter of the first division and another win this time against Norwich City 2-1 at St. Andrews. We were soon brought down to earth by Sheffield Utd who beat us 3-1 at Brammall Lane and Blues were now in 6th place. Next up was a local derby against West Brom at St. Andrews and 25,025 saw Blues win 2-1 which was followed up the next week by an away win at Preston 2-0 which took Blues back to 4th spot in the league and Cardiff beckoned.

I headed to Heroes bar in Abu Dhabi to watch the final with Steve, who was currently onshore, and his mate from work. I had my Blues shirt on as usual and Heroes was packed with people who had come to watch the game. There were a few red shirts but all of the neutrals were supporting Birmingham, including of course Steve, who was being ribbed by his mates as he knew almost as much about the current Blues team as me! Well, he did have a very good teacher and had been listening to me for the last couple of years. 'I don't believe you' said his mate as Steve informed him that Geoff Horsefield used to be a brickie.

The match got underway and I was forced to down a few pints to calm my nerves. Blues were by far the better team but a cracking shot from Robbie Fowler put them ahead. My sister

Annette and her boyfriend Steve had travelled to the game and I had already had a few drunken phone conversations with her. It was a really dramatic final and not long before the end Blues were awarded a penalty. The pub went silent and I was bag of nerves as Darren Purse stepped up and held his nerve to score from the spot to take the game to extra time. The pub exploded as everyone jumped in the air and I dived on Steve in celebration and his mate was also celebrating wildly. I think Blues had touched the hearts of everyone in the pub as the game went to extra time.

In extra time Blues should have had a clear cut penalty as Andy Johnson was brought down in the area but the referee waved play on. The match was finally decided in a penalty shootout with Blues missing out by the narrowest of margins as Andy Johnson's spot kick was saved. We gave Liverpool a good game but Blues really should have won. Some of the Liverpool fans said that the journey back had been subdued as many of them felt that it should have been Birmingham's cup. Robbed by the scousers once again was my message to Annette when we spoke after the game as she was enjoying a pint in a pub in Cardiff before they headed back to Birmingham. Liverpool went on the win the treble of cups but it was Birmingham City that pushed them the hardest. There were 73,500 inside the Millennium Stadium that day and the three tiers occupied by the Bluenoses was a sea of Blue and white flags and scarves as once again they did us proud.

I was worried that we would now struggle to bounce back in the league and I was relieved as Blues won the next home game against Watford 2-0, won at Crystal Palace 2-1 and then beat Crewe at St. Andrews 2-0 to claim 3rd spot. Then, as an expectant crowd of 29,250 packed into St. Andrews to see Blues take on Blackburn Rovers we slipped up and lost the game2-0 sliding back to 4th place. This was followed by another defeat away at Stockport County 2-0 and after an away draw at Grimsby 1-1, we again lost to Sheffield Wednesday 2-1 at St. Andrews and 1-0 to Wolves. I was beginning to get worried and my fears got worse as Blues continued to lose away at Wimbledon 3-1 and away Tranmere 1-0.

This poor run of form was halted at Bolton as Blues drew 2-2 then drew the next game 0-0 at home against Portsmouth. The next game was away at Burnley and I was once again heading back to Birmingham and was planning the trip to Burnley with Julie, Stephen and Annette.

I was back in Birmingham and was travelling to Burnley in Julie's car with Stephen and Annette. Annette's boyfriend Steve was travelling on the coach with his mates from Harborne and they were going to meet us in Burnley. We had a nice drive up to Burnley and it wasn't long before we found a small pub on the outskirts and made our way inside. There were a couple of Burnley fans playing pool and after a few pints we soon got some banter going with them. We were all having a good laugh around the pool table when Annette's phone rang with the old Nokia ring tone. Stephen and I shouted 'Hello' as per the Ali G sketch and both fell about laughing. It was Steve asking us where we were and how to get to the pub we were in. Annette, having downed a couple of pints handed the phone to a Burnley fan which of course went down like a lead balloon with Steve. He found his way to us and not long after we were off to the ground.

Once inside Steve and Annette, who had left ahead of us, were already there so I set about ringing her to find out where she was sitting as the Blues end was packed. After shouting our seat and row number down the phone, I noticed a whole row of blokes stand up and head to where I was. They all came and stood around me and I discovered they were Steve's mates, Fiddler and Co. I thought it was really funny as did Annette who followed them up not long afterwards. Apparently they asked Annette where I was sitting and then she said they all just got up and left. Brilliant. It was great to see them and the atmosphere was brilliant. Blues were singing 'you're just a small town in Blackburn!' to the Burnley fans who seemed to be taking great offence to this. Then it was a chant of 'you'll get it, you'll get foot and mouth!' which seemed to go on for ages and also annoyed the Burnely fans. It was brilliant in amongst the Bluenoses but the game finished in a draw 0-0 and Blues were down to 5th but still in a playoff place. As we headed back to the car we were penned it by police horses for a while as the Burnley fans left. Then the police decided to let us through a few at a time which meant squeezing past the police horse at the front and as Annette passed the horse he snorted white stuff over her. I sang 'you'll get it, you'll get foot and mouth" as we all fell about laughing. Stephen thought it was really funny.

Next up was a game against Grimsby Town and I was off down St. Andrews to soak up the atmosphere that I had missed so much. I met up with Dave and the lads again for a few drinks and this time we made the kick off and saw Blues beat Grimsby 1-0 with a goal from Curtis Woodhouse. It was a great day and I was looking forward to my last game and the last game of the season away at Huddersfield.

The trip to Huddersfield brought back fantastic memories of the season that we won the second division championship at their ground. Stephen and I went by car with Julie and Annette went with Steve and his mates on a coach and we met up at the ground. I saw loads of people I knew inside the ground and so did Annette and Steve which meant that they spent the whole of the second half up the back in the bar getting very drunk and did not see any of the second half. Stephen couldn't work out why they would travel all that way for a match and then spend most of it in the bar. I must admit I could not enlighten him on the matter either. In fact , Steve thought the game finished 1-0 to Blues as that was the score last time he was in his seat! The game did in fact finish 2-1 to Blues and due to a strange set of other results at the last minute Huddersfield were dragged from nearly halfway up the table to be relegated. We were rubbing it in by singing 'we'll meet again, don't know where, don't know when but I know we'll meet again some sunny day' whilst waving to them.

Hence, when we got outside after the game there were a lot of pissed off Huddersfield fans and Julie had parked her car right in the middle of them. So, whilst the other Bluenoses got a police escort we had to head into enemy territory to get to the car. As we passed the Blues coach I saw Grainger on the bus with the door open so I said hello to him and asked if there was any chance of a lift to avoid the angry mob in front of us. 'You'll be okay don't worry' he said to us. Alright for him to say, I though as we headed to the car. It was quite sad really to see the Huddersfield fans as some of them were really devastated. I saw people just sitting behind the wheel of their cars crying. I know how that feels being a Bluenose. But today was a happy day for Blues as we were in the play offs and due to play Preston with the first leg at St. Andrews and I was heading back to the Middle East.

The play offs again brought heartbreak as the two legs finished all square and the second leg at Preston went to the deadly penalty shootout. I watched live as Trevor Francis took his players off the field in disgust when they refused to allow the penalties to be taken at the empty neutral end of the ground after previously agreeing that this is where they would be taken. It took a while for him to bring the players back on and agree to continue but I think that the players had already been unsettled by this and once again we were knocked out on penalties. I was once again devastated. Always next year I thought in despair. Overall though Blues had had a very good season, finishing in the playoff position and reaching a major cup final for the first time since 1963 and giving Liverpool more than a run for their money.

Fulham were crowned champions of Division One and Blackburn finished in second place with Bolton also promoted after winning the play off final. Huddersfield Town, Queens Park Rangers and Tranmere Rovers were relegated to the Second Division. The FA Cup was won by Liverpool who beat Arsenal 2-1 and as I stated earlier Liverpool also won the League Cup Beating Birmingham City on penalties 5-4.

CHAPTER TWENTY – Play Off Final!

As another season was about to begin, I was still working at the Corniche Hospital in Abu Dhabi and I was still seeing Steve – the Manchester Utd fan that I had been going out with since we met in Ruwais in 1997. I must admit that I was enjoying living in the sunshine; I had a membership for the nearby Sheraton Hotel where I enjoyed sunbathing and chilling out on the beach or in the pool on my days off. When Steve was offshore I would get out and about with my mates, particularly Alex and we would drink in various bars such as Finnegan's – which would later close and be relocated nearby as PJ O'Reillys. We would also visit the Marina club on a Friday night as this was the 'in' place for westerners to go on a Friday. It was a Disco on the beach near to the pool and it was always really exotic. I would also take Steve when he was in or we would head off for a few days away either in Dubai or sometimes to a lovely hotel in the mountains near Oman called Hatta Fort Hotel. It was really quiet there and really romantic and we would pack the cooler box with champagne and food and head off in my little black sporty Peugeot 206. It was fun times. We would often pass camels on the journey as we headed into the desert and we would stop and take pictures and laugh together.

The start of the 2001 to 2002 season began with an away trip to Wimbledon, which unfortunately Blues lost 3-1, not a good start. However, we got our season underway with a good 4-1 win over Millwall in our first home game of the season at St. Andrews and followed this up a few days later with a 3-0 home win over Southend in the first leg of the league cup. Blues continued in a winning vein by beating Walsall in a local derby away 2-1 and then beat Stockport at home 2-1 to claim 3rd spot in the league. Things were looking good and I was heading home again for another of my visits.

I flew to Birmingham on 30th august and had to wait over a week for my first game, which would be at St. Andrews to see Blues take on Sheffield Wednesday. It was great to be back and I met up with Dave and the lads again in the pub before heading into a buzzing St. Andrews to watch Blues win 2-0 with goals from Bryan Hughes and Andrew Johnson. What a great start to my trip.

As always I was enjoying being home and looking forward to my last match before returning to Abu Dhabi which would be a cup tie against Bristol Rovers away. I was really looking forward to this game as my brother Neil and his wife Sue were taking us to Bristol for the game. The game was on 11th September 2001 and as I was getting ready for the trip I turned the TV onto sky news only to be shocked by what was unveiling in New York as terrorists flew two airliners into the twin towers causing them to collapse killing thousands of people. I was in shock. All air traffic was grounded and the skies were silent. I was due to fly back in two days time! So it was in a state of shock that I headed to Bristol for the cup tie against Bristol Rovers that night.

Neil, Sue and Nicola dropped Stephen and I at the ground and headed off to shop or get something to eat. Stephen and I headed into the small Bristol Rovers ground and we were soon mingling amongst the thousands of Bluenoses who had also made the trip. Everyone did seem a bit subdued but they soon got a bit of cup atmosphere going. I was pleased to bump into Alan again and I sat by him and we chatted about football and the events of the day. The game got under way and Blues soon raced into a 2-0 lead. With a few minutes to go to half time Stephen needed the toilet so we headed down towards the toilets that were situated at the back of a little terraced area populated by Blues fans. With a minute to go to half time Stephen asked if he would be okay to go to the toilet or did I think we would score again. 'You will be okay' I replied 'there's not enough time left to score another', so off he went. Within seconds of him going into the toilets Blues scored a third! He'll kill me I thought! As I celebrated he came running out and the look on his face was a picture. He burst into a smile and we both fell about laughing as we celebrated madly. The game finished 3-0 and Blues were through to the 3rd round of the league cup as we headed out of the little ground to meet up with the others to head back to Birmingham.

Two days later I headed to Birmingham International Airport to fly back to Abu Dhabi. The airports were open again but security was red hot causing all flights to be delayed by at least a couple of hours. I was a bit worried about going back to a middle eastern country as I didn't know what the fall out would be like – especially as it was reported that some of the terrorists had UAE passports. I was quite glad of the extra security measures as it made me feel a bit safer about flying even though I was not looking forward to going back.

After our good run of results Blues again slipped up, this time away at Manchester City, losing 3-0, followed by defeats at home against Burnley 3-2, Preston 1-0, before we drew away at Watford 3-3 and Crewe 0-0. Then came our biggest defeat in a long time and we crashed out of the league cup in embarrassing fashion 6-0 away at Manchester City. This was our lowest point for a while.

However, I am ever the optimist and the following week Blues won away at Barnsley 3-1 although we were now in 12th place. Following a draw at Nottingham Forest 0-0 and wins at St. Andrews against Bradford City 4-0 and Gillingham 2-1 we were back up to 5th spot. Following Blues is a bit like being on a roller coaster though and we followed the wins with a loss at Grimsby 3-1 and draws at Portsmouth 1-1 and Rotherham Utd 2-2 and defeats by West Brom 1-0 at St. Andrews and 4-0 away at Sheffield Utd saw Blues slip to 12th place in the table again.

This run of wins followed by losses followed again by wins kept Blues yo-yoing up and down the league table. Our manager Trevor Francis resigned in November and it was rumoured that Steve Bruce would be our next manager as he went on 'gardening leave' from Crystal Palace. Sure enough, in December, Steve Bruce became our next manager. Promotion was looking a lost cause but we still had the FA Cup to look forward to.

In January Blues took 9,000 Bluenoses to Anfield to watch Blues take on Liverpool in the 3rd round of the FA Cup but they witnessed a 3-0 defeat which saw our interest in the FA Cup finished for another year. We still had promotion to aim for though and we were currently in 7th place.

I was planning a trip to America for my 40th birthday celebrations. As always, Steve could not be relied upon to make any holiday plans, so I made plans to go with my mate Lani from Australia. We planned to hire a car and travel around California and planned to spend my birthday at Caesars palace hotel. It would also be Lani's birthday on the day we were due to fly back so we would celebrate both of our birthdays in the USA. I was really looking forward to it as I had always wanted to visit America and it would be a holiday of a lifetime for me.

We arrived in Los Angeles a few days before my birthday – which is on the 24th January, and as it was late we booked into a motel for the night. The following day we picked up our hire car and it was decided that I would drive to start with as I was used to driving on the right as I already do this in Abu Dhabi. Then we set off for LasVegas where after a long drive we booked into Circus Circus for our first night there.

It was just like being in the film Thelma and Louise as I drove through the desert to get to Las Vegas and I was enjoying being in America. We checked into Circus Circus which was really nice and then headed out to explore Las Vegas. It was really spectacular at night as all the hotels were lit up and there was loads to see. Most hotels had shows happening outside at certain times such as a volcano that erupts fire and the water display at the famous hotels. One hotel – Treasure Island, was situated with real Old Style Ships outside and they staged a pirate fight at certain times during the evening. There was so much to see that it would take a couple of weeks at least in Las Vegas to see everything.

Inside the hotels there was also entertainment as well as all the casinos. Underneath Caesars Palace it was set out like the old roman cities and there was a show that was on at certain times in throughout the evening. Even the ceilings were painted like the sky. The room we stayed in was a luxury room with a massive double bathroom which incorporated two bathrooms including fabulous Jacuzzi. I began my birthday celebrations from the luxury of drinking champagne in the Jacuzzi before heading downstairs to the Chinese restaurant before heading to 'Shadows' bar downstairs where we embarked on cocktails made by a cute barman putting on a great show whilst making them. I must admit to having more cocktails than I should have done as I enjoyed watching him make them!

After two nights in Vegas we headed off again, this time we were faced with a really long journey up to Lake Tahoe where Lani wanted to go skiing. It was during this trip that I got pulled for speeding – doing 85mph in a 55mph area. It was only after a bollocking by a Police Officer on a Motorbike that I headed into the state of Nevada to the snowy Lake Tahoe. It was really beautiful there and there was two foot of snow overnight and I was amazed by the sight of so much extra snow when I got up the next morning. Lani headed off skiing and I headed off for the casino's and then for a massage as I've never been skiing and didn't fancy breaking anything. The snow was so bad that we had to have snow chains put on the car heels when we left a couple of days later, not before I had already managed to crash the car though, after sliding in the snow! Not much damage done though and I was sure the hire company wouldn't even notice.

Next we headed to San Francisco and we stopped in a small motel down by the Wharf. I enjoyed a ride on the Tram that travels up and down the really steep roads and I also took a trip across the Golden Gate Bridge. I also went on a trip across to Alcatraz prison. Lani had already done this trip on a previous visit so I headed across on the boat on my own. It was really great though and with headphones and commentary throughout I found it really interesting. I have to say it is great to experience and I thoroughly enjoyed it. I was also sending my mom, Annette and

Neil and Family a post card from everywhere I was visiting – which seemed to be loads and I knew they would enjoy getting them.

From San Francisco we headed down the coast road back towards Los Angeles and although it was a longer route, the views were spectacular. We even saw oil rigs offshore and Seals on the beaches, and we stopped at night fall about half way into our journey at a small place and checked into a motel. It was really nice and the next morning we recommenced our journey which took us past Los Angeles on to San Diego. I really loved San Diego, it is a place I could live, it has a large bay and housed America's navy and air force and many war ships could be seem and submarines. We checked into a motel for the night and Lani said she wanted to cross the border the next morning into Mexico. I wasn't so keen on this as I wanted to go on a boat trip around the bay (Lani doesn't like boats), but I agreed to go into Mexico in the morning and Lani would drop me at the bay afterwards where I could embark on my trip.

It was easy crossing the border into Mexico but not so easy getting back as there were longs queues of people trying to gain access to America. I must admit I didn't like Mexico at all, there were too many beggars and it seemed quite dirty and scruffy and I was glad to be back in America. My boat rip proved to be a roaring success too as I downed quite a few 'Long Island' cocktails during my two hour trip. I even saw a whale which had got trapped in the bay and Lani laughed as she came to pick me up and I staggered off the boat!

Then it was back to Los Angeles after stopping off at Disney Land in Arnhem. I really enjoyed that trip and went on many of the rides and saw some interesting Disney Characters. I even had my picture taken with the hunky 'Hercules' as well as Mini Mouse, Pluto the Baby character from one of the movies.

To complete our trip in Los Angeles we headed to Universal Studios and this was probably my favourite part. It was really brilliant and the rides were fabulous, I heartily recommend a visit.

During a trip to Venice Beach we were give free tickets for shows that they were filming that week and we managed to attend one of the late night talk shows and also the filming of one of the episodes of 'Becker' which was really good. They have a comedian to entertain the audience during breaks which was great. We also saw a car chase on the Freeway on the way home which was then on live TV when we got back to our motel.

Then it was time to fly back on Lani's Birthday, so we started early with breakfast at a local bar/restaurant sitting outside and celebrated with a bottle of champagne. Very nice!

Back in Abu Dhabi at the end of February and Blues were now in 9th place following wins against Barnsley 1-0, Watford 3-2 and away at Burnley 1-0. Of course we followed this by two defeats and a draw before winning again away at Bradford City 3-1 and at Norwich City 1-0 and we were one place off a play off place. Following a 1-1 draw at Coventry and a 4-0 home win over Grimsby, Blues were in 6th place and a playoff spot. Things were looking good under our new manager Steve Bruce. Then came two draws against Crystal Palace away and at home against Portsmouth before a home win against Crewe 3-1 which took us up to 4th spot. It was getting really exciting and following a 2-2 draw away at Rotherham and a final day home win against Sheffield Utd 2-0 in front of 29,178 fans, Birmingham City finished the season in 5th place and once again in the Playoff Semi finals. Could this be our year? I once again thought!

Blues were to play Millwall in the semi finals and the first leg would be at St. Andrews on 1st May. Unfortunately I couldn't make it home for the match so I had to make do with updates from Annette who informed me of the final score which ended in a 1-1 draw leaving things all square for the second leg at Millwall just a few days later. This meant that Millwall had the advantage of being at home and I was more than a little nervous especially with our recent history of losing in the last 3 playoff semi finals.

On the night of the match I was in Dubai with Steve as he was onshore and we decided to go out and watch the match at the Irish

Village where it was being shown live. I decided to wear my Blues home shirt and was surprised by how many guys came up to me and wished Blues luck against Millwall. Everyone wanted Blues to win and Steve was surprised by how much attention I got in Blues shirt. I downed a couple of Vodkas to settle my nerves and as the game was nearing the end and the dreaded penalty shootout, up popped Stern John to score for Blues. The pub erupted and I jumped about wildly in celebration! Before I knew it the final whistle had sounded and Blues were in the Final at Cardiff just over a week later.

I was so happy and decided there and then that I would fly home for the Final. It would be our greatest chance ever of returning to the top flight for the first time in 16 years.

A day after the semi final win I was still in Dubai for a concert by UB40 and Steve and I headed to the Dubai Tennis Stadium where they were performing. As everyone knows, UB40 are big Birmingham City fans and I went to the concert in my Blues home shirt. Once inside the stadium we obtained beers and we ere soon approached by some guys who were from a British nuclear submarine which was currently in Dubai for repairs and they had a large union jack with 'Blues On Tour' on it. We were soon joined by another Bluenose and his girlfriend who also spotted my Blues shirt and came over to chat and we all watched the concert together. We were quite close to the front and I decided to get onto Steve's shoulders so that Ali Campbell and Co could see my Blues shirt. The other girl with us decided to do the same and got up on her boyfriend's shoulders to join me and we held aloft the 'Blues On Tour' flag. Ali Campbell soon spotted us and looked over during his singing and I moved the flag to one side to proudly display my Blues shirt. He looked at my shirt and smiled as he sang. I began waving at him as he continued to look over at our flag and Blues colours and eventually, much to my delight he waved back at me! I shouted down to Steve 'did you see Ali Campbell wave at me?' to which he replied 'no, your bloody handbag is in my face!' and sure enough my shoulder bag was swinging in front of his face! I had to laugh, and I did move the bag then.

When the concert was over and people were leaving we made our way to the stage to chat to the support crew who remembered me from the concert they had done in Abu Dhabi a couple of years before when I had also got on someone's shoulders clad in my Blues shirt. They gave me the drum stick that the group had been using and Steve asked them if they would sign my shirt as I was going to the Millennium Stadium for the Final next week. I did a quick shirt swap with Steve and they took my shirt for the band to sign. It was brilliant when they bought it back to me. They had all signed it and written messages of good luck to Blues for the final. It was the shirt with the phones 4 U on it and Astra had used the U and made it into 'ZULU' which looked really good. Ali Campbell had written 'were on our way' on it, which as all Bluenoses know, was our song at the time and we had sung it in anticipation for being on our way to the Premier league. I have since had the shirt framed and it sits proudly on my wall!

It was soon time for me to head back to England for the Play Off final between Birmingham City and Norwich City at the Millennium Stadium in Cardiff and I was so excited. From the minute I set foot back in Birmingham all the talk was of the upcoming final in Cardiff and luckily Steve (Annette's boyfriend) had managed to get tickets for all of us to go which meant Annette and my mom would be coming as well as Stephen and I and Steve and his boys. Steve had hired and minivan for the day and it would be full for the trip to Cardiff.

On a sunny morning on 12th May 2002 we gathered at my mom's getting ready for the exciting day ahead. Sue (my sister in law) brought Stephen over, bright and early and I was pleased to see he had dyed his blonde hair blue for the occasion. He also had on his blues shirt and had bought a Blues flag along with him as well. Annette, mom and myself all had Blues shirts on and I also had a Blues flag. I had bought a crate of Smirnoff Ice for the trip and as Steve pulled up with the mini bus and his sons on board, I loaded the drinks and sandwiches which mom had made and we all boarded. Annette sat up front with Steve, who was driving, and Stephen, mom and I sat together in the row behind them with Stephen ensconced at the window.

We headed off towards Harborne and collected the rest of the lads on the way, and then it was off to Cardiff. We set off really early and it was only about 7.45am when we headed out. Several hisses were heard at the back of the van as the lads opened cans of beer and one voice piped up with 'has any one got a bottle opener?' Much to everyone's surprise I waved a bottle opener in the air and everyone cheered! I then decided to crack open a bottle myself, much to my mom's horror as she pointed out it was only 8am. I reassured her that I would pace myself as I passed Annette a bottle. Stephen informed me that his mom had said he could have some also so I let him have a couple of sips from my bottle, although not entirely convinced that he was telling me the truth!

Everyone chatted and sang on the journey and before long we had reached the 'Welcome to Wales' sign which was by now draped in Birmingham Flags and scarves, probably put there by other Bluenoses who had set out before us. I thought this was really amusing and it added to the excitement of the day. By now I had loads of butterflies in my stomach. I needed the Smirnoff Ice to calm me down. Stephen was just as excited also and the two of us soaked up the atmosphere of the day. It was the biggest match that Stephen had ever been to.

Steve had decided to park up just outside of Cardiff and get the local train into the city centre. This was because of the nightmare of last year's Cup Final appearance when traffic was at a standstill both in before the match and out afterwards due to poor arrangements for the final. We parked the van in a side street near the station and headed off to catch a train into Cardiff. As we headed for a subway we spotted three Norwich supporters in their yellow shirts coming out of the subway and after one look at us clad in our Blues gear they did a complete about turn and disappeared rather quickly back the way they had come. I had to laugh at this as did Stephen and Annette.

Once we arrived at the local station we discovered that it was packed with Bluenoses who had obviously had the same idea and we ended up squashed amongst them as we made our way to the platform. Because of the large numbers there were police on the doors to the platforms allowing a few through at a time and we all had to battle to stay together. It was great on the platform where all the Bluenoses were in full voice and I enjoyed joining in. 'were on our way!' rang out loud and clear and it carried on onto the train as we boarded. The train was soon packed and Stephen and I found ourselves sitting in the baggage shelves whilst mom and Annette had to make do with standing. It wasn't too long before we were pulling into Cardiff though and we all surged out as one blue mass.

As we came out the station we were met by an amazing sight. It was blue and white as far as the eye could see. The city centre around the Millennium stadium had been divided into two sides and the Blue half was extremely impressive. There were already thousands of Bluenoses who were happily playing football in the streets and drinking beer either outside the many bars or from cans obtained from the local shops. We headed for the nearest chippie and after consuming chips and gravy we headed to a pub for a drink. All the pubs were packed so after a quick drink that followed queuing for an extremely long time, we decided to head towards the stadium that could be seen from where we were and try to find an off licence.

The Millennium Stadium was really impressive as we walked passed it and crossed the river to find a shop. Once we had obtained beers we headed for the river bank where we chatted and mom dished out the massive bag of sandwiches she had bought with her. The lads were well pleased and tucked in to various sandwiches washed down with cans of beer. I bought a play off final 2002 Birmingham City scarf as a souvenir and we soaked up the atmosphere which was absolutely brilliant. We also took lots of photos and were soon approached by a reporter who Steve called over and pointed out our 'Abu Dhabi Blues' St. Georges flag! He asked me how far I had travelled for the game and when I told him I had travelled 3,500 miles he was very impressed and took some photos for the Sunday Mercury the next day.

We headed into the ground early to soak up the atmosphere and due to the fact that the demand for tickets was so high (around 50,000 Blues were there), our tickets were in different areas. I was with Stephen in the lower tier and mom, Annette, Steve and his lads were in the third tier. Blues had the biggest end and the majority of the stadium and it was just a mass of blue and white with a smaller section of yellow and green at the other end. It was brilliant, the noise levels were tremendous. Stephen and I were seated at the back of the stand underneath the second tier and we wondered down to the front to take some photos and look around in total awe at the Blue support. I felt tears in my eyes and felt so proud and lucky at being able to be part of it. It is a feeling that you just cannot put into words but it was one of the best days of my life. We had waited 16 years to get here and the possibility of playing in the Premier league was right in front of us. I prayed we could do it. I was so used to disappointment though after the last four years that I was petrified we would miss out again. As I looked up at the many flags and banners, I laughed as I saw one that said 'Beckham bends it like Grainger' – brilliant. For those who don't already know, Martin Grainger is our left back who scores great goals from free kicks. I also saw a massive banner which read 'Goodbye Division One!'

We went to our seats just before the players came out onto the pitch and shared a few words with the people around us. There was a man in front of me who looked at least 80 and had these dark sunglasses on and he kept looking around excitedly and we would share a smile and thumbs up. Then the players came out to a crescendo of noise and once again I could feel tears in my eyes and I felt the emotions of the day. I looked at Stephen and he looked as excited and nervous as me.

The game got underway and the noise level remained pretty much the same as the Bluenoses sang our hearts out. Oh, how I hoped they would not be broken by the end of the match. It was an exciting game and both sides had good chances but 90 minutes ended with the scores still level at 0-0 and another 30 minutes of extra time. It was nerve wracking stuff and not long into the first half of extra time Norwich scored – right in front of our end, we were losing 1-0. We were shocked and our hearts were breaking. I could not believe it. The Blues fans refused to give up though and immediately sang out 'Keep Right On' to spur our team on.

Blues surged into the Norwich half and there was big Geoff Horsefield to smash the ball into the back of the Norwich net – 1-1! The Blues end erupted and everyone was jumping on each other. The old man in front of me turned around with his fists in the air in celebration and a massive smile on his face. I lifted Stephen in the air and everyone else seemed to jump on us too. It was a mad celebration and I can't begin to explain both the joy and the relief that I felt. At least now we still had hope. As the game carried on we missed a couple of really good chances and Michael Johnson hit the post for Blues right in front of the Blues fans with only three minutes to go. The whistle for full time blew and it finished 1-1. This meant the dreaded penalty shoot and my heart began to sink. We all knew Blues record at penalty shoot outs and in fact I had never seen Blues win in a penalty shootout. I was by now extremely stressed and worried I might have a heart attack!

The toss was made and Blues surprisingly won and chose to take the penalties at our end in front of the Blue Army. Was this a good sign? I debated it with Stephen. Norwich were to take the first penalty and scored putting them in the lead 1-0. Then it was Blues turn and up stepped Stern John as the rest of the Blues team stood huddled with their arms around each other's shoulders. I was a bit nervous as Stern John can often miss chances like this. Behind me someone said 'not Stern John, he's fucking shit that Stern John' as he stepped forward. I could barely look but I am glad I did as the ball smashed into the back of the net! The same voice said 'he's fucking brilliant that Stern John!' much to my amusement, and the Blues fans went wild. It was now 1-1.

Then it was the turn of Norwich again to a crescendo of whistles from the Blues fans behind the goal. The Blues fans celebrated wildly as our goalkeeper Nico Vassen made a brilliant save giving Blues the advantage. Still 1-1. Then it was the turn of Paul Devlin, a true Bluenose and he smashed an unstoppable shot into the bottom right hand corner. 2-1. Then it was the turn of Norwich again and unbelievably Nico Vassen made another great save! Blues fans went wild and Norwich fans heads were now in their hands.

Up stepped Stan Lazaridis for the fourth penalty and he also smashed it into the net! I couldn't believe my eyes, I began to feel that we may actually do it and I joined the others in celebration. Then Norwich stepped up again and they had to score because if they missed then Blues would be promoted! There were whistles from all the Blues fans but despite Nicò Vassen getting a hand to it, Norwich scored and it was now 3-2. However, if Blues scored from the next penalty then it would be Birmingham City who would be promoted to the Premier League.

Darren Carter, our 18 year old Bluenose, who had sat in the stand at Cardiff last year to watch Blues in the League Cup final against Liverpool, stepped forward to take the 40 million pound penalty. He asked the referee 'if this goes in are we up?' and the referee replied "yes'

As he stepped up to take it the commentator remarked 'Darren Carter for the Premiership' and our 18year old hero coolly smashed the ball into the back of the net to begin absolutely wild celebrations amongst both the fans and the players. As he ran towards the Blues fans he was mobbed by Blues players and Andy Johnson was first to get to him and he jumped on his back to be carried to the Blues fans, then it was Jeff Kenna and Paul Devlin that caught up and mobbed him. By now I was crying and jumping on everyone and the old guy in front of me turned around and took his glasses off and tears were streaming down his face. All around me grown men were crying with joy and it just seemed so right. 50.000 Bluenoses began singing 'we are Premier League, say we are Premier League' and that was when it really hit me. We were back in the top flight after an absence of 16 years! I was ecstatic along with everyone else and we celebrated and sang our hearts out. It was probably the best day of my life and I couldn't begin to describe how I felt. Unless of course you were there and then you would know what it felt like.

Over excited Bluenoses spilled onto the pitch to celebrate and had to be asked to leave the pitch in order for the presentations to be made. Darren Carter looked stunned and Nico Vassen Jumped on a beaming Steve Bruce as he was about to be interviewed. As Darren Carter was interviewed he told how he was sitting up in the stands last year and he couldn't believe he had scored the winning penalty in a strong Brummie accent. He said he didn't think he would be able to sleep for days and it was just unbelievable.

When they came to interview Paul Devlin, also a Bluenose, he was too overcome to speak. Michael Johnson put on a blues jester hat and danced around blowing a horn – classic! Nico Vassen was running around with a'We're Going Up' flag as 'shit on the villa' rang out from the Blues end. The trophy was bought out onto the pitch and it looked fabulous draped in Blue and White and the fans were going wild as the Blues players did a lap of honour before going over to collect their winners medals. 'Keep Right On' rang out so proudly and the trophy was award to Birmingham City and the fireworks lit up the stadium and the streamers rained down. It was a crescendo of noise as Jeff Kenna lifted the trophy high in the air in a mass of Blue and White. Even Beau Brummie (our mascot) was on the pitch celebrating with the players and fans. Birmingham City are back in the Premier League!

As we headed out of the stadium following long celebrations, we met up with the others and headed back to Newport where we enjoyed a couple of celebratory drinks in one of the local pubs. By the time we headed back to Birmingham the traffic had lessened and we were still in full celebratory mode! We sang our hearts out all the way back to Birmingham and I went to bed a very exhausted but happy person. At last we were in the Premier league and I could not have been any happier.

The civic reception was being held in the city centre and I would still be here for it so I put on my away Blues shirt this time (the yellow shirt) and headed into town with Stephen, who bunked off school for a dental appointment! Along with thousands of other school kids who also had 'dental appointments', and with

Annette and Steve. We went into a pub on Broad Street before hand and had a beer or two before heading into Chamberlin square to see our heroes returning with the trophy. Stephen and I had big 'Birmingham City Promoted' flags and we waved them proudly as we joined the crowds and took loads of photos for the album. It was a lovely sunny day and it was great to see the lads celebrating and holding aloft the trophy. Steve Bruce had done really well to achieve promotion after coming late in the season and leading Blues on such a great run of results which took us to the play off finals. I was so proud and happy and we had another couple of beers in a pub on Broad Street before heading home. It was another great day.

Manchester City were champions of the First Division and West Brom were promoted as runners up along with Birmingham City as Play Off Final winners. Crewe, Barnsley and Stockport County were relegated to Division Two. The FA Cup Final was won by Arsenal who beat Chelsea 2-0 and the League Cup was won by Blackburn Rovers who beat Tottenham Hotspur 2-1.

We are Premier League, say we are Premier League.......

CHAPTER TWENTY-ONE – The Premier League!

I was back in the sunshine of Abu Dhabi and I was really looking forward to Birmingham City's first season in the Premier League. I scanned the fixture list when it came out in June as I eagerly anticipated the local derby with the villa after an absence of 16 years. I was also looking forward to the big games against the likes of Manchester Utd and Liverpool and they didn't come much bigger than the first game of the season. The computer had dealt Blues a daunting away trip to the home of the current Premier League champions Arsenal. What a prospect, and as I had cable TV I would be able to see this game live.

So on the 18th august the 2002 to 2003 season got underway and I sat in front of the TV in my Blues shirt to watch the Arsenal game. Blues played really well and I thought we were really unlucky, especially when Ashley Cole dived and our new signing Aliou Cisse was sent off on his debut. The replay showed that there was absolutely no contact and that Ashley Cole had dived, in fact in the following weeks the red card was rescinded! But the damage was done and with only ten men left on the field against the mighty Arsenal we did extremely well but still lost 2-0. Our first game in the Premiership and Blues could hold their heads high after such a display.

A few days a later and our first match at St. Andrews saw Blues lose 1-0 in front of a packed St. Andrews and a fantastic atmosphere. Even the commentator remarked that it was good to have Birmingham City in the premiership as our support and atmosphere brought something special to the Premiership which is sadly lacking these days.

Then it was away to Everton where Stern John put Blues 1-0 ahead before Everton, somewhat luckily scrapped an equaliser and the game finished 1-1 and we were still awaiting our first win in the Premiership. That was to come on the 31st august at St. Andrews in front of 27,164 who watched a brilliant goal from Damien Johnson help Blues to a 2-1 win over Leeds Utd. I celebrated wildly as I ran around my living room. Blues were 14th in the Premier League and next up was a daunting trip to Anfield to take on the mighty reds of Liverpool. Annette and Steve were going to this game and I really envied them and wished I could be with them. As was probably expected Blues were soon losing 2-0 although the Bluenoses could be heard really loudly singing their hearts out. I think their support began to lift the team and with the game in the last quarter Clinton Morrison pulled a goal back, scoring right in front of the Blue Army and I could see them celebrating madly. It was now 2-1 and Blues were battling hard to get something out of the game and with a few minutes left, up popped Clinton Morrison again to score and shock the reds of Liverpool. The Bluenoses were in heaven and as I looked at the TV I spotted Annette celebrating amongst the Blues fans. It was a brilliant result and it certainly shocked a few people who were expecting us to struggle in the Premiership.

Next up was the one that every Blues fan was looking forward to and that was the match against Aston Villa. It was to be a night game on 16th September and would be our first league game against them for 16 years. I stayed up late to watch it (we were 4 hours ahead) even though I had work the next day. There were 29,505inside St. Andrews, a full house, and the atmosphere was like nothing I have ever heard before, or since. The commentator remarked on how hostile it was and that he had never experienced anything like it before. The match kicked off and I admit to being a bag of nerves as I watched Blues put on a display like their lives depended on it. When the ball fell to Clinton Morrison just inside the area and he smashed it into the villa net the ground exploded. Robbie Savage jumped on him and then he was mobbed by the Blues players and the fans running on the pitch in their excitement. Steve Bruce jumped in the air just before a Blues fan jumped on him and Blues fans were invading the pitch for all sides in a wild celebration. It was brilliant and I was running around the room enjoying my celebrations. It took a few minutes and a tanoy announcement to clear the pitch of the celebrating Blues fans before the game could get underway again.

At half time it was 1-0 to Blues and I was excited and hoping that we could keep it that way. The second half got underway and the atmosphere was brilliant. 'Shit on the Villa' rang out so loudly and 'Keep Right On' was also belted out on several occasions. As the game drew on, Villa were desperate to get a goal back and not concede again. When they had a throw in their own half everyone watched in amazement as Mellburg (known as smellburg to Bluenoses) threw the ball back to his keeper only for Enckleman to attempt to stop it with his foot. As we all know the ball just clipped his foot, going under his boot and trickled across the line into the back of the villa net! Que absolute wild celebrations from the Blues fans and a second pitch invasion. Steve Bruce's face was a picture as he realised what had happened and celebrated whilst also enjoying a good laugh. I fell about laughing and ran around the room again madly. Brilliant, not only were Blues now 2-0 up but Villa had just made a laughing stock of themselves too. One Blues fan ran onto the pitch, tapped their Goalkeeper Enckleman (who was looking extremely sick) on the forehead and did the wanker sign to him. I must admit to a little giggle at this even though the fan in question ended up going to jail for this.

I was in heaven and when Geoff Horsefield seized onto a defensive error to run on to goal and smash the ball into the bottom corner of the Villa net for number three, I was absolutely ecstatic. Unbelievable, 3-0 and 'can we play you every week?' rang out loudly around St. Andrews as the Villa fans were streaming out. Following the third pitch invasion of the day, the game got underway again and the final whistle was soon sounding to an eruption of noise as the match finished Birmingham City 3 Aston Villa 0! What a brilliant result and there was no way I was going to be able to get to sleep after that! Annette bought me a t-shirt with 'Midland Massacre' and a big 3-0 on it. Blues were now 9th in the premier league and causing a few raised eyebrows.

The following week Blues lost 1-0 at Middlesbrough and then lost 2-0 against Newcastle Utd at St. Andrews before getting back to winning ways in the League Cup 2nd round against Leyton Orient 3-2 in London with Stern john getting a hat trick. Blues then achieved a great win away at West Ham Utd 2-1 with 2,704 Bluenoses making the trip south. This meant that Blues were now 12th in the Premiership and I was happy with our form so far this season. The local derby against West Brom at the Hawthorns was up next and we came away with a 1-1 draw. Then Manchester City came to St. Andrews and left with all 3 points after beating us 2-0 in front of a packed house.

I was still optimistic that Blues could do well in the top flight and my optimism was rewarded in the next game as Blues beat Bolton at St. Andrews 3-1. Unfortunately we slipped up again in the next game which was in the League Cup 3rd round against lower league opposition in the form of Preston North End who came away with a 2-0 win at St. Andrews. Why is it that Blues always seem to lose to lower league teams in the cup?

Next up were Chelsea who were riding high in the league and we came away beaten 3-0 at Stamford Bridge. This was followed by a home draw against Fulham 0-0 before we got back to winning ways by winning 1-0 in the Stadium of Light against Sunderland.

In January Blues travelled to Old Trafford and gave a really good account of ourselves before going down 2-0 to Manchester Utd. Then our participation in the FA Cup came to an end at Fulham in the 3rd round as Blues went down 3-1 only a few weeks after winning 1-0 at Fulham in the Premier. In fact we didn't get many points in the first few weeks of the year as we came up against all the big teams, losing 4-0 to Arsenal, 1-0 to Manchester Utd in the return leg and losing 3-1 to Chelsea, also in the return fixture. When it came to Liverpool at home we were again expecting to get beat. What a fantastic surprise then when Blues put on a great display and beat Liverpool 2-1 with Clemence and Morrison getting the goals in front of a packed St. Andrews.

Then in it was Villa again in the return fixture and once again I was a nervous wreck. It would be much harder on their patch, and I would happily settle for a draw. Just not to lose really as I hate losing to Villa and hadn't had to experience that feeling now for a long while. So once again I was clad in my Blues shirt in front of the TV as the match kicked off inside a packed Villa Park where the Blues fans could be heard singing loudly. It was a mass of blue and white behind the goal at the Witton end of the ground. It was 3rd March 2003.

The game got underway with Blues attacking the Witton end where the Blues fans were situated and it wasn't long before Clinton Morrison headed the ball just over the Villa crossbar. I was feeling so nervous. Shit on the Villa could be heard really loudly over the TV and I was soon on my feet as Christophe Duggary hit a great shot from 25 yards which was only just over the bar. Then in the second half Dion Dublin made a disgraceful tackle on Robbie Savage and then as Robbie Savage got up the claret and blue wanker actually head butted Robbie and was shown a straight red card as the Blues players surrounded him. Deservedly so too. It was disgraceful and how he expected to get away with it was beyond me!

Revenge was gained as Blues raced up field and Damien Johnson crossed the ball into the penalty area to be met by Stan Lazaridis who smashed the ball into the Villa net 1-0! The Blues end erupted and the players mobbed Lazaridis.

Not long after this I was in heaven as Geoff Horsefield ran onto a through ball and rounded the Villa keeper to put the ball into the Villa net and the Blues end erupted once again. Aston Villa 0 Birmingham City 2! What a game. The Blues end was a mass of celebration and Annette said she saw one Blues fan who was waving a five pound not at a policeman guarding the pitch, saying 'a fiver mate, if we score again I'm on that pitch' with the policeman just shaking his head at him. 'I'm telling you mate, if we score again I'm on that pitch' he kept repeating as he waved his five pound note at him. Excellent!

With ten minutes left the match really boiled over as Gudjohnson put in a disgraceful two footed challenge on Damien Johnson which left him on the ground. This resulted in what almost became a mass brawl between the two teams as the Blues players rushed over to revenge this atrocity. As the commentator remarked on what a stupid irresponsible tackle it had been and could have done some serious damage, the referee produced the second red card of the game and sent the Villa player off. Blues ended up down to 10 men as our keeper got injured and we had used our subs, so Geoff Horsefield ended the game in goal. So six points gained against the Villa and I was extremely happy and I was once again heading back to Birmingham to visit and was looking forward to seeing Blues play live in the Premier League for the first time.

My first game back would be a trip to Maine Road to see Blues take on Manchester City and I was lucky that Steve managed to get me a ticket as the demand for tickets for away games was massive for our first season back in the top flight. I travelled to the game with Stephen and this time we travelled on the coaches from the St.Andrews Tavern. It was great, a couple of drinks and a bacon buttie in the St. Andrews Tavern before we left and then we were on our way. It was a really nice day and before we knew it we were arriving in Manchester and were soon inside the ground. We were sitting next to a couple of Steve's mates who had got the tickets for us and I soon got chatting to them and they gave me some chocolate that they had bought with them as he works in Cadbury's. Stephen soon ate his as the match got underway. The 2,000 Bluenoses sang loudly but the Manchester City supporters were silent and soon the Blues fans were singing 'it's just like being in church, it's just like being in church'. After gaining no response from the Mancs, the Bluenoses turned our attention to their new signing Robbie Fowler who had done nothing up to now as we sang 'what a waste of money' to him. I should have known that this would come back to bite us on the bum as he bloody scored the winner right in front of us as the

Mancs now taunted us with chants of 'what a waste of money'. Oh well, can't win them all and off we headed back to catch the coach having lost the game 1-0.

Blues were down in 16th place now and we really needed to win in the local derby against West Brom at St. Andrews which would be my last game before I headed back. West Brom were in deeper trouble than us and stood a big chance of being relegated if we beat them. It was a lovely sunny day and Stephen, Annette and I made our way into St. Andrews. We had tickets for the paddock area of the main stand near the Tilton end and it was really close to the pitch and we were basking in the sunshine in our Blues shirts. It was a brilliant atmosphere and the Bluenoses were in great voice. There were 29.445 inside the ground and 'Keep Right On' rang out so loudly. The game seemed to be heading for a draw and we really really needed to win. Then in the last few minutes up popped Geoff Horsefield to score and send the Bluenoses into mass celebration. Annette, Stephen and I all jumped on each other as we celebrated and the West Brom players dropped to the ground in despair. Blues fans now sang 'going down, going down, going down' to the West Brom fans situated in the Railway end. Then the final whistle blew and the ground once more erupted in celebrations.

Then I was heading back to Abu Dhabi and I would have to make do with watching the odd game live on TV, which is not the same as actually being there. I miss the live games so much, which is why I never miss a match whenever I am home in the UK. The following game saw Blues lose at Tottenham 2-1 before a great home win against Sunderland 2-0 which in fact relegated Sunderland to the First Division with five games to go.

Blues were now in 15th place and following a good away win at Charlton 2-0 and at home against Southampton 3-2 we were up to 13th place in the Premiership. Duggary was on great form having scored against Sunderland, Charlton and now two against Southampton. It was no surprise then when he scored again in the next game against Middlesbrough at St. Andrews as Blues achieved another win this time 3-0. Blues then lost away at

Newcastle Utd 1-0 and then it was the last game of the season at St. Andrews against West Ham Utd. West Ham had to win to stay up but goals from Stern John and Geoff Horsefield saw Blues draw 2-2 and send West Ham into the First Division.

It had been a great season for Blues and for me, back in the top flight. Blues finished in 13th place and the highest place midland team for the first time since 1906. I was just happy to have stayed in the Premier League and of course to do the double over our rivals Aston Villa!

Manchester Utd were crowned Premier League Champions with Arsenal the runners up. West Ham Utd, West Brom and Sunderland were relegated to the First Division. The FA Cup was won by Arsenal as they beat Southampton 1-0 and the League Cup was won by Liverpool who beat Manchester Utd 2-0.

CHAPTER TWENTY-TWO – Villa Park

Apart from it being extremely hot, I had a nice summer and I had another season of Premiership football to look forward to in August. Steve had changed jobs once again and his new job involved him travelling offshore from Qatar and so in July I headed over to Qatar to spend a few days with him before he went offshore again. It is only about a forty minute flight from Abu Dhabi to Qatar and Steve had told me to pick up a bottle of vodka from duty free in Abu Dhabi airport which I duly did. This proved to be a big mistake though as I was stopped in Qatar airport as it is not allowed to take alcohol into the country. Thanks for that one Steve, it took me a while to talk my way out of that one! I thought I was going to end up in jail.

Once through the airport I was met by Steve and we got a taxi back to his hotel. We went to the hotel bar in the evening and it was awful, full of men, mostly Indian and a couple of Filipino girls. I was the only blonde western woman in there and I felt very conspicuous. I was glad when it was time to leave. When we got back to the room I ordered two vodka and cokes and when they arrived I signed for them without checking the tray he had brought, only to discover after the waiter had left that he had brought two cans of coke and two half bottles of vodka!

I have to say that I really didn't like Qatar much to be honest and the only reason I was sad when I left was because I would miss Steve. Mind you, he called to say that he was back in Qatar two days later and could I come back for another couple of days. Fool that I am, I returned two days later for two days and we did have a nice time together, relaxing by the pool and a couple of beers on the night time.

Steve was offshore for less than a month and then I went back to Qatar at the beginning of August to spend another couple of days with him. It was a nice break but I wouldn't want to do it all the time I must admit. It gets expensive after awhile also.

The 2003 to 2004 season got underway on 16th august with a home game against Tottenham and Blues won 1-0 to go 6th in the table. Great start and a full St. Andrews for the game also. Then it was time for me to head back to England and sunny Birmingham for another visit. I was doing a lot of travelling this year and was getting a bit fed up of airports but I always love to go home.

My first game back in blighty was a trip down south to see Blues play Southampton at their new St. Mary's stadium. This would be a new ground for me as I had only ever been to their old ground, which had had the worst away end I had ever been in. Anyway, it was a lovely sunny day as Stephen and I set off on the St. Andrews Tavern coach following a bacon buttie and a cider in the pub prior to setting off. As we arrived at the ground the sun was shining and loads of lads had their shirts off and were wandering around in the sunshine drinking beers and eating chips. Stephen and I got off the coach and headed to the nearby chippie van where we obtained chips and cans of pop. It really was a lovely day and there were Blues shirts everywhere.

Once we had eaten our chips we headed into the ground and the Blues end was full as 2,356 Bluenoses had made the trip. The atmosphere was electric and Blues fans were singing loudly and were in good spirits. The noise from the Blues end was amazing and it was as if Blues were at home. Then the players came out to a crescendo of cheers from the Blues contingent. It was brilliant and once the match got underway Blues played great and really should have won the match. One chance in particular should have resulted in a goal much to the dismay of the Blues fans as it hit the post but some knob head behind me kicked the back of my seat (the whole Blues section stood for the entire game) and my seat shot down hitting me in the backs of my legs. Lucky it wasn't Stephens's seat as he is only young and slim and it would have done some serious harm. As it was I had terrible bruising on both my legs the next day and I never bruise! The match ended 0-0 and Blues were still up in the top half in 6th place.

Next up was a trip to Newcastle and I was really looking forward to this trip as I had never been to St. James Park in Newcastle and it would be another new ground for me. Once again Stephen and I had booked to travel on the coaches from the St. Andrews Tavern and Neil dropped us at the pub early and we enjoyed our usual bacon buttie and a cider before setting off. As it was a long trip we set off early and made good time, therefore the coaches stopped half way at two pubs situated across the road from each other. Each coach pulled into one of the pubs car parks and the Bluenoses poured off and into one of the pubs. It was quite funny really as the pubs were only small and in the middle of the countryside, so when loads of Blues fans poured into the pubs the owners were taken by surprise. The pub we headed into had two elderly people behind the small bar and the look on their faces was a picture. They called in the back for help and we had to queue for a while to get our drinks – hence I got two and some crisps and a coke for Stephen. We were both really enjoying the trip so far.

The Bluenoses on our coach were in really good voice on the trip and as we set off again they were singing all sorts of songs such as 'I would rather be a pastie than a pie!' which I admit to joining in. It was great fun, but we encountered some traffic and by the time we had been met by our police escort it was getting near to kick off time. The police stopped all the traffic and rushed us to the ground with their sirens blaring and their blue lights flashing. We had already been boarded and searched by the police when they met our coach and it was quite amusing when one of the coppers said he hoped we beat them as he was a Middlesbrough fan! Of course we gave them some stick as usual.

We arrived at the ground with minutes to spare before kickoff and as Stephen and I ran towards the ground, I dropped my ray ban sunglasses causing them to be scratched. I was well pissed off as they were new and expensive. I just hoped the day would be worth it. Once inside we headed to our seats and as any away fan who has been to Newcastle knows, the away section is at the top of a very high stand and by the time we had dashed to the top I was looking around for an oxygen mask! I was bloody knackered but once inside the atmosphere was brilliant. There were 2,500 Blues fans who were trying to out sing 50,000 noisy Geordies. It was great. Blues fans having a great sense of humour were singing 'shit ground, no noise' to the amusement of the Newcastle fans. Blues also broke into a chorus of 'my garden shed is bigger than this' to great amusing from the Geordies who were fast warming to us. I sent a text to Craig (Newcastle fan) who was currently off shore, to tell him that I was at the match but I didn't receive a reply.

The match got underway and Blues were playing really well. Before long a Blues player was brought down in the area and a penalty was awarded. It was at the opposite end of the pitch to where we were sitting in the away section be we had quite a good view even though we were in clouds. David Dunn stepped up to take it and it was saved by the keeper but Dunn reacted the quickest to put the ball into the Newcastle net – 1-0 to Blues. The Blues end erupted and we celebrated madly and sang our hearts out. Just before half time as the referee was running backwards and as he put out his arm to indicate a decision he hit our Robbie Savage full in the face knocking him out. As Robbie lay flat out on the pitch Alan Shearer came over to the referee, picked up the cards that had fell from his pocket and showed the referee the Red Card. This was really funny and everyone laughed. Poor Robbie was helped to his feet but even he had a little smile after seeing the funny side. He said afterwards that he was sure many referees would have liked to have knocked him out.

At half time it was still 1-0 to Blues and I texted Craig to inform him of the score and I headed to the bar downstairs. As I was obtaining beers I bumped into Dave and we got chatting about the game and stuff. It was good to see him and he always makes me laugh. Then we said goodbye and headed to our seats to watch the second half.

The second half Blues continued to play well and we sang our hearts out in support and in our celebration. The game finished Newcastle Utd 0 Birmingham City 1, and it was great to witness such a win in this fabulous stadium. It's always good winning on other teams turf and it doesn't come much better than winning at the big clubs such as Newcastle. As we got outside I couldn't believe how many Blues coaches were lined up along the road. There looked to be about 30 of them and we had to walk along them for ages until we came to ours. Most Bluenoses were boarding the coaches or getting into cars but I did notice two brave Bluenoses in Blues shirts heading into a pub in the middle of the Newcastle fans. As we headed out of Newcastle the police escort had stopped all the traffic and I noticed loads of Sunderland fans getting out of their cars and as they stood with their arms in the air they started bowing to our coaches because we had just beaten their rivals. It was really funny. We just waved back at them and laughed.

On the long trip back to Birmingham we continued to sing and Stephen and I chatted and read our programmes until we arrived back at the St. Andrews Tavern whereby we went inside to await Neil's arrival to take us home.

My last game before I headed back was at St. Andrews against Fulham and once again I met up with Dave and the lads in the Greenways for a pre match vodka or two. As always inside Stan's the atmosphere was brilliant and I sat on the Kop with Stephen and watched excitedly as Forssell scored twice in at 2-2 draw. As I left the stadium I was a bit sad that it would be my last live game for a little while again.

When I arrived back in Abu Dhabi I was again excited as I was due to fly to Hong Kong for a short trip a week after my return from England. Just before I left though, Blues had a good away win at Leeds Utd 2-0 and were now 7th in the league. Then on the

22nd September I flew to Hong Kong with my mates Roxy and Janine for a short trip that would last five days and four nights. It was great, I really loved Hong Kong. We would cross over to Hong Kong every day on the old ferry's that crossed over frequently and cost the equivalent of 20 pence. We saw all the sights such as the Aberdeen docks and the street markets. We even visited the leisure park and rode on the cable cars to the top, which was very high and an amazing sight to behold. I had a really great time and came back laden with gifts and souvenirs. While we were away Blues were again knocked out of the League Cup by lower league opposition, this time in the form of Blackpool away 1-0.

Blues got back to winning ways in the next game at home against Portsmouth 2-0 and this took us as high as 4th in the Premier League and a champion's league spot! Could we dare dream? This meant that our next game at Old Trafford against Manchester Utd was a top of the table clash! It was what dreams are made of, unfortunately the referee didn't see it the same way and sent our goalkeeper off very harshly and turned the match in the Reds favour. Blues went on the lose the game 3-0 following a brilliant goal by David Beckham, but it could have been so much different had we kept 11 men on the field. The 3,009 Blues that made the journey (including Annette and Steve) made loads of noise and out sang the Mancs for most of the game. My flat mate at the time was a Man Utd fan and I refused to speak to her for ages after the game.

Next up was Chelsea at St. Andrews and a very credible 0-0 draw was gained which took us back up to 4th in the league. Then it was the local derby against the Villa and once again I sat in to watch it as I was too nervous to go out and watch it. The Villa fans reckoned it didn't mean anything to them but from the reaction of their fans to the 0-0 draw – it was like they had won the league! That's how relieved they were not to have been beaten again.

Blues then travelled to Bolton, which I watched live and I was amazed as Blues again won away from home, this time 1-0 and we were still riding high in the Premiership! Of course we still barley got a mention on any of the sports programmes. We were brought down to earth in the next game though when we were beaten at home by Charlton 2-1 but 5 days later we travelled to local rivals Wolves and drew 1-1.

Three days after the Wolves game I was off on my holiday, this time to Singapore for a month where I would be joining Steve. Steve was now stationed in Singapore and would be onshore for a least a month before he again went offshore. He was staying in a lovely hotel/apartment just off the main street in Singapore and I moved in with him and set about having a great time. Whilst he was working during the week I would head out and about and sight see or shop. When he wasn't working we would go out for meals and also a bit of sightseeing. On one of his weekends off I managed to drag him across to visit Santosa Island which was fab. We travelled over to the island on the glass bottom cable car. It was a bit scary but great and we spent the day on the island and had a thoroughly great time.

On Sundays Steve would play football for his works team and on one Sunday I went with him to watch. As happens in Singapore the heavens opened and there was a tropical downpour in the middle of the game. It was so bad that play stopped and the teams ran for cover under nearby trees. I hadn't seen anything like it before and watched in amazement under a massive golf umbrella that Steve had given me. It was funny watching them play, when they returned to the pitch it was well and truly waterlogged but they battled on bravely. Steve even scored a goal so I cheered him loudly as only a girlfriend can, and he looked rather pleased with himself and proud of me. Then we headed back for him to dry off and get changed before heading out for a meal at the Hard Rock Cafe nearby.

Whilst I was in Singapore Blues lost at home to Arsenal 3-0 and then we were playing at Anfield again as we prepared to take on Liverpool. This was on really late in Singapore but I decided to stay up and watch it and Steve decided to stay up for the first half and then go to bed as he had work the next day. It was brilliant when Forssell scored for Blues right in front of the Kop and I celebrated with Steve, who was also very happy as he is a Manc and hates Liverpool. One of his mates back home was a Liverpool fan so he sent him a copy of my Birmingham City screensaver just to rub it in. Once again my celebrations were premature though and as Steve went off to bed I was left alone to watch Blues concede three goals and end the match losing 3-1. Oh well, can't win them all.

With Christmas fast approaching, Steve had his works Christmas party which was held in our hotel/ apartment complex and I met a few of his colleagues and their wives/ girlfriends and we had a really nice time. The rugby world cup was also being played at this time and I watched as England beat Australia in the final in their own back yard and won the World Cup. England were world champions. I couldn't wait to rub that in with the rather big headed Aussies back in Abu Dhabi. My mate Roxy was locked out of her apartment by her Aussie flatmate when she returned home after celebrating the win. Bad losers that's what I say. Anyway, Steve and I celebrated England's win in style over in Singapore.

Just before I was due to leave Singapore, Blues played Blackburn Rovers at home and lost 4-0 and were now in 9th place but still in the top half of the table so I was relatively happy. I must admit though I was really sad to be leaving Steve after spending so long with him and I didn't know when I would him again. I cried a lot in the taxi to the airport but then I picked myself up and got on with it. My visa had run out by two days but nobody seemed to notice and I flew back to Dubai before heading on to Abu Dhabi.

Two days after I arrived back Blues travelled to Leicester City and came back with a 2-0 win and we were having a great season. I was still missing Steve terribly and Christmas was only two weeks away. On Boxing Day Blues took on Manchester City at St. Andrews and won 2-1 then it was away to Everton where we lost 1-0.

The New Year started with Blues gaining revenge over Blackburn for their 4-0 win over us as we knocked them out of the FA Cup 4-0. Sweet revenge and we were rewarded with a home draw against Wimbledon in the 4th round. We then came unstuck at Tottenham losing 4-1 before getting back to winning ways against Southampton at St. Andrews 2-1. Next up was an away trip to Chelsea and a 0-0 draw which was a really good result. Blues were in really high spirits for the FA Cup match against Wimbledon on my birthday (24th January) and Bryan Hughes scored the only goal of the game as Blues progressed to the next round with a 1-0 win. The draw for the 5th round produced an away fixture at Sunderland on the 14th February and I would be home for this match. The last game before I travelled home was the home Fixture against Newcastle Utd and ended in a 1-1 draw.

Before my trip home I was again travelling to Singapore to see Steve, this time though it would only be for four days. I was really excited about seeing Steve again and as he would be working when I arrived I made my way to his hotel (he had been moved out of the apartment and into the Concorde Hotel). I had travelled overnight and was in bed in his room when he arrived in from work. It was great to see him though and he gave me big hug and looked pleased to see me.

We had a great time while I was there, especially when we went out for a meal in the new brazilain restaurant, which was really nice and we both enjoyed it. It was soon over though and once again I was sad to leave. I had bought loads of gifts to take home to my family as I was going to England two days after arriving back in Abu Dhabi. I had so much stuff that Steve had to pack my case nicely for me, as he is so neat and tidy! He had bought me a DVD player for my birthday so he packed that in safely for me. Little did I know but this would be the last time I would see Steve as his job moved to Brazil and he never had the nerve to tell me. He just disappeared off the radar slowly as his emails and calls and excuses got less and less. He does keep in touch even now though as he seems to think we are just on a break!

Anyway, on the 4th February 2004 I again headed back to the UK to see my family and the Blues and my first game was another trip to Maine Road to see Blues take on Manchester City. This would be my last ever trip to Maine Road as it was being closed and Manchester City were moving to a new stadium called the City Of Manchester Stadium. Stephen and I again travelled with the St. Andrews Tavern Coaches and we had a good trip with Blues coming away with a 0-0 draw. Our goalkeeper Maik Taylor had made a stunning double save and then Blues had missed a brilliant chance to win the game in the last few minutes but a point was good and we were now 10th in the table and looking good. I was really pleased with how the season was going so far.

Everton were the next team to take on Blues and I set off for St. Andrews in good spirits. It was great watching a Blues team that seemed to play together so well and I could see that the team were enjoying playing together. The players were often smiling and laughing amongst each other especially when Robbie Savage set up Forsell for Blues 3rd goal, as he ran to him and lifted him over his shoulder and carried him for a few feet with a smile on his face. The Blues lads were really enjoying their football and it was good to see. Johnson and Lazaridis scored our other goals in a great 3-0 win that took Blues up to 9th in the Premiership inside a packed St. Andrews.

Following Blues 4th round win against Wimbledon in the FA Cup, we had been drawn to play away at Sunderland in the 5th round. This would be another long trip for Stephen and I and we travelled on the coaches once again. Loads of Bluenoses made the trip and there were 2,429 of us inside the Stadium of Light making loads of noise. The Sunderland support were also noisy but there were large empty sections of seating in the home area. Sunderland had been relegated the previous season and the Blues fans rubbed this in by singing 'we are premier league!' to them. It was a good game and a great atmosphere and the fact that our manager Steve Bruce is from Newcastle, did not go unnoticed by Sunderland who are big rivals with the Geordies. They sang 'there's only one fat Geordie' to him on a couple of occasions. This came back to haunt them though when Forsell scored a brilliant goal for Blues and all the Bluenoses began singing '1-0 to the fat Geordie!' I thought this was really funny and it certainly wiped the smiles of the faces of the Sunderland fans. However, Sunderland managed to score an equalizer which meant that the game ended 1-1 and would need a reply at St. Andrews to settle the tie.

The last match before I went back was the big one against the old enemy from across the city, and it was at Villa Park. I was so looking forward to this game as I had not seen Blues play Villa live for over 17 years. I was also really nervous as I could not stand the thought of losing to them. They game had been made a noon kick off to avoid trouble and for live TV viewing, and this does tend to take the edge of games. Not this match though! Annette, Steve, Stephen and I were inside a pub in harborne at around 10am even though pubs don't open till 12 on a Sunday. We popped into McDonalds to pick up breakfast first as saw a couple of vile fans in their drab colours. They looked in our direction and we glared back. Then it was round the back of one of the pubs that was only letting in Bluenoses of course, and pre match drinks began. We met the usual crew such as Brendan, Graham etc and chatted to them whilst downing beers.

As we had left it a bit late we decided to get a taxi to Villa Park and 5 of us piled into a black cab and off we set. As we approached the away end at Villa Park the roads became really busy, so with the ground in sight but the taxi stuck in traffic, we disembarked and walked the rest of the way to the ground. Steve told me to keep quiet with all the villa fans around but you know me. I remarked to Stephen, 'can you smell something?' and he innocently replied 'like what?' to which I answered 'smells like shit!' Stephen laughed but the others looked around worriedly.

Once inside the ground the atmosphere was brilliant. Just as I had remembered and the Bluenoses were in full voice with 'shit on the villa' being sang at full blast by the 3,000 Blues in the away end. The blues end behind the goal was packed and everyone was standing and singing. Annette and Steve had tickets away from us but when we got to our seats there was a few empty next to us and everyone remained standing anyway so I made a mental note to get Annette and Steve to come and stand with us for the second half.

The match got under way and Blues just never got started. They looked awful in the first half and it was no surprise when Villa took the lead. The villa fans were going wild as we looked on in despair. Before half time it was 2-0 to Villa and Blues had just not turned up. Losing is bad enough in the local derby but when the lads on the pitch do not put in the effort then it makes it worse. The Villa fans were enjoying it and it was obvious that they were confident that they had already won the game. The games not over yet though, I thought.

Blues came out with all guns firing in the second half and were unlucky on a number of occasions. It didn't seem like it was going to be our day though but the Bluenoses never stopped singing. Then Forsell scored a cracking goal right in front of the Blue army and the away ended exploded with celebrations. Annette and Steve were now standing next to us and Annette, Stephen and I all jumped around madly, hoping that perhaps we could get something out of this game. I just did not want to lose today and I just could not bear that thought.

The game reached the 90 minute mark and the 4th official held up the board informing us that there would be 4 minutes of injury time. My heart was in my mouth by now and the Villa fans were taunting us and celebrating their win. In the 93rd minute Clinton Morrison got the ball just on the edge of the area and has he ran into the penalty area he unleashed a shot that their keeper dived to his right to save but he only parried the ball to the inrushing Stern John with the goal at his mercy. Time seemed to freeze as well as everyone in the ground and my heart stopped as I fully expected him to blast over but to my utter delight he blasted the ball into the top of the Villa net! Yeeeeessss, 2-2 in the last minute of stoppage time. Stern John pulled his shirt off and ran to the ecstatic Blues end and was mobbed just as he reached us. This had all happened right in front of us and I lifted Stephen in the air as Annette jumped on me from the other side. Everyone was jumping on everyone else – it was unbelievable, it was like we had won. Instantly a chant went up from the Bluenoses '2-0 and you fucked it up, 2-0 and you fucked it up!' Brilliant! The Villa fans looked absolutely gutted. They could not believe it, their faces were a picture as they looked totally defeated. Then the Blues fans started singing 'beat the Blues you're having a laugh, beat the Blues you're having a laugh!'

When they interviewed our Finish striker Forssell after the game, he said it was incredible celebrations, just like we had won the league or something. I was over the moon as I watched the Villa fans stream out silently and the Blues fans leaving the ground singing 'Beat the Blues, you're having a laugh, beat the Blues, you're having a laugh'. The trains leaving Aston were silent apart from the singing Bluenoses. Someone remarked that you could tell who were Bluenoses as they couldn't wipe the smiles from their faces. What a brilliant day, and we went on to Harbrone to celebrate our win in the Stores pub. I could hold my head up high as we still had bragging rights in the city and I could head back a very happy girl.

A few days after I got back Blues were knocked out of the FA Cup by Sunderland in the replay 2-0 and our cup interest was over for another season. We followed this with a home game against Middlesbrough who were riding high after winning the League cup and Blues played brilliant to record a 3-1 win that took us up to 7th in Premiership. Three days later Blue did even better by beating Bolton 2-0 at St. Andrews and moving up to 5th in the Premiership. These were great days and I was dreaming of a champion's league place for next season.

I should know better really though and my dreams being dashed in the next game when we lost at home against Leicester City 1-0 and then went to Middlesbrough for the return fixture and lost in a really bizarre game 5-3. Having watched the game live I though we were the better team and extremely unlucky to lose. We did get back to winning ways at the end of March as Blues beat Leeds Utd 4-1 at St. Andrews and it was followed by a 0-0 draw away at Fulham. The big boys from Manchester were next at St. Andrews and Blues were really unlucky to lose 2-1, then we lost away at Portsmouth 3-1 before drawing with Charlton away 1-1, wolves at home 2-2 and Arsenal away 0-0. Unfortunately we lost our last home game against Liverpool 3-0 and drew the last game of the season away at Blackburn 1-1 which meant Blues finished the season in 10th place in the Premiership. This was still great though and was our highest finish for some time, and was especially good considering that most promoted teams get relegated in their second season in the top flight. Blues had survived and put up a great show and I was proud of them.

Arsenal were crowned champions, which made our 0-0 draw at their ground all that much better, and Chelsea were runners up. Leicester City, Leeds Utd and Wolves were relegated to the First Division. The FA Cup was won my Manchester Utd who beat Millwall 3-0 and Middlesbrough won the League Cup beating Bolton 2-1.

CHAPTER TWENTY-THREE – End of the Dream

The 2004 – 2005 season got underway on the 14th august away at Portsmouth. I was still living and working in the sunshine of Abu Dhabi and things were going well. I was now working as a Sister after gaining promotion and was enjoying life. I watched the first game against Portsmouth live and was impressed with a brilliant free kick by Robbie Savage that flew into the Portsmouth net to put Blues 1-0 up. The game finished 1-1 but all in all it was a good start to the new season.

I had already taken all my leave for 2004 so would not get to see any games live for the rest of the year. As 2004 drew to a close Blues were 9th in the Premiership and were out of the League cup following a win against Lincoln City 3-1 in the 2nd round and then defeat at home against Fulham 1-0. However, Blues had already had brilliant wins in the local derbies against Aston Villa 2-1 at Villa Park and a week later we beat West Brom 4-0 at St. Andrews. I had watched this game in Heroes in Abu Dhabi and had the pleasure of taunting a West Brom fan (Justin, the local DJ) as Blues smashed four past them. Blues had also had a fantastic win over Liverpool at the mighty Anfield 1-0 with a goal from Darren Anderton (sick note). I had been at a Dessert Diamond party at the time and it was on live with Arabic commentary. I was watching it with Deb, a Liverpool fan, so I enjoyed that one! I was really enjoying the Premiership party. Blues finished the year with a good away win at Fulham 3-2 which took Blues to 9th in the table.

I didn't have any holiday booked until September so this meant that I would not be able to see any live games this season but I made sure I watched every time Blues were on Live TV. Blues had a good season with some good wins and I was happy with life in the top flight. We were knocked out of the FA Cup in the 4th round by Chelsea 2-0, following our win in the 3rd round over Leeds Utd 3-0. Blues also did the double over Liverpool after winning the return fixture 2-0 at St. Andrews. The best 'double' though was the one we achieved 'again' over local rivals Aston Villa as Blues won the return fixture at St. Andrews 2-0 and 'can we play you every week?' was sang along with 'beat the Blues you're having a laugh', 'shit on the villa' and 'Keep Right On'. We still had the bragging rights of the City.

Blues also gave champions elect Chelsea a scare at Stamford Bridge and a goal from Walter Pandiani took Blues to a within a few minutes of bringing Chelsea's very long unbeaten home record to an end. It was only a goal from Drogba with minutes remaining that saved a draw for Chelsea as the game finished 1-1. I was gutted when they equalised as I watched the game live with my mom who was visiting at the time, but I was also very proud of our lads after gaining such a good result.

The last game of the season was a cracker and I watched it live as Blues shocked everyone with Heskey scoring the winner as the game finished Birmingham City 2 Arsenal 1. What a great result and a great end to a really good season that saw Blues finish in 12th place with some very good wins under our belt. Chelsea finished the season as Premiership champions with Arsenal the runners up. Crystal Palace, Norwich City and Southampton were relegated to the second tier. The FA Cup was won by Arsenal on penalties after the game finished 0-0 against Manchester Utd. The League Cup was won by Chelsea who beat Liverpool 3-2 after extra time.

I had brought a new car in January, a lovely red convertible sports car and I loved it. It was great to drive around in the lovely weather with the roof down and I proudly displayed my Birmingham City car sticker in the front windscreen. In February I moved into a lovely two bedroom apartment in the city centre and was now living alone as I now had single accommodation due to my promotion as a Sister. It was a newly built apartment block as was lovely, with floor to ceiling windows in the living room and one of the bedrooms. I was really happy and was looking forward to my family coming to stay as they often did. Life was good. My friends and I had also been discussing plans to travel to Germany for the 2006 World Cup Finals to follow England so we were making plans for that as the 2005 – 2006 season approached.

The satellite TV that I currently had (South African) had lost the rights to screen the English Premier League so I changed to the local one, Showtime, which had all the Premier games on. This was even better as it showed every Premier game being shown on different channels. This meant that I would be able to watch every single Blues game for the coming season. I was so excited and I was really looking forward to our fourth season back in the top flight.

The season kicked off with an away draw at Fulham 0-0, which I watched live on my new satellite channel. Unhappily, Blues then lost in their next game at home against Manchester City 2-1 and a few days later we lost again at home against Middlesbrough 3-0. I was getting a bit worried but then Blues travelled across to West Brom and got our first win of the season 3-2 to raise my hopes again. And then I was off home again and the prospect of seeing Blues live again. It felt like ages since I had been home and I was really looking forward to it.

My first game was on the 10th September at St. Andrews against Charlton and Stephen and I had tickets in the new railway stand again. I thought Blues played really well and were unlucky to lose 1-0. Steve thought Blues had played crap but I disagreed and I thought Blues had a good side with real promise.

The following week Blues were away at Portsmouth and Neil had said that himself, sue and Nicola would take Stephen and I to Portsmouth and enjoy a day out at the same time. This was great news and I was really happy to travel with them. It was a lovely sunny day too, and we set out early to have the whole day down in Portsmouth. When we arrived we headed to the City centre for a look around before heading to a local pub for a drink. We found a nice city centre pub and were soon joined by other Bluenoses who were also down for the match. Then we headed off to get some food, I fancied chips for a change. Neil had a really nice England top on with a union jack and someone stopped him and asked where he got it from. I thought it was quite funny when he told them he got it in Blackpool. 'Bit far to go really', the bloke replied with a smile.

Just before kickoff, Neil dropped Stephen and me at the ground and they headed off to the sea front. Stephen and I headed into the away end, with no roof, but for once it was a lovely day and we sat down in lovely sunshine. We were only a few seats from the front and had a great view. Hence we had a great view of Butt has he got sent off for a foul on a Pompey player right in front of us. I turned to Stephen 'what the bloody hell did he do that for?' as we looked on amazed. Now Blues were really up against it and Portsmouth scored to take a 1-0 lead.

Blues got a corner as the Pompey fans were in full voice. 'This will shut them up' I said to Stephen, and sure enough the ball came across for Jarosik to score our equaliser. We jumped up and celebrated as the away end was a mass of celebration. Even though Blues only had 10 men we played really well for the rest of the game and it finished all square at 1-1 and we were off to meet up with the others for the journey back. We stopped at a small motel on the way back for a drink and a meal and all in all we had had a very nice day out at the seaside. It was nice to be home and to be with my family.

Blues had drawn Scunthorpe away in the second round of the League cup but as Stephen was at school I didn't have anyone to go with so I wasn't planning to travel. However, as it got closer it was getting harder for me to imagine missing it. It was a night match and when I got up early on the day of the game and the sun was shining it was killing me to think of missing it. I decided to ring Alan and see if he was travelling and if he had room in his car if he was. Alan said he was going and he did have room to take me if I wanted to go. I decided I did and headed off to St.

Andrews to get a ticket. Luckily there were tickets still available so I purchased one and Alan came by to pick me up before heading off to pick the others up for the trip.

By the time we set off for Scunthorpe the car was full and I had met more new Blues fans that I would be travelling with. We stopped on the way for sandwiches etc and before long we were arriving in Scunthorpe. We stopped at a really nice large pub within walking distance from the ground, which could clearly be seen nearby. There was a sign outside saying no football shirts allowed. Great, I had mine on, so I had to do my jacket right up and it was quite warm inside. Mind you, before long the pub filled up with Bluenoses wearing Blues shirts! Hence my jacket was soon removed and I joined with the other Bluenoses in a pre match drink. The lads I had travelled with were great and bought me drinks as we all chatted. I looked around and it was a mass of Blue and White with only two Scunthorpe shirts on display. The atmosphere was a happy one and Alan headed off to park the car near the ground as we arranged to meet up with him in the ground after having a couple more drinks.

Then we headed into the ground and Blues had one end of the ground behind the goal and it was now filling with Blues fans that had made the trip. It was a little cold to be honest, but I joined in with the singing and chatted to other Bluenoses as we waited for kick off. The match got under way and Blues were soon ahead with a nicely taken goal be Forsell and we all celebrated. Forsell scored his second before half time and we celebrated again as Blues took a 2-0 lead. At half time I headed to the toilets and when I got back the lads had bought me a sausage roll and said 'get that down yer love' which I thought was really nice of them. They were real gents and looked after me for the whole of the trip. The match finished with a 2-0 win for Blues and we were in the next round of the League Cup. The trip home didn't seem to take too long even though we were all tired and Alan dropped me home, which was really nice as he lives the other side of Birmingham to me. Alan is one of life's gentlemen and has always looked after me over many years of watching the Blues. He is the most ardent, loyal Blues fan I have ever met.

My last game before travelling back was a big one as Blues took on Liverpool at St. Andrews. Liverpool had won the Champions League this year and were the current holders. This gave us Bluenoses the chance to give them some stick as Blues played really well and we sang 'champions league, you're having a laugh, champions league, you're having a laugh!' it was really funny. It was really great when Walter Pandiani scored to put Blues 1-0 up and we celebrated loudly. Liverpool fans sang at us 'you've never won fuck all' to which the Blues fans sang back 'we've never won fuck all' which left them speechless. Once again, I thought this was really funny. At least Bluenoses have a great sense of humour despite everything. Unfortunately Liverpool equalised and then went 2-1 ahead. Poor Kilkenny who had played brilliant on his debut, decided to play goalkeeper and made a good one handed save only to give away a penalty and get sent off. Even though we were now losing, the Blues fans never stopped singing and the lads continued to play well. Stephen and I were sitting on the Kop near the corner and we watched as a Blues corner was swung into the penalty area in front of us and a Liverpool player managed to direct a header into his own net. Brilliant! 2-2 and we celebrated by jumping on each other and waving our arms madly. It was no more than Blues deserved and the game finished 2-2. Although we were in 15th place and in the bottom half I was sure we were too good to go down. Then I was off back to Abu Dhabi again having had a wonderful time once again.

The first game after arriving back in Abu Dhabi was another big match, this time against Arsenal, who were riding high in the table at this time. It was away at Arsenal and Blues did well I thought only losing 1-0. The real blow came in the next game when we were really unlucky to lose at home to our rivals Villa 1-0. I was gutted by our first defeat in 20 years against them but the less said the better. Blues then lost away at Blackburn 2-0 and we were slipping down the table into 18th place. I was still not worried though, as there was still a long way to go and I thought we were by far too good to go down as did everyone else.

It was back to cup action towards the end of October as Blues took on Norwich City at St. Andrews in the 3rd round of the League Cup. Jermaine Pennant and Jarosik scored the goals in a 2-1 win which saw us through to the 4th round and a tie against Millwall away. Not a pleasant place to travel to either.

The next two games ended in defeat against Everton at home 1-0 and away at Newcastle 1-0. Things then picked up with a really good away win as Sunderland 1-0 although Blues were now in 19th place. Three days later it was a break from league action when we again played Cup football as we travelled to Millwall and following a 2-2 draw, Blues won the penalty shootout 4-3 and progressed to the 5th round where we were rewarded by a daunting home tie against Manchester Utd. Mind you, I was still confident as always. The following week Blues against lost at home this time against West Ham Utd 2-1 and things were not looking too good as I again headed home to Birmingham and the prospect of more live football.

It was great to see all my family again and it was great to be home during the run up to Christmas as this was the first time I had been back in the UK around Christmas for six years. My first match was to be at St. Andrews against Fulham. I met up with everyone as usual and I had a great day out at Blues beat Fulham 1-0 with a goal by Nicky Butt. The relief was audible around St. Andrews when Butt scored and when the final whistle went to signal celebrations of our win. I would only get to see two games whilst I was home and the next game would be away at Manchester City at their new City of Manchester Stadium, so it was another new ground for me.

It was a night game and Stephen and I were again travelling on the coach from the St. Andrews Tavern pub. We had a couple of pre match drinks before setting off into what was becoming a very cold night. The trip was enjoyable as always when travelling with Bluenoses and we were soon arriving in a wet Manchester. I must admit I was quite impressed with the City of Manchester Stadium though I did wonder what on earth the strange looking monument type thing was just outside the ground. I was later to go out with the guy who designed it and he did explain what it was but it was obviously not memorable as I can't remember what on earth it is.

Anyway, once inside the ground it was really cold but as we downed another pre match drink under the stands with the away Blues support, the atmosphere was brilliant. Blues were singing whilst consuming their food and drinks and it was really loud and echoed underneath the stand where we were congregated before kickoff. The Bluenoses were singing 'shit on the villa' and 'Keep Right On' over and over. It was great. Just before kickoff we made our way up to our seats and I was very impressed with the stadium. Blues had a large section just behind the goal next to the Manchester City fans and the Blues faithful were in good voice despite the cold. The game got under way and we conceded four goals very quickly really but it didn't stop us singing, much to the amazement of the Man City fans. As the game dragged on and hope began to fade, Jarosik scored a brilliant goal right in front of us and we all began celebrating in the hope it would warm us up and lead to a fight back. Blues fans began singing 'we're gonna win 5-4, we're gonna win 5-4, we're gonna win 5-4!' which was quite funny really. That's one of the things I love about Bluenoses, we have such a great sense of humour even when things are going against us. Even though we lost the game 4-1 I left the ground with a feeling of warmth from the brilliant Blues fans who always make me feel better. Then it was onto the coach and back to Birmingham and my last couple of days before I had to head back to the sunshine.

Although I was sad to leave all my family just before Christmas, the sunshine and heat was a welcome relief after the rain and cold in England. I still missed it though and I sat up late despite the four hour time difference to watch Blues get beaten by Manchester Utd 3-1 in the 5th round of the League Cup a couple of days after arriving back. So Blues were out of the League cup and sitting in the bottom three in the Premier League and I was a little worried. On Boxing Day Blues travelled to Tottenham and I watched the game live as we lost 2-0 and I again watched as Blues drew at home against Manchester Utd 2-2. This was a far better game and one that I though Blues should have won. Then it was away at Chelsea where we lost 2-0 and home against Wigan when we got back to winning ways beating them 2-0. Still in the bottom three though and an away draw at Torquay Utd in the FA Cup. I was concerned about this game as I thought it could be a potential banana skin for us. I was relieved when the game finished 0-0 meaning there would be a replay two weeks later at St. Andrews.

As January progressed, Blues lost again away at Charlton 2-0 and then beat Torquay in the FA Cup 3rd round replay to bring some cheer to all of us Bluenoses just when we needed it. The draw for the 4th round paired us with Reading away, who were currently top of the Championship and running away with it. No problem, I thought, as I watched Blues demolish Portsmouth 5-0 in a very important match at the bottom of the table. Blues played really well at Reading in the 4th round of the FA Cup and gained a replay after drawing 1-1 up in Reading. Then it was off to Anfield where we always seem to do well and I watched a very exciting game as Blues again came away with a good result drawing 1-1 and we were now 3rd from bottom but with hope in our hearts.

At the beginning of February we were brought back down to earth when Arsenal came to St. Andrews and took all 3 points as they beat us 2-0 but a few days later we were cheered up once again as we progressed into the 5th round of the FA cup after beating Reading 2-1 in the replay at St. Andrews.

The roller coaster ride continued as Blues lost the next match away at West Ham 3-0 and then went and won a place in the quarter finals of the FA Cup as we beat Stoke City away 1-0 with a Forssell goal. I was really happy and couldn't believe that Blues were in the Quarter Final of the FA Cup for the first time in ages. My hopes of seeing Blues run out in the FA Cup final were once again high. Still on the crest of a wave Blues went into the next relegation battle against Sunderland at St. Andrews full of confidence and won the game 1-0 thereby sending Sunderland into the Championship in the process.

It was getting really nervy as we went into March and an away defeat against Middlesbrough 1-0 did nothing to calm those nerves. Next up was West Brom at home and we only drew 0-0 before losing against Tottenham 2-0 and we remained third from bottom and in a relegation place. I wouldn't be able to get home for any of the remaining games as I had booked most of my leave in June to go to the world cup finals with England. So it was with much hope that I stayed up late to watch the FA Cup Quarter Final game against Liverpool. I soon began to wish I hadn't bothered though as it was awful and Liverpool began a demolition job on us. When the score got to 6-0 I gave up in disgust and went to bed. It was only the next morning that I discovered it had got even worse and we had lost 7-0 in utter disgrace. How can a team get to the Quarter Final of the FA Cup and lose 7-0? To this day I will never know.

Blues had a tough run in to the end of the season and I guess it was no surprise when we lost 3-0 away at Manchester Utd in the next game. We played much better in the next game against champions elect Chelsea when we deserved at least the 0-0 draw that we got. I went to watch the next game live at the British Club in Abu Dhabi with the guy I was going out with who was a Manchester Utd fan from Bolton named Lee. He used to support Bolton so he had a bit of a soft spot for them but even he was impressed with the brilliant goal from Jarosik that sent me celebrating despite the funny looks around me. Lee just smiled at me and Blues won the game 1-0 and moved out of the bottom three. 'Don't worry', he said, 'you are too good to go down'.

Then it was away at Wigan and a 1-1 draw before more horrors as we lost at the Vile again 3-1 and I watched this game with my brother and family who were visiting me. As we watched the game in Heroes Bar I was driven to drink and ended up downing many pints of Cider before we headed off to the Captains Arms to smoke Shisha (which I never do!). Blues did recover to beat Blackburn 2-1 in the next game and we were once again one place off the bottom three. It was getting really nerve wracking with only three games remaining. The next game was away at Everton and we really needed to win. Disaster though as only a 0-0 draw was achieved and we were back in the bottom three. This meant that we had to beat Newcastle at home in the next game.

Annette and Steve were flying out to visit me on the fateful day when Blues took on Newcastle so they would arrived at mine not knowing it we were down or still in with a chance with a game remaining. I sat and watched the game in my Blues shirt and my pint of Cider in my Birmingham City pint glass and was shaking with nerves. Blues played really well but just couldn't score. As the time ticked by I got more and more despondent and when the final whistle blew with the game at 0-0 I burst into tears as Blues were condemned to relegation with a game to go. I was distraught and when I opened the door to Annette and Steve all I could say in way of welcome was 'we're down!' To this day Annette has never forgotten that. I didn't even say hello or welcome them, just the words 'we're down'. It was a very sad day but at least I was cheered up a bit by having Annette there with me.

The last game just seemed to be pointless but it would still be good to win our last game and I watched live and had a giggle at all the Bluenoses that had travelled to Bolton in fancy dress as they were determined to go down in style. It's a shame the players couldn't have had the same attitude as they lost 1-0 as the Bluenoses sang 'Blues go down, Blues go down, we all go down together, come back up, win the cup, kick fuck out the villa!'. We would be back, of that I had no doubt. Our supporters deserve to be in the Premiership with our brilliant sense of humour, our fantastic support and our deep love of the club that has yet to repay us. As our anthem says, we will "Keep Right On!'.

Chelsea were crowned Champions again, with Manchester Utd as runners up. Relegated were Birmingham City (much to everyone's surprise), West Brom and Sunderland. The FA Cup was won by Liverpool on penalties after a fantastic game against West Ham with finished 3-3 after extra time. The League Cup was won my Manchester Utd who beat Wigan easily 4-0. And I was planning my forthcoming invasion of Germany in 2006 where I hoped to see England lift the world cup.

CHAPTER TWENTY-FOUR – Invasion of Germany 2006

In June 2006 the World Cup finals were being held in Germany and along with four of my mates, I planned to be there to watch England hopefully lift the world cup for the first time since we won it in 1966. We had booked the trip well in advance and arranged for us all to take our holidays at the same time. We had booked a nice hotel in Cologne for 8 days followed by two weeks in a sort of hostel in Berlin for the remainder. I was planning the trip with Roxy, Carolyn and Janine and we were really looking forward to it.

Because we could only take three weeks holiday we had to decide whether to miss the first two group games and still be there for the final or assume we would not reach the final and be there for all the group games. Ever the optimists we decided that England would indeed win the world cup so we opted to miss the first two group games in order to be there for the final itself.

I was really excited about going to Germany for the finals and had obtained face paint, England tattoos, a large England hand sent to be by my mom and a large St. George flag with 'ABU DHABI BLUES' on it. I was all prepared. First though, we had to suffer watching the first two matches in Abu Dhabi. The first game on 10th June in Frankfurt saw England take on Paraguay and the girls and I, dressed in England shirts, flags and England flags tattooed on our faces, set out to watch the game in one of our local pubs named PJ'O'Reilly's. I had been to the hairdressers the day before and had my hair dyed with a thick red cross in my hair (across the top of my head and down each side, back and front). It looked quite cool when I lowered my head as my hair is blonde and I had blown it straight so that it was clear it was a St. George's cross!

Anyway, to be honest there wasn't much atmosphere in Abu Dhabi this time for the world Cup so as much as we jumped about and celebrated England's 1-0 win against Paraguay, we couldn't wait to actually be in Germany soaking up the atmosphere. The next game on 15th June was a little better for atmosphere as we watched it in Heroes Bar this time and there were loads of England fans there. We were all dressed up in our England gear complete with our St. George's flags and we jumped around like lunatics as England beat Trinidad & Tobago 2-0. The next England game we would be in Germany for – fantastic!

A few days later on 19th June, my sister Annette's birthday, we set off for Germany. I was up at 3.30am and ready for the journey ahead that would take us on to German soil for the English invasion of Germany 2006!

Carolyn, Janine and I were picked up by a courtesy limo at 4.40am and headed to Dubai for our long flight to Dusseldorf that was due to depart at 8.30am. We arrived in Dubai with time to spare and headed into the Irish village in Dubai airport for a fab breakfast and our first drink of the holiday – Smirnoff Ice!

Our flight finally took off at 9.20am and we were on our way! It was a nice flight, as I listened to my iPod, chatted and had a few holiday drinks. Janine and I did a rendition of the dam busters as we came in to land at Dusseldorf much to Carolyn's horror! – Which amused us immensely. There were a few other footie fans on the plane, English and Japanese, dressed in their footie shirts!

We disembarked quite easily at Dusseldorf airport and after obtaining German SIMMs cards for our phones we headed to the train station for rail passes. Then it was on to the train and off to Cologne where we would be staying for the next 8 nights. We arrived at our hotel in Cologne, put our stuff in our rooms and headed downstairs to the local pub on the corner (conveniently right underneath our hotel – or so we thought!). There were England fans everywhere – oh, and the odd Sweden fan. Inside the bar there were more England fans clad in England shirts and flags everywhere. Fantastic!

Janine had already decorated the window in her room with a big England flag which we traipsed across the road to see if we could see – we could! Then after consuming food and drink we headed back to our rooms for a rest before the night ahead. I phoned snowy (bluenose!) about the tickets he had promised us for the Sweden game only to find that he and the lads were currently in Dortmund for a game but were heading back to Cologne later whereby we could meet up.

Our other mate Roxy arrived from the UK at about 7pm and we began to get ready to head out on the town. Roxy and I were ready first so we headed off to another bar just up the road to wait for the others. We were having a nice time sitting outside when the heavens opened and it pissed down! And I mean pissed down! Living in the Middle East we are not used to this! Never mind, we moved inside, had a drink and by the time the others joined us it had stopped raining.

We were supposed to meet snowy and the lads (bluenoses) in the square, but I couldn't raise him on the phone so we headed to the square anyway. It was only one stop on the train and as we came through the main station we were greeted by the sight of England fans everywhere and West Midlands police! The police were friendly and it was nice to see their presence in Germany. We headed out of the station and went in the general direction of the singing.

The main square was full of England fans (and the odd Swede) who were singing loudly in a group and waving flags. The German police stood around watching them and appeared amused by the whole thing. There were chants of "I am England till I die", "it's coming home", "I would rather be a cabbage than a Swede!" (I quite liked that one!) And, probably the best one "there were 10 German bombers in the air – and the RAF from England shot one down!"

A drunken Swedish girl with a Sweden flag wondered into the middle of them – which was probably a big mistake (which she took time to realise!) as the lads sang "get yer tits out for the lads" which she did and was then followed by a loud rendition of "fuck off back to Sweden!" All good fun eh!

As the night wore on thousands more England fans joined them, including Swedish and Switzerland fans. I couldn't get hold of snowy at all as his phone was turned off and I was getting a bit worried about the tickets for tomorrow's game. We chatted to a few England lads, bought 'invasion of Germany – 2006' badges then headed back towards the train station at about 1.30am.

There were English police everywhere chatting to the fans. Inside the station there were fans sleeping everywhere and loud renditions of 'en-ger-land' could be heard. Great! We got on our train with Swedish and German fans. This was fun. One lad told us he supported Italy, so the 4 of us gave a loud rendition of "you're just a small town in Europe" which appeared to impress the others on the train! We then went on to do "Italy, Italy give us a song" which completely stumped him. His mate then informed us that he supported Brazil! And they had Ronaldino. We then sang loudly "you can stick your Ronaldino up your arse!" So a fun time was had.

We got off the train and ran into several Sweden fans, to whom we sang "I would rather be a cabbage than a Swede". Don't think they completely understood that one to be honest. We ran into more England fans and then arrived back at our hotel safe and sound. What a fab day! We went to sleep to the sound of the England fans singing outside our window (which was directly above the pub!)!

I was up at 9am and I headed down to breakfast with Roxy and the others joined us. The restaurant was full of England fans as well as 4 Swedish girls, and breakfast was lovely. We then headed back to our rooms to get ready for the big day ahead. I still could not get hold of Snowy. I was now really worried!

We were now ready, we had all donned war pain and got into our England gear and were ready for the day ahead! By one o'clock all 4 of us were kitted out and ready to go, complete with face paint, hat's flags, England shirts and invasion of Germany badges. We all looked really cool and stopped for a photo in the lobby on the way out. We walked into town having fun waving our blow up England hand (which Carolyn later lost!), flag's and scarves at everyone we passed. There was England fans everywhere.

When we arrived at the cathedral and the steps were a sea of red and white along with a few Swedes and Germans. Fantastic! The open topped England bus and the Sun bus were there and the big England flag that had been signed by everyone prior to the finals.

We had our photo taken by a photographer for the Yahoo web page with my 'Abu Dhabi Blues' flag! I then got an England v Sweden fanzine (Free Lions) as we made our way to the square. I saw some bluenoses on the way. There were England Flags everywhere. It was a great atmosphere!

There were loads in the square making it very difficult to get a drink. I think each bar only had one barman/woman! We waited for ages to get served only to be told that they had run out of vodka! I thought they were joking but I was informed that we had drunk all the vodka last night (obviously not prepared for us English eh!)! Bummer! I had to make do with Bacardi and coke – 50/50 measures that nearly blew my head off! However, I got 2 in case and Carolyn helped me out while we waited for Roxy and Janine who were getting beer from the ice cream shop!

Whilst we were waiting for the girls we spotted Snowy and the lads! I'd given up hope after being informed that there were over 100,000 England fans in Cologne! However, it was bad news as Snowy informed us that his mate had let us all down and that no tickets were forth coming. He was gutted too but at least we were here amongst the fans and the atmosphere. The other bluenoses, including Fiddler, were there too so we sank a few beers with them and took a few pics. There was a great group shot of us with my Abu Dhabi Blues St. George's cross flag. There was a group of QPR fans nearby who had 'sussed' the German bar staff situation and had bought their own crates of beer, vodka etc!

There were now thousands in the square and the atmosphere was great – we even met superman wearing England face paint and with an England Flag! Four Brazilian guys wondered past with 'will shag 4 ticket!' T-shirts and I was very quick to spot a photo opportunity!

So, on we went with our pub-crawl heading towards the England fan fest on the other side of the river. There was England flags hanging from everywhere you looked including across the main bridge! A funny incident occurred when we passed a pub full of guys dressed as 118 with curly wigs and moustaches, as they spotted Snowy in his England shirt, shorts and socks they began singing "there's only one Paul Parker!" loudly and everyone burst out laughing (he did look like him to be honest!). Even Snowy laughed when he realised they were singing it to him! Then they sang "Parker, Parker

Give us a wave" to which snowy responded with a wave and was greeted with cheers from the lads. Very funny!

So, on we went across the bridge to the fan zone where it looked like there were between 30-40,000 England fans already there (the guy on stage later said there were 70,000 inside). It was jammed but fun. There were guys with the blow up England 'missile' which they were throwing about and also a bloke in a blow up 'fat man' outfit. Very funny! Lots of people were seeing how thigh they could kick footballs into the air and where (or on whom) they would land! Occasionally they would land on tables and beer would fly everywhere to the sound of a big cheer! (Makes a change from a fight whenever beer is spilled!).

Snowy launched the ball into the air and promptly fell on his arse – amid cheers of "he fell over!" At this point, I discovering they only sell beer (which I'm sad to say I don't drink!) and the queues were about 10 deep, so Janine, Snowy and I decided to head back to the bars along the river to get a decent drink and watch the match. Roxy and Carolyn decided to stay in the fan zone.

The walk back was fun as we passed a few Germans and gave a good rendition of "5-1, in your own back yard!" and "5-1, even Heskey scored!" Very amusing! We finally made our way to one pub in particular where the singing was the loudest and got drinks and settled to watch the match. All the bars had tables and big screens outside and were packed with England fans, a few Swedes and a few German fans. Sweden fans were funny. They were singing "we've got a man on the inside". England fans (when they stopped laughing at this!) replied with "Rooney's gonna get ya!" and "I would rather be a cabbage than a Swede!" followed by "you can stick your IKEA up your arse!"

When England scored there was a massive cheer all along the riverside pubs and the square! There wasn't much of a sound when Sweden scored to be honest. Anyway, match over, a 2-2 draw and our objective was achieved with passage to the next round, and the celebrations really began! Dancing and singing everywhere. Our bar was the main celebration area and we sang "10 German bombers in the air – and the RAF from England shot one down" for about 2 hours solid! Brilliant! Even a film crew came and filmed it. A couple of Germans joined in too!

We also sang "we hope Sweden beat the Germans" which really pleased the Swedes in the area. We also sang the Steve Gerard song several times too. Then the 'let's go fucking mental!' singing started and lots of beer was getting thrown in the air! Fun but we all got a beer shampoo! Someone then started 'let's all do the conga' and off they went down the street!

We then went into the square and the cathedral steps were still a sea of red and white with flag's everywhere and lots of broken glass. Police were standing back and watching the fun (got a great pic of 2 English coppers sticking their thumbs up to the camera – great!). After a few songs' photo's etc – we headed to the station, which was buzzing, and headed back to our hotel! What a fantastic day!!!

I woke early and managed to make it down for breakfast, all be it a little the worse for wear! There were several hung-over looking England fans who had also made it to breakfast and were sitting around the restaurant. Roxy and I managed to drag ourselves out and headed outside to explore the local shops. We obtained Top-up cards for our phones and got our photos printed off in a nearby shop. The 43 photos we had already taken were fab! It was great to see them. This done, Roxy and I headed into the square, which now appeared empty without the thousands for England fans from the day before!

I bought an England/Sweden cologne 2006 scarf for my collection then we decided to do the Rhine River cruise. There wasn't much to see to be honest (except the chocolate factory), although we passed several camper vans and tents with England flags on the banks of the river. Then we headed back to the hotel and down to the local bar to watch the Holland v Argentina game. Carolyn and Janine had headed off to their room early and crashed (lightweights) so a quiet day was had by all of us, but we were all recovering from yesterday!

The next day we were off on a trip to Frankfurt to stay with friends of Roxy's, so we were up early for breakfast and off to the station to catch the ICE (fast train) to Frankfurt. These trains are fab and travel at 190 mph. We had a nice journey and arrived in Frankfurt full of the joys of spring, put our overnight bags in one of the station lockers and head into town to explore.

Roxy's friends, Lisa, Pete and Sandeep were working till six so we would catch up with them later. The weather was lovely and sunny and we soon found our way to the river and the old square. It was very nice and pretty and I bought some post cards, then we sat outside one of the bars and had a cool drink in the sun. After we finished our drinks we decided to wander around the shops and the German market so off we went. I had my photo taken outside the "Birmingham Pub" – cool.

Suddenly the place seemed to be invaded by hundreds of singing and flag waving Italians who had just booked their place in the last 16. They were quite excited. Some of them were hanging out of cars and there were horns blaring everywhere. There was also a group of celebrating Ghana fans that had just qualified!!! They were very colorful and looked to be having a better time that the Italians!

At this point, following a phone conversation with Lisa, we headed back to the square to meet up with the others. We found a seat outside one of the bars currently occupied by the Czech Republic fans – a nice bunch I must say. Even though they had missed out on qualification they were having a good time (again I have to say better than the Italians!). A group of celebrating Italians arrived and proceeded to taunt the Czech's, with a couple of girls standing on their table singing (I'd have knocked em off if it had been our table!). Then the police arrived and took one of the Italians aside to give him a warning before it got out of hand as it looked like it was about too.

Then Sandeep, Lisa, Pete and Toby arrived and I decided that I had to buy a new England flag as mine was back in cologne. I felt the time was right to stand up and be counted, and the Italians were getting on my nerves to be honest. I thought I'd show them that the English were also there! I waved my new flag around for a bit and got told by the Czech's that we were great and that they hope that England won the world cup. Me too!

We decided to go to the fan zone to see the massive screen in the middle of the river. It was very impressive. We all stood and watched the first half of the Japan v Brazil game before heading for the pubs on the other side of the river the watch the 2nd half. I did a bit of flag waving and singing with a bunch of England fans we spotted on the way and reminded a few Germans of the '5-1 in your own backyard' score line, before getting a kebab and heading back to our friends flat to get some sleep. I must say, the kebabs in Germany are the best I have ever had! I was absolutely knackered!

I must admit I didn't feel too well when I woke up as I had a sore throat and a cold. The sore throat was probably not helped by the singing from the night before mind you! However, I'm on world cup duty so I struggled on. Lisa came to collect us at about 13.30 after the girls had been on a breakfast adventure to the shops and come back with all sorts of goodies. Janine had managed to fall out of the string hammock on the balcony after breakfast which was funny. Roxy had managed to capture it on camera which was pretty cool! I just sat on the balcony in my England pj's struggling through breakfast and laughing at Janine's antics.

Then we all got into Lisa's car and headed off to the local train station where we promptly got a train to the main Frankfurt station (hangover and all!). Our bags were once again shoved into lockers and we set off to explore some more of Frankfurt. We made our way to the tall tower with a viewing gallery on the top (can't remember the name of it) – 55 floors!! Very high up and a fantastic view! We all took pictures and could see the football stadium in the distance. There was a film crew and a reporter up there filming some report – weather maybe?

There were certainly no wags in sight! We were now called swags – supporters without a game!!! Or so I had been informed! Not for long though! Then we headed off again back to the station via the kebab shop. Fantastic kebabs! Then we spotted it - there on the corner (calling us) was an Irish pub – O'Reilly's, by the station. So in we wandered ordered a beer (or in my case a vodie!) and sat down to watch the Spain v Saudi game. Unfortunately due to exhaustion most of us couldn't keep our eyes open so when half time came we made our way out of the pub (which was packed) and over the road to the station. We collected our bags and jumped on the ICE train back to Cologne. The train was packed (didn't they know the Spain v Saudi game was on!! Ha) as it was heading to Amsterdam but we managed to find seats and collapsed into them. Better not fall asleep eh!

We arrived back in cologne and decided that we fancied a nice sit down meal at one of the restuarants along the river where we could watch the Togo v France game that was being played in cologne and also catch the atmosphere. So we went back to the hotel, showered dressed and ready to party we headed out to the riverside bars. We did see the odd french fan but not many. Nothing like when england played a couple of nights ago. It was eerily like being on the moon! (not that ive been on the moon of course but I have been to old trafford! – just kidding janine!). oh well, we had a nice meal, watched the game and awaited the arrival of the celebrating french – who must be heading to town to celebrate – right?

I think they must have got lost though, cos they never arrived! Well, a couple of them maybe. I must say though, they have no idea how to celebrate and I hoped they would go home soon and leave the real fans to it! So, somewhat disappointed, we all wandered back to our hotel and our beds to dream of seeing our boys holding aloft the world cup! No, I wasn't that drunk!

The next morning I was up early once again and off to get a train to Dusseldorf for the day (good job we have a world cup rail pass eh!). We had decided that we would watch the Germany v Sweden game (5pm kick off) in Dusseldorf and then head home to cologne for an early night prior to the big match tomorrow. Well, that was the plan anyway!

We arrived in Dusseldorf and wandered around the city a bit before we headed to the nearest bar for cocktails. The cocktails were pretty bloody potent to be honest! I only got it because it was blue and I'm a Birmingham fan!

As we were sitting outside the bar we noticed loads of German fans heading past, so we decided to drink up and head in the same direction to see where they would be watching the match. We stopped off at a pizza place for food and a beer along the way before continuing on our journey which led us to the river where there were several outside bars with big screens. The whole place was packed with singing Germans and it was bloody hot! However, it looked like fun so we got beers, vodka etc and joined in the proceedings.

Can you believe the Germans love singing the three lions song – its coming home – IN ENGLISH!! Word for word! Do you think they know what they are singing? Probably not – or they are very very drunk! They also sang vindaloo – again in English! I couldn't believe my ears. Daft bastards or what! We did join in though – after all, they were our songs!

The bar staff were running around with massive trays with about 20 pints of beer etc in plastic glasses on them and people would just stop them and buy one. Fantastic! I didn't think I would like to carry the trays though, and the bars were packed! It was so bloody hot too. This freak heat wave was killing us (we have air-conditioning back in the Abu Dhabi).

Anyway, the Germans won 2-0 and they were in a great mood. The party had begun so we decided to walk along the river front pubs and see what was happening.

A few bars further down I spotted a fan in an England shirt dancing on a table – I couldn't miss an opportunity like this so I dragged the girls in to join the England lads for a spot of partying! The lads turned out to be from Birmingham like myself, although unfortunately most were vile fans (Aston villa for those of you from outside brum). Still, got to stick together when surrounded by about 500 drunken Germans eh (yeah, I know it was a close call! The vile or the Germans!). They turned out to be okay really and were also heading to Stuttgart tomorrow for the England game. Their names were Andy, Gary, martin, Geoff, Gary and John from Sutton Coldfield.

It seemed like the right time to get my England flag out – so I did and stood on the table waving it about. The lads went a bit pale but supported us all the same and a few Germans with flags and face paint came over to join in the fun.

They turned out to be good fun really and I got some good photos of us together with the flags! I taught one German fan the Steve Gerard song – which he picked up quite well and the "St. George in my heart" song too! Needless to say we never left early. People kept disappearing and reappearing and then we lost

Carolyn (not that unusual though). Turns out she had gone on one of her food finding missions that she always goes on at the end of the night when she is pissed!

So we said our goodbyes to the lads and headed off in search of Carolyn. As we suspected we found her at the last pizza place we had been to (I got a kebab) and we headed off to the station. Somehow, we managed to get the train that took the longest possible route back to Cologne that stopped at every bloody small station in between Dusseldorf and Cologne! A twenty-minute journey turned into a one hour and fifteen minute journey and we were all pissed and tired. We arrived back around midnight and fell into an exhausted sleep. Oh, yeah, and set alarms for our early start in the morning for the big one! ENGLAND!!

The next morning our alarm went off at 8am and we all jumped out of bed with excitement. Roxy headed down for breakfast whilst I tried to clear my head in the shower. Never again before a big match! After breakfast we all piled into Carolyn's room with presents and cards, as it was her birthday. She liked the world cup book I got her and all of her cards and presents were really nice. We (or rather me!) then sang happy birthday followed closely by three lions!

So, with our kit on, flags wrapped around our waists, badges and face paint applied, we made our way to the train station to catch the 9.54am train to Stuttgart. It was fantastic when we got to the station. The station and our train in particular was jammed with England fans. Brilliant! I was so looking forward to the day ahead. We found our reserved seats on the train and out came the beers. Fantastic – we are on our way!!!

Lisa and Pete called to say that they were on their way up from Frankfurt (driving) and would meet us there. Fantastic! The train journey wasn't that bad really – 2 hours and 15 minutes and we joined a sea of red and white heading out of the Stuttgart station. We even saw our good old English plod – sorry – police presence in and around the station. They were a pleasant bunch thought, I must say. There were England fans everywhere! So, we headed to the first pub across the road from the station!

The girls plonked themselves down on a window ledge outside the pub as it was packed inside and we looked around - there were England fans everywhere! Since I was the only one without a drink (the girls all had beers), I headed into the pub to get a vodie and coke. The bar was packed and it took bloody ages to get a drink but I got chatting to a cockney couple while I was waiting to be served. They were a nice couple and they had tickets to the game – lucky sods. So, with hope in my heart I got my drink and headed outside to find the girls chatting to a couple of guys who just happened to share Carolyn's birthday! What a coincidence eh! One guy was in a lot of pain with his back so I gave him panadol and talked to him for a while.

There was a cute little lad with them that kept kicking a football at us (or perhaps the wall behind us?). He managed to sell the 'Free' England fanzine 'Free Lions' to an England fan for 2 Euro. What a hero eh! He tried to persuade me to kiss the guy he was with for a Euro – I told him I would for 2 Euro! Cheeky bugger said he would give me 2 Euro if I kissed him twice! How could I resist eh? I kissed the guy twice and let the cute little lad keep his 2 Euro. He was well pleased with himself.

It was now time to start thinking of tickets. I asked a passing England fan if he could get any tickets and was informed that he could for 450 Euro – 300 quid! I must admit I thought about it for a bit but the girls decided it was a bit too much so off we headed towards the square and the fan zone. It was really hot – 36 degrees according to the weather report. On the way to the fan zone we were stopped by a guy from capitol radio who interviewed Janine (the rest of us declined as were weren't pissed enough yet!) He asked about the heat and how the lads would cope. Janine said they were professionals and should be able to cope.

Personally, after Paraguay and being half-dead in the heat myself, I thought they would struggle. By now Lisa and Pete had joined us outside the pub and were looking well cool in their England gear. Pete had a blow up hand, which looked good. By now, everyone was necking beers as we walked along except Lisa and me, as both of us are not beer drinkers. Just up ahead we spotted a little shop with a queue coming out of it – must be serving alcohol I thought! Just to be safe though I shouted into the shop – got any vodka mate? Yeah, he shouted back – so worth queuing I thought. An England lad came out laughing and said – good old English girls eh – know what they want. We bought a small bottle of vodka and a few bottles of coke – sod these bloody beer only fan zone stalls eh! Cost 20 Euro too – robbing bastards!

Lisa and Pete bought an England flag for 3 Euro! We arrived at the fan zone in the square and there were loads of English singing on the steps! Fantastic! I saw a flag with 'Fletch 0n Tour' hanging from a building (for those of you who don't know me that is my nickname). I was impressed, as I am known as fletch. I even got a picture of it.

Anyway, we got to the fan zone only to find everyone getting searched and no bottles allowed in (or drinks!). No problem. We sent the others in and then Lisa and I slipped the vodka through the fence to Roxy and then went in ourselves. It was really big inside with 3 massive screens. There were already 25,000 people in at the front where some kind of show was going on, on a stage. We stayed at the back with the 2 big screens near the bars where there was more room. It was so bloody hot in here and no shelter from the heat. Lisa – the sensible one amongst us – pulled out some sunscreen and we all put some on.

I decided that I could take no more and pulled up my England shirt and tied it up just under my boobs whilst Pete painted a St George's cross on my stomach! While the others 'set up camp' (on Janine's big flag) Carolyn and I headed to the bandstand at the back for a bit of shade. Janine had already beaten us to it and was mingling with the lads. The bandstand was full of completely pissed England fans.

As my England shirt was now cropped, I was immediately singled out for a loud rendition of 'get yer tits out if you're English'! Bastards! Whilst I debated getting them out or telling them to fuck off, Carolyn gave them some abuse on my behalf! Anyway, it was good fun inside the bandstand I must say. Some of the lads were kicking a blow up England beach ball around whilst others were throwing around a blow up spitfire! Great!

We got chatting to some lads and while our backs were turned Carolyn and I got drenched as someone threw a bucket of water into the bandstand. Bastards! Still, once we realised it wasn't beer and we had actually escaped another beer shampoo we felt a little better – and cooler! At this point a mental bloody German fan wandered straight into the middle singing 'Germany'. He was quickly led outside before any serious damage could be inflicted on him!

After a couple of texts from Roxy asking 'where are you?' we headed back to the others just as the guys in the bandstand were burning a German shirt! (At least there was no one inside it at the time!). Oh, yeah, we sang 'ten German bombers' a few times too. That was fun. It was really loud and I called my mom in England so she could hear it, and when they got to 'and the RAF from England shot one down' she thought it was really funny!!

We finally found our lot again and perched ourselves on our giant flag and prepared for the match. Lisa and I had discovered – much to our delight that they served vodka at the bars. Mind you – we had a big enough bottle already to get through and what with the heat and alcohol we were already steaming! I didn't know where Janine and Carolyn were but the rest of our gang were present so we topped up our drinks and continued singing.

The match was not really much to write home about but when Beckham curled a free kick into the back of the net the place went wild!!! Funny thing was, about a minute before the goal I had said to everyone – "put your drinks down –we are gonna score!" So they did and up popped Beckham and sent us into hysteria! He struck it beautifully and - yes believe it or not the fucking screen went blank!!!! A few seconds later the screen came back on and there was Beckham getting mobbed and the England fans in the stadium going mental! No explanation was needed and we promptly jumped all over each other. Fantastic!!! We then continued to play crap so Roxy and I sang 'we're shit – but we'll win the cup'.

As expected the next day was a hangover day and not much was achieved by any of us really. Roxy headed off to join her boyfriend in Glasgow so we were reduced to 3 and felt sad that she was leaving and would miss the rest of the world cup. Janine and I went downstairs to the pub to watch the Italy v Australia match and then I headed off for an early night halfway through the Ukraine game. I was knackered and needed to recharge my batteries!

The next morning I woke up somewhat refreshed, packed my things and met up with the girls to check out of our cologne hotel. I must admit I will miss the place! I have really enjoyed my time in Cologne. So, checkout completed, we headed off to the train station and after obtaining food and booze for the long journey ahead, we boarded our ICE train to Berlin.

We arrived in Berlin over an hour late (we were given forms to fill in on the train by the ticket inspector to claim for the delay!!) and we then set about trying to find our way to get the local train to get to our destination, whilst loaded up with suitcases! This proved to be a nightmare as the screens, timetables and staff sent us to various platforms – non-of which were correct! Anyway, we finally arrived at our destination after convincing a taxi driver at the local station that he could get the three of us plus our luggage into his car!

The accommodation was very basic – especially after cologne, but it was cheap and suited our purpose.

We dumped our cases etc in our room and headed to the pub to watch the Spain v France game. The taxi driver had already informed us that Brazil had beaten Ghana 3-0 – no surprises there then eh! The bar itself was okay but the drinks were really expensive (6 pounds for a vodka and coke!) but that was pretty normal around Germany (maybe world cup prices?). The food however, was disgusting – the pasta was uncooked and I left the entire meal. We watched France beat Spain 3-1 and headed off to unpack and get a good night sleep.

After a bit of a lie in we headed off to the Internet café to sort out some accommodation for England's quarterfinal game in Gelsenkirchen against Portugal. We had decided it was too long a trip to make just for the game (around 5-6 hours each way). We eventually found a really nice hotel in Dusseldorf – which is very close to Gelsenkirchen, and booked two nights stay there. Gelsenkirchen was totally booked up, as it is only a small town. Dusseldorf would be great though and only thirty minutes away by train.

So, this achieved, we headed off to reserve seats on the train for this trip and then off to see the sights. I had a great time at the Berlin wall/museum and at checkpoint Charlie. Janine tried on a pair of world war two flying goggles from a local seller. They looked fab – I must say!

The next day was spent shopping and sightseeing really. We visited the Brandenburg gate, the Berlin Wall memorial, for those who died trying to cross the river, the Berlin wall and checkpoint Charlie again where various souvenirs were obtained. Then, after a few drinks in a nearby bar and a few in our room we called it a night. Tomorrow would be a big day! Today we had been SWAGS – supporters without a game!

The next day we were up early, our overnight bags were packed and we headed off to Berlin train station to catch our train to Dusseldorf. Once again food and drink was obtained for the journey and we were on our way!

We arrived in Dusseldorf around 3pm and already there were a good few England fans scattered around as we made our way to our hotel. It was already really hot, so because we had our bags, we treated ourselves to a taxi. I must say, the hotel was fab! Best so far. Our room had a massive plasma TV screen! Not that we would be in to watch it of course! So after a very quick change of clothes – into our England tops we headed out to find a pub to watch the Germany v Argentina game via the pizza/kebab shop.

The atmosphere was great (nowhere near as good as when England play though!) and we wandered around till we found a bar that was not too packed where we could sit outside (in the shade). It was very hot and we wanted a good view of the TV. Drinks were promptly ordered and before long various England fans – who were attracted to our England shirts – joined us and there became quite a group on us!

We soon got chatting to a group of lads from London who were very impressed that 3 girls had travelled to the world cup (without boyfriends/husbands is what they meant). I explained that it was perfectly acceptable to leave the bloke at home to go and watch footie instead of vice versa with the men leaving the women at home! Don't think they were fully convinced to be honest. However, they were impressed!

As the day wore on the west ham fan became annoying though as he was constantly singing west ham songs despite being told by everyone that domestics are not brought to internationals. It was only my threat of cracking his pint glass over his head and kicking him in the bollocks that bought an end to his west ham songs. He said that he knew that me being a Birmingham City fan I would carry out my threat if he carried on! He was a bit more tolerable after that.

The game kicked off and the Germans became quite excited – that was until Argentina scored – silence! Even us England fans were not impressed! As the game (and silent German fans) progressed and the drink flowed, some of the more drunken England fans amongst us began singing '5-1 in your own backyard!' etc. We were so outnumbered it was scary. The German police started wandering around and watching us and I could see that if Germany lost there would be big trouble. Just as we were drawing up battle plans – Germany equalised! And so into extra time.

Phew! Even the England fans were cheering (I guess we really do hate the argies!). Another group of lads arrived and one tall lad was the spit of Pete Crouch (in an England Shirt too!). I couldn't help myself and started singing 'let's all do the crouchy' whilst doing his robotics and all the England lads joined in. His mates laughed and he just looked like it wasn't the first time this had happened to him.

I got talking to a scouser who taught me the Wayne Rooney song – fantastic! As Janine continued to wind the lads up, I got chatting to a couple of England fans who had driven over for the weekend for the quarterfinal. This is where fate threw a bloody spanner in the works as I ended up getting together with one on the guys, Mark, and our relationship continued well after Germany. Unfortunately, he was a Leeds fan, although he says his team is Lincoln City (lower leagues), and he lived in Weston-Super-Mare! He was with his 17year old son who was extremely pissed and quite amusing. Weston-Super-Mare as we all know is Birmingham's beach.

So, the game finished 1-1 and went to the dreaded penalty shootout. This could be fun, I thought! And it was – especially as the Germans beat the cheating argie bastards – fantastic! And so the party went on into the night. Mark asked for my number as he wanted to meet up with me the next day in Gelsenkirchen and I game him my German number. As it got late everyone was moved inside the bars by the bouncers except Marks son who wasn't old enough and it wasn't long before we were called outside because he had sat under a tree in a drunken stupor and someone had called an ambulance, once that was resolved I headed back to our hotel and fell into bed.

The next day I was feeling extremely unwell as I am sure were the others as a result of our drinking antics from the previous night. It was the big day though, and we set off to catch the train to Gelsenkirchen for the quarter final tie with Portugal. We obtained beers in the station to consume on the train in an effort to cure our hangovers. The train was packed with England fans and I was really looking forward to the day ahead. Mark texted me to see if I would meet up with him once we got there and he seemed surprised that I gave him the correct phone number!

Anyway, we were soon arriving in Gelsenkirchen after a short train journey and as we came out of the station it was just a mass of red & white clad England fans. They were everywhere, there must have been thousands (over 100,000 we later learned) and mark was now calling me to meet him at the fan zone. Loads of the England fans were boarding the many buses that had been put on to take the England fans to the fan zone so we boarded one of the buses along with the others. They were long bendy buses and ours soon filled up with loads of fans standing also. Once it was packed the bus set off and I must admit it was a brilliant journey with the England fans singing really loudly. We were singing and swaying and our bus was swaying from side to side. As we passed people in the streets we could see everyone looking and waving and they must have been able to hear us also cos as we sang '10 Germany bombers' all the England fans we passed could be seen joining in. It was absolutely brilliant and something that I will remember forever. I can't even begin to describe the atmosphere.

We arrived at the fan zone and headed to get a couple of drinks before we went inside. Mark had said he was at the pub just outside the fan zone but I couldn't find him so headed inside once we had finished our drinks. Loads of lads were kicking footballs in the air and the atmosphere was excellent. Once inside there were thousands of England fans and mark was repeatedly calling me to arrange somewhere to meet him now that he was also inside the fan zone. It took about half an hour and loads of phone calls before I realised that the fan zone he was describing was not the fan zone that I was in! Apparently there were two fan zones quite far from each other so we would now have to watch the game separately.

There were loads on bars that looked a bit like round huts with a roof and it wasn't long before many of the England fans had climbed up onto the roofs with their beers. It looked funny but scary as the roofs began to shake. Many were clad in world war two attire with England flags painted on the helmets. They looked brilliant. The bar staff were looking really worried though, in case the roof fell in. We headed to the back to obtain food and found a bar that served cocktails – excellent! I even got filmed by sky news as I waved my 'Abu Dhabi Blues' flag around – don't know if anyone saw me back home though. I wasn't exactly sober at the time.

The fan zone was full and it was only England fans inside, which made it much better. Just as the teams were about to kick off the big screened was turned off and it was announced that it would not be turned back on until the fans came down off the roof's. This pissed everyone off and as everyone else threw their beers up at the fans on the roof, the reluctantly climbed down and the screen came back to life just as the teams kicked off.

The game got under way and it proved to be extremely stressful. England were by far the better team and really should have won easily but everything changed when that bloody lady boy – Christiano Ronaldo got Wayne Rooney sent off by cheating. It was utterly disgraceful, especially as he winked at the Portugal bench as Rooney went off. He is a cheat of the worst kind and I, along with hundreds of thousand England fans, will never forgive him and I for one will hate him until the day I die.

With England now down to 10 men and up against it, they put on a magnificent performance and still had chances to win the game but it was not to be and the game finished level and it would go to the dreaded penalty shootout. I was a nervous wreck along with thousands of England fans but I was sure we would win the shoot out on the law of averages and we had lost all the previous shoot outs in previous competitions. I could hardly look as I stood watching with Janine, having lost Carolyn somewhere. It was so painful to watch and it finally came down to Portugal having to score their last penalty to knock us out. I was so traumatised that I could not watch. I turned my back and stood facing Janine. Silence in the fan zone and from the look on Janine's face I knew we were out. 'They've scored it' she said and put arms around me as I cried on her shoulder. I couldn't believe it, as I looked around many people were crying or sitting on the ground with their heads in their hands. I crumpled to the ground and couldn't move for quite a while as I came to terms with the devastation I felt.

After a while I turned to Janine and said 'right that's it now, we've been sad and now we will celebrate the fact that we are here in Germany and we have had a great tournament and a great time, so I got up off the ground and we headed for the bar at the back. We wandered about chatting to people and I found Carolyn but lost Janine. As I was walking at the back along the bars a big cage like trolley came shooting out in front of me, being pushed by some lads and standing on it, arms outstretched – titanic like, was Janine! It hit a bump and she gracefully flew off and landed perfectly upright on her feet. I burst out laughing, I couldn't believe it, it was so funny and really cheered me up. The lads had a go at it themselves afterwards but they kept ending up on their arses on the grass. Well done Janine!

Janine and I decided we should now head back to Dusseldorf for some celebrations before the buses taking people back to the station stopped. Also mark had been phoning loads and he had headed back to Dusseldorf and wanted me to meet them. Carolyn was happily chatting to the only German in the fan zone and it was proving impossible to move her as she was extremely pissed. Janine and I tried for ages but just got pissed off waiting so decided to head back without her if she wanted to stay so much!

It was a great atmosphere on the bus, with everyone singing 'there's a hundred thousand English on the piss!' And there was over 100,000 English in Gelsenkirchen, it was brilliant. Once back at the station we had to wait for a train and the one we got on was packed and took hours to get back. I have never seen so many people jammed onto a train in all my life. It was impossible to move and only just possible to breath, it was awful. To make things worse one of the England fans got into a fight with another England fan and attacked him for no reason, biting him and there was blood everywhere. The train was then stopped at the next small station and the police got everyone off and arrested the fan who had attacked the other lad. It was disgraceful really and he got loads of abuse from the other fans as he was led away by the police.

By the time we arrived back in Dusseldorf, Carolyn was on the train behind and Janine was so pissed off that she just wanted to get a pizza and go back to the hotel. I was still on for partying though and mark wanted me to meet him, so I left Janine to get a pizza and I headed off to meet mark. Mark and I partied until the early hours of the morning and I snuck back in at about 6am, having got the receptionist to let me into the room with their spare key so that I wouldn't wake Janine and Carolyn, and they wouldn't know how late back I was! Mark had wanted me to leave Germany now that England were out and go back to England with him but my bags were still in Berlin and I couldn't leave the girls, so I headed back to Berlin with them the next morning.

We had over a week left in Germany and neither Janine nor I wanted to stay now that England were out. We both wanted to go home and see our families so we discussed it with Carolyn and decided to get flights across to the UK. Mark was glad to hear this and we said we would meet up once I got to England. We did manage to do a bit more sightseeing before we left and before long I was touching down in Liverpool as this was the first flight I could get back and my mom had driven up to meet me.

I had a lovely time at home; my mom was really pleased to see me especially as this was a surprise visit so a bit of bonus really. I met up with mark and we headed to Blackpool for 3 or 4 days and that was where I watched the World Cup Final, in Blackpool with mark. Both of us had lost interest a little now that England were not in it but we watched it anyhow and then headed off to have some fun at the fair. I had a great time in Blackpool and at home in Birmingham and I was sad when it came time to go back. Not as sad as mark though, he was gutted and didn't want me to go back. He soon arranged to come out to visit me in a few weeks time though, so we had that to look forward. Looking back though, I wish I hadn't bothered as he turned out to be a right wanker. Oh well, I had a great time in Germany and I did have fun with mark while it lasted!

I was back in Abu Dhabi and looking forward to next season even if Blues were back in the championship. Every the optimist I was sure that Blues could bounce back at the first attempt and I was looking forward to winning more matches that we had been previously. Unfortunately I would not be able to get to many games if any next season because I had already had all my leave for the year.

CHAPTER TWENTY-FIVE – Bouncing Back!

The 2006 – 2007 season got underway on 5th August with Blues taking on Colchester Utd at St.Andrews but I would have to be content to listen to the game live as I would have to do for the majority of games this coming season now that Blues were playing in the championship. It was really hard to listen to but despite being reduced to 10 men for much of the game Blues chalked up a good 2-1 win thereby opening our account for the season with a win. I was confident that Blues could get promotion this season and my hope grew as Blues achieved some good results at the start of the season, beating Sunderland away 1-0, drawing with Stoke City 0-0, beating Crystal Palace 2-1 at St. Andrews and winning in the League Cup 1-0 against Shrewsbury Town.

Our unbeaten run came to an end at fellow promotion hopefuls, Cardiff City where Blues lost 2-0. Blues were back to winning ways the following week though, beating Hull City 2-1 at St. Andrews, winning away at Queens Park Rangers 2-0, drawing with Ipswich Town 2-2 at St. Andrews and then winning in the League Cup against Wrexham 4-1 at home.

It always seems to be a bit of a rollercoaster ride with Blues though and the downward ride began with an away defeat at Leeds Utd 3-2. We then held Leicester City to a 1-1 draw at St. Andrews before again losing, this time at Luton Town 3-2 followed by our real low point of the season as we lost 1-0 at home to Norwich City. The fans were becoming restless and were calling for manager Steve Bruce's head. I personally like Steve Bruce and though we should stick with him.

My confidence was not misplaced as Blues travelled to Derby County in the next game and won 1-0 and this proved to be the turning point of the season. Next up was League cup action and a trip to Premiership side Sheffield Utd in the next round where Blues put on a brilliant display to come away 4-2 winners and a place in the next round where we were drawn against another Premiership team Liverpool.

Back to league action and a good win against local rivals West Brom 2-0 at St. Andrews followed by another win against local rivals Coventry City away 1-0 before travelling to Plymouth and again winning 1-0. We were on fire but were brought down to earth again in the League Cup where we lost at home to Liverpool 1-0, which was a big improvement on the previous season where we had lost 7-0 to them in the Quarter final.

Blues picked themselves up again a few days later beating Barnsley 2-0 at St. Andrews, drawing against Wolves 1-1, winning at Burnley 2-1 before losing at Southampton in a really thrilling game which finished 4-3 and we were very unlucky to lose. We then went on a great run, winning five on the trot and scoring 15 goals in the process, against Plymouth at home 3-0, Preston at home 3-1, Sheffield Wednesday away 3-0, Southend away 4-0 and Queens Park Rangers 2-1 in our 100th year at St. Andrews testimonial at a packed St. Andrews on the 26th December.

Blues ended 2006 with a home draw against Luton Town 2-2 where a Luton player broke his leg and was taken to hospital in Birmingham and ended up on my sister's ward! 2007 began with a rare defeat against Ipswich Town away 1-0 on New Year's Day and then it was onto FA Cup action against Newcastle Utd from the Premiership. This game was on live to I was able to watch as Blues played brilliant and were soon 1-0 ahead, but then we had a player sent off and Newcastle got back into the game 1-1 and then Newcastle went 2-1 ahead. Blues refused to give up though and when Larsson put the ball in the net for the equaliser the ground erupted. So it would be a replay at Newcastle in couple of week's time.

It was a cold January and due to weather conditions there were no more league games able to be played, therefore the next game would be the replay against Newcastle at St. James Park on 17th January and this was to be shown live. It was a night game and I sat up for it and what a game it was. Craig had been texting me form offshore asking me if I was ready for the thrashing that Newcastle would bestow on us. I think this was what everyone was expecting so it was a shock for them when we quickly went 1-0 ahead, and at this point it could easily have been 3-0 to us. I text Craig some stick but at 2-0 to Blues he went quiet and stopped texting. Newcastle then pulled a goal back but almost immediately Blues scored again and it was 3-1. It was brilliant and the best Blues had played all season and I ran around the room in celebration at the 4th goal went in and when Campbell scored our 5th I was in heaven. We had beaten the Premiership big boys in their own back yard 5-1! What a night, certainly worth staying up for!

Due to the weather still being very bad there were still no games until the next round of the FA Cup when we took on Reading in the fourth round at St. Andrews. Reading were also doing very well in the Premiership and despite playing well Blues cup run came to an end as we lost 3-2. So it was back to our promotion battle, but a very disappointing display saw us lose at home to Southend 3-1 followed by and away draw at Colchester Utd 1-1.

I was beginning to fear that we would mess it up and it was getting really stressful to listen to the games on live commentary but Blues won the next game against Stoke City 1-0 at St. Andrews and then beat Crystal Palace 1-0 away before drawing 1-1 at home against Sunderland who were now also in a good position for promotion. Then there was a small cloud on the horizon as we lost 2-0 away at Hull City but we were soon back to winning ways against Leeds Utd 1-0 at St. Andrews, followed by a very good win over promotion rivals Cardiff City 1-0 at home then another good home win against Derby County 1-0.

Norwich City again spoiled the party with a 1-0 win over us at their place but we followed this win a 1-1 draw away at West Brom before winning 3-0 at home against Coventry City. It was getting really nervy as we approached the end of the season and the nerves began to show over the Easter weekend as Blues lost surprisingly at home to Burnley 1-0 and then away at Barnsley 1-0 watched by 8,000 Bluenoses that had made the trip! I had Neil, Sue, Stephen and Nicola visiting at the time and we had just returned from a trip to Dubai when we learned of the score. Stephen summed it up when he said 'you can always rely on Blues to ruin your weekend!'

There were only five games left now and I was extremely worried that we had messed it up and would miss out on the automatic promotion places. I was convinced that if we ended up in the play offs we would miss out. My nerves were calmed a little with the next game as Blues beat Southampton 2-1 at St. Andrews and then won away at Leicester City 2-1.

Mom, Annette and Steve then came out to visit me and we would be able to watch the next game against Wolves away as it was due to be shown live. We all usually go sunbathing at the Sheraton Hotel which is situated right next door to the hospital where I work and the game would be on live at the hospital social club so we decided to watch it there. I put my Blues shirt on and Annette, Steve and I headed for the social club, leaving my mom sunbathing at the Sheraton next door. This was a really big game and I was really nervous. Francis the social club barman, who I had known many years, served up pre match drinks and turned the volume up for the game. There was also a Sunderland fan there to watch the game and he wanted us to lose as Sunderland were up there fighting us for promotion.

What a stressful but brilliant game of football got underway. Blues scored the first goal and I was up and running round the social club. The Sunderland fan laughed and thought we were great fun and also though we were playing well – as did Francis the barman. Then Wolves equalised and we were silent. Then they scored a second and wolves were 2-1 ahead – silence in the social club! I was gutted, we were about to lose out at the final hurdle once again. I couldn't believe it and I sat silently. Then Bendtner jumped for a Blues corner and powered a header into the top corner of the Wolves net! 2-2 and I was off again running around the social club. My hopes were raised and when Cameron Jerome went on a run in the last few minutes and shot past the Wolves keeper and into the net to make it 3-2, I went wild. I ran one way, Annette ran another and Steve ran in another direction. Mad celebrations were going on by the three of us and the Sunderland ran laughed.

Unbelievable, but then in the last minute the bloody referee awarded Wolves a very very dubious looking penalty. To this day I do not think it was a penalty and I was devastated. The kick would be the last kick of the game and I held my breath and prayed as Steve shouted abuse at the screen. I added a few choice words myself and then up stepped the Wolves player and our keeper dived and saved it! Absolutely fantastic and the three of us were off again on a run around the social club. It was one of the most exciting, nerve wracking games I had ever watched and it ended in at 3-2 win by Blues. Two games remaining and we could do it!

Mom, Annette and Steve were still with me for the next game against Sheffield Wednesday at St. Andrews and if Blues won and Crystal Palace beat Derby the next day then Blues would be promoted back to the Premiership. We had to listen to this game on the radio and I was ready early (as we were going out afterwards) and I listened as the others were getting ready. I was so stressed and when Blues had a player sent off early on I thought our chance was gone and we just had to try to hang on for a draw and take it to the last game of the season next week against Preston away.

When Jerome latched onto a ball in the penalty area in the second half all I could hear from the commentator was GOOOOOOOAAAAAAAAAAAAL! And Steve came running out from the bathroom asking 'who's scored?' BLUES!' I shouted as I ran around the room and my mom laughed. Please let us hang on I thought as the game continued with Blues down to 10 men. Then Larson got the ball on the half way line and ran, and ran, and ran, and shot – GOOOOOOOOOAAAAAAAAAL! The commentator was going mad and so was I as I ran around the room again. I could hear St. Andrews exploding with celebrations from 3,500 miles away! Oh, how I wished I was there. The game finished 2-0 to Blues and the Crystal Palace v Derby game could confirm our promotion the following day.

I was more excited that nervous the next day as I knew even if Derby did win we could still get promotion on the last day although I really didn't want it to go to the last game. Then news filtered through that our old boy Clinton Morrison had scored for Crystal Palace and Blues were promoted back to the Premiership at our first attempt. And so we all headed off out to celebrate! I was so happy – 'we are Premier League!'

This also meant that Blues only had to win away at Preston to win the championship and the game would be on live. I should have know we would mess that up and as Sunderland won 5-1 at relegated Luton Town, Blues lost 1-0 at Preston having hit the woodwork a few times and missing numerous chances, the Blues faithful were denied that which we should have had – the Championship Title which went to Sunderland. Oh well, at least we were back in the Premier league, although I couldn't help but feel disappointed as we really should have won it. That's the Blues though and I love them.

So Sunderland were promoted as Champions with Birmingham City promoted in second place with Derby County who won in the Play Offs. Southend Utd, Luton Town and surprisingly Leeds Utd were relegated to the third tier. The FA Cup was won by Chelsea who beat Manchester Utd 1-0 after extra time and the League Cup was also won by Chelsea who beat Arsenal 2-1.

CHAPTER TWENTY-SIX - The long way round!

The new season back in the Premiership got underway on 12th august 2007 with an away trip to Chelsea the current league champions. Well, it couldn't get much harder that this one, I thought. I had decided to go out to watch the game at the social club with Pamela, a Scottish friend of mine who supported Glasgow Rangers. We got pints of cider in before the game (a decision I was to regret the next morning!) and we sat down to watch Blues take on the mighty Chelsea at Stamford Bridge. Much to my utter amazement Blues scored through Forsell and we were winning 1-0 at Chelsea! I knew it was too good to last though and Chelsea scored to equalise. However, a brilliant goal from our new signing Kapo put Blues ahead again and I ran around the social club in celebration. My joy was to be dashed though as Chelsea scored twice more and beat us 3-2. I wasn't too despondent though as our performance was a credit to the Blues and I had high hopes for the forthcoming season.

Next up was a home game against Sunderland which was drawn 2-2 but then we lost the next game against West Ham Utd 1-0. I was having mixed emotions watching the Blues live on TV again this season but I was filled with joy as I watched Cameron Jerome score in the first minute of the next game away at Derby County. Jerome also scored a second as we got back to winning ways beating Derby 2-1 and moving up to 11th place in the league. Then it was League Cup action as Blues beat Hereford Utd 2-1 at St. Andrews to progress to the next round and a tie against Blackburn Rovers away.

There was just time for one more match before I was to head back to Birmingham, and it was against Middlesbrough away. It wasn't a very good game and I was disappointed as we lost the game 2-0. Blues were down to 16th in the table but I was really looking forward to watching the next game live in Birmingham.

I was really excited as I got up at 4am to get a taxi to Dubai airport at the start of my holiday. I was about to spend four weeks at home in Birmingham, England with my family, and get in as many Birmingham City matches as was possible. I must admit, I started as I meant to go on, and after a seven hour flight (which was almost an hour late) I disembarked at Birmingham airport at 1.30pm to be picked up by my brother Neil, my mum and my niece Nicola. My mum had a ticket for me for the Bolton game at St. Andrews and the plan was to drop me straight there and they would take my bags on home.

As soon as we got close to the ground and I could see all the blue and white clad supporters heading for the match I became really excited. Due to work commitments and the fact that last year's holiday had been in Germany for the World Cup Finals with England, I had not been to a live Blues match for nearly two years! The longest ever and I was withdrawing something terrible! As we got closer to St Andrews I told Neil "anywhere here will do!" "Will you be okay?" my mum said as I hopped out. "Fantastic, I will see you later," I said as I joined the mass of blue and white. My mum later said that I looked like a kid in a sweet shop as I headed off without a care in the world.

I headed straight for the Birmingham City shop where I purchased the new home shirt and the new away shirt. Then it was off to the turnstile with my ticket clutched proudly in my hand and into the ground I went. First stop was the toilets where I duly changed into my new home shirt before heading to my seat which would be next to Steve, my sister's boyfriend, who had got the ticket for me originally. My seat was in the corner of the Kop by the railway end – right next to the away supporters and as I came in and up the steps I gave them the two-finger salute in my current state of happiness at being back in my 'home!'

I found my seat and said hello to Steve before looking around me and taking in the fantastic atmosphere. The prices had been reduced for today's game, therefore the ground was full of real supporters instead of the prawn sandwiches and they were singing their hearts out. As Steve Bruce once said – you could smell the hotdogs! The level of noise was really high and when the team ran out onto the lovely green pitch, it went up an octave with the usual clapping to the song that is played when they come out onto the pitch.

It was a lovely sunny day and as the game kicked off and 'Keep Right On' rang out around the stadium I felt butterflies in my stomach for the first time in ages. I really enjoyed the game and when Oliver Kapo scored the only goal of the game right in front of us, I jumped up in jubilation. The away fans were becoming restless and sang 'you don't know what you're doing' to their manager. The Blues fans quite enjoyed this and joined in with them in agreement that indeed Sammy Lee did not know what he was doing. We sang, we stood when we sang 'stand up if you love the Blues' and we thoroughly enjoyed the day. The end of the game was greeted with cheers from the Blues fans and the players were applauded off the pitch.

My first game was over and on my way home in the car; I was already looking forward to next week's away trip to Anfield.

It was Saturday 22nd September and I was up early and looking forward to my trip to Anfield to see Blues play title chasers Liverpool on their own turf. I was quite optimistic as we have had a few good results against them during our time in the premier league, although the odds were firmly stacked against us! So at around 08.45am, Annette, Steve – known to is mates as Stegga, Stephen and I left the house with our packed lunch, made by mom, and headed down the road to catch the bus to town.

Steve had already booked our train tickets and planned the trip, so we arrived at New Street station with time to spare and after obtaining newspapers for the trip, we went to the off licence to obtain beers. Meanwhile, Steve disappeared off in search for a corkscrew (which were on sale in the off licence in the station that we were waiting for him in!). We had cans of beer, bottles of wine and plastic cups and so off we set to board the first train that was leaving for Glasgow at 10.03.

The train was already on the platform and we got on and found four seats with a table, so jackets off – I had my new white away Blues shirt on, and we settled down for the journey. There were quite a few more Bluenoses on the train, all with the required carrier bags containing sandwiches and beer for the journey. As this was probably the only journey we would get a decent seat on, we made a start on the sandwiches and opened the beers and had a look through the newspapers. We chatted and drank and ate and soon arrived at our first destination – Crewe station, after our 50 minute journey and disembarked along with the other Bluenoses.

We soon discovered that there was a train leaving another platform quite soon heading for Chester, our next destination. Another Bluenose came up and asked if I knew where we got the next train from, was it this station or another one. I asked him if he was going the Chester way, and he said yes, and I told him it was this station but I was unsure which platform we were going from. Then everyone seemed to head to the same platform and off we went and boarded the local train to Chester.

This journey only took about 20 minutes and we soon arrived at Chester only to see waiting police who were obviously intent on stopping any fans slipping out into Chester itself. We were not to be stopped though and I zipped up my jacket and so hiding my shirt and we slipped out into Chester and across the road from the station into a pub called the Town Crier that was opposite the Queen hotel on the corner. It was a good sized pub and quite nice inside where we obtained drinks and took them outside into the beer garden as the weather was quite nice. More supporters wandered in and there was now a group of fans with Newcastle and Manchester United shirts sitting opposite us. A couple of Liverpool fans came in too but didn't stay long. Four supporters came in and I thought they were Sunderland fans, Stephen said he thought that they were Brentford fans because they had championship numbers on the back of their shirts. Annette and I said 'Brentford!' at exactly the same time and burst out laughing. Stephen then got the paper to check who was playing and informed us that it was in fact Brentford who were due to play Chester and he delighted in sticking his two fingers up at us, causing me and Annette to burst out laughing again.

I headed inside to the bar to get more drinks with Annette and Nobby's nuts for Stephen. It was quite funny because I asked the barman what nuts he had and he said salted or dry roasted so I asked him had he got Nobby's nuts, so I guess I walked into his answer of 'no, I've got my own!'. After serving our drinks he remarked 'I'll tell Nobby you was asking after him' as he walked away, leaving me and Annette in fits of laughter again. Quite an entertaining hour there really.

After finishing our drinks we headed back into the station and boarded the local train to Liverpool Central. Bloody hell, it stopped at loads of stations and was jam packed – and late! It took almost an hour to get to Liverpool and by the time we reached there we were in desperate need to find toilets (as this local train had none). Steve had decided that we should get the soccer bus that ran directly to the ground as he said it would be the only way we could get back after the game, so we got another local train to sandhills station and headed for the soccer bus. I must admit I did not enjoy this part of the journey one bit, as it was not much fun being the only person on a Liverpool football special bus with a Blues shirt on I can tell you! It didn't help much when Steve's phone rang and he chatted away loudly with a broad brummie accent. Annette and Stephen had been pretending they didn't know me at this point and now we all pretended we didn't know Steve!

I had already obtained my programme for the game whilst queuing to board the soccer bus, and we soon got off the bus by Stanley Park and headed for the Blue House on Steve's instructions. As we were walking past a pub full of Liverpool fans called the Abbey, Steve saw two of him mates Craig and Graham, who informed him that the Blue House was closed so we went into the Abbey for a pre match drink or two with them. As this was one of their main pubs I don't think the Liverpool fans were too impressed by having us gate crashing their party in a Blues shirt, but I lived to tell the tale. It was full of Reds with not a single Bluenose in sight, not a comfortable place to be for me really. I downed a few pints though and was comforted by the fact that I was next to the door should a quick exit be required!

I had to laugh when Craig and Graham went to the bar and ordered two 'wicked's' and the barmaid asked red or blue? The pub went quiet as everyone awaited their reply and I thought ooooh! Especially when they answered Blue!

At twenty to three we left the pub and headed through Stanley Park towards the Anfield road stand where we had tickets for the away section. There was still loads of people milling around outside and we headed through the turnstiles and into the ground. Our seats were great, they were right at the front in row two and we had a great view. The sun had come out as well, and the Bluenoses were in full voice. 'Keep Right On' rang out loud and proud as always. The Liverpool fans were silent and remained so for most of the game, only singing once. Blues were singing 'it's just like being in church'.

As always the Bluenoses created the atmosphere and it was quite funny when they began singing 'you're on a day trip from Belfast' to the scousers. We also sang 'sign on, sign on, with pen in your hand and you'll never work again!' to the tune of you'll never walk alone, several times quite loudly.

The game kicked off and we all got quite excited. Especially when the ball came flying in the direction of my face, very fast, but luckily hit the edge of the boarding just missing the head of the steward who jumped a mile! He recovered quite quickly and with a smile I said 'I shit myself then!' Stephen, who was sitting next to me had also ducked and laughed before admitting that he nearly shit himself too.

Blues were playing quite well in defence and when a Liverpool player blasted over the fans sang du du du du, fucking useless!

They also sang, 'we'd forgot that you were here' when the scouser sang once. There were also several renditions of 'shit on the villa' and when Liverpool finally bought on their expensive signing Torres, all the Blues fans sang 'who are ya? Who are ya?'. Even the stewards smiled at that. The Blues fans certainly kept the stewards busy, and they had to move into the crowd a few times, you could see from their faces that they wished they had avoided this shift! The Blues fans sang 'get a proper job, get a proper job' to the tune of where's your mamma gone. We had a laugh at half time as my sister and I headed to the toilets. We were both singing 'I hate villa more that you!' to each other from adjoining cubicles.

The Blues did really well, and if McSheffrey had done better when we caught them on the break, we may even have snatched a win, but a draw was an excellent result. Liverpool have never beaten us in the premier league under Rafa Benitez. We have a good recent record against the scousers and we were jubilant when the final whistle went. Blues broke into a chorus of 'were gonna win the league, were gonna win the league, and now you're gonna believe us, were gonna win the league!' Quality! The players came over to applaud the Bluenoses and we rewarded them with a loud rendition of Keep Right On and applauded our players for their effort.

It was great leaving the ground as all the Bluenoses were still singing loudly and all appeared in good spirits. We headed in the opposite direction to the other bluenoses towards the soccer special back to sand hills to get the train back. There was a queue for the soccer bus back to town and we joined the end, I promptly zipped up my jacket in the hope of avoiding getting my head kicked in. Before long we were on the bus and we sat quietly until we arrived at sand hills station where we boarded the local train back to Liverpool Central station.

Once back in Liverpool Central we wandered outside as we couldn't decide whether to eat in Liverpool or carry on to Chester to eat. As we left the station two Blues fans ran past us singing 'sign on, sign on, with pen in your hand and you'll never work again!' They were laughing but I'm not sure if they were just having a laugh or running from scousers – it was really funny anyway. We had a bit of a laugh at that before deciding that we were better heading back to Chester for food, because at least we would have got the worst train journey over with and could relax a little bit.

We returned back to Central station and boarded the train to Chester via about two hundred stops! Forty minutes later we arrived in Chester station and after zipping up my jacket and hiding my shirt, we left the station and went into the Town Crier pub across the road from the station. The pub had filled up since we had left and there was now a hen night partying in there. Never mind, we ordered food and beer and sat down to enjoy our visit. It was quite busy in there now, and after enjoying our food we drank up and headed back to the station to catch the train back to Crewe.

The train arrived shortly and we got on board followed by a load of lads who were on the piss from Stoke. One of the blokes was talking on his mobile and was obviously being asked who Stoke were playing, to which he answered, 'were not playing anyone, we are just on the piss in Chester!'

Before long we were back in Crewe and after asking the staff we were informed that the train to Birmingham was not for another 45 minutes, so off we headed out of the station to try to find a supply of alcohol for the rest of the journey. We left the station and headed down the road past Crewe's ground and past the pub on the corner where we were informed by some locals that we needed to go back in the other direction towards the petrol station, to obtain supplies for the train. So, we turned around and went back, past the station. Steve asked the police standing outside, where the nearest off licence was. The police officer said 'I don't know mate, I'm from Birmingham and I am only here for the football!'

Once we had replenished our stocks from the local garage, we headed back to the station where there were now lots of Bluenoses waiting to get the train back to Brum. One bloke was asleep on a bench in a bizarre position and lots of Bluenoses were taking pictures on their mobile phones and laughing. I had to laugh when someone said 'that's how Blues fans get a bad name!'

It wasn't long before the train pulled up at the platform and we pilled on board. We were in the 'quiet zone' and before long our carriage was jammed with Bluenoses and the party began. The journey was brilliant and the singing and drinking began in earnest. Annette and I had a bottle of Jacobs Creek between us and Steve and Stephen had a six pack of beer. There were a few Bluenoses standing just behind us and they were really good fun, singing and cheering for the whole trip. Both ends of the carriage were singing 'we hate villa more that you!' to each other as well as doing a few renditions of Keep Right on. The lads sang quite a few funny songs that I had not heard before including a song about Liam Ridgewell and a song about Steve Bruce being a Zulu. Some Blues fans started singing 'if I die at Aston Street, no, no, if I die at Aston Street there'll be ten villa bastards at my feet!' I liked that one!

Suddenly the train stopped and one of the fans standing was bashed against the wall. Next thing we knew the driver appeared and asked 'did one of you lot pull the cord?' to which the reply was 'I don't even know where the fucker is!' We all laughed as the driver pointed out where it was. 'I know where it is next time then' was the reply. Someone said 'that's it, blame the football supporters!' I don't know who pulled the cord but it wasn't anyone in our carriage.

As we journeyed on someone pointed out that we were about to pass through Wolverhampton and instantaneously a chorus of 'always shit on the old gold and black' to the tune of always look on the bright side of life, broke out. It was really funny. As the train pulled into New Street station, Keep Right On was belted out at full volume to announce our arrival and it sounded brilliant.

We disembarked and as we all headed up the stairs into the Station everyone started singing 'were Birmingham, were

Birmingham, were Birmingham City!' really loud and it echoed around the station, alerting the waiting police, amongst others, that the Blues were back in town. All those in the local station pub looked around and the police arrived from everywhere to make sure we left peacefully. It had been a great day and a great result and as we headed for a taxi back home I contemplated the adventure I had just been on. 9 hours of travelling, 8 trains, 2 soccer special buses full of scousers – what a day! Next time I will take the direct route and not the long way round! I think we all went home happy.

The following Saturday Blues were to take on the might of Manchester United at St. Andrews and I had tickets to see it! I must add, though, the tickets were outrageously priced at 45 pounds! I was going to the match with Stephen, my nephew, and at four o'clock my brother arrived to give s a lift to the game. It was a 5.15 kick off as it was live on Sky.

We were both excited about the game, although no one gave us any chance of getting anything out

of the game. I was hopeful of at least a draw, and I believed that we were due a win due to the fact that we hadn't beaten them since 1978 when we won 5-1 and 'hopelessly devoted to you' by Olivia Newton John was top of the pop charts!

St. Andrews was surrounded with Blue and White clad supporters when we arrived and we mingled amongst them and headed to the programme seller and obtained two programmes priced at £3.50 each. How expensive it is nowadays for the ordinary supporter. Programmes obtained, we headed for the turnstiles and in towards our seats on the Kop. As we entered the ground I was tempted to place a bet on the game and as I was feeling brave I put £2 on Kapo to score the first goal and Birmingham City to win 2-1. A brave bet but with odds of 175 to 1, I just couldn't resist.

We headed to our seats that were well placed on the lower section of the Kop towards the Tilton goal. Great view. I was struck by the fact that our seats were not far from where Dave, a good friend and Bluenose of ours, had his season ticket. Tragically two weeks before, Dave had passed away tragically whilst on holiday in Tenerife and I was sad that he couldn't be here and missed the fact that I always used to meet up with him before the games for a pint. He will be sadly missed by a lot of people, and it was Dave that came up with the title for my book when I told him that I was writing it.

Rest in peace Dave.

The sun was shining and the atmosphere inside St. Andrews was buzzing. There were a lot of Manchester United fans and they were making quite a bit of noise. Blues were also singing and Keep Right On belted out loud and clear. The match got underway, and I have to say Blues were by far the better team and Utd were very lucky to go in at half time level. We had a lot of chances and should have put at least a couple away. As is always the case though, in the second half Blues made one mistake and Utd jumped on it and scored the only goal of the game with their only real chance of the game. Bloody typical. They are beginning to call Man Utd the 1-0 team this season as they are always just scraping 1-0 wins. Blues were by far the better team as everyone agreed after the game including players, managers and the press. Even Alex Ferguson said he was happy just to get to half time level. He also said that we were the best team that Man Utd had played this season!

The atmosphere had been great with Blues singing 'we support our local team' to the Man Utd fans, along with 'Cockney scum, get out of Brum'. Ronaldo (the cheating Portuguese player) was booed by fans whenever he touched the ball and when McSheffrey barged him off the ball and landed him on his cheating arse the biggest cheer of the game rang out. He had already angered the Blues fans with one of his trademark dives earlier in the game.

Although Blues lost against the run of play, the fans were in good heart by the display the Blues team put on and the applause rang out loud and proud at the end of the game. The fans sang

Keep Right On loudly as the players walked round the pitch applauding the Blues fans for their support.

As we headed towards the exit we saw Mike, a family member and waved across at him before heading out to find Steve, my sister's boyfriend who was also at the game and was giving us a lift home. As we headed round the back of the Railway Stand toward the road that would lead us down toward Steve's car, we ran into a load of trouble. A gang of about 20 Manchester Utd supporters were causing trouble and were picking on ordinary Blues supporters with families. A few Birmingham fans were having a go back and it took quite a while until a load of police arrived in riot gear to surround the Red's fans that were causing the trouble.

We soon arrived at Steve's car and after informing him about the troubles, we set off home. It had been a really good game and a great day out but we had just been well and truly robbed by the manc's.

A week later and I was off on my travels again. This time to Blackburn to see Birmingham take on Blackburn Rovers at Ewood Park. I had not been to Ewood Park since it had been made all seated. In fact, the last time I had been there it had been to stand on the old terraces, so I was really looking forward to this trip. Also it would be my last game before I had to fly back to my home in Abu Dhabi in the United Arab Emirates, and my niece Nicola was coming with me for her first away trip.

It was a bit cloudy when Steve called to pick us up at 9.15am but at least it wasn't raining. Steve was going to drop us at St. Andrews where we would board the supporter's coaches that were due to leave at 10.15. Nicola and I were really excited and had our packed lunch that my mum had made up the night before for the two of us, along with several other goodies all packed in a carrier bag for the coach.

We arrived in plenty of time, stood in the queue for the coaches and were soon on board and waiting to leave. Nicola had her mini iPod with her and I had a newspaper for the journey. I was wearing my new white Away shirt, which looked fab, so I thought. The coaches set off on time and it wasn't too long before we were pulling up at the service station for a forty minute stop. Nicola and I disembarked

to use the toilets and saw a few Tottenham fans and a couple of Liverpool fans standing outside the services. They looked surprised to see so many Birmingham City fans descending on them. It looked quite funny when we came out of the toilets as there were Blues fans everywhere! The shop and restaurants were full of fans wearing Birmingham shirts. It looked great and Nicola was well impressed. We headed back on the coach and spent the rest of the time eating sandwiches, chatting and waiting for the others to return so that we could recommence on our journey.

It wasn't too long before we were being met by our police escort on the outskirts of Blackburn and being led towards the ground. As the coach was pulling into the car park next to the ground, I noticed a nice big pub on the corner with tables and benches outside that seemed to be full of Birmingham fans, so I decided to head over to this pub once we disembarked.

Once Nicola and I were off the coach we headed back up the road and into the large pub called the Fernhouse. The outside area and large car park were already filled with Blues fans and as we headed inside the bouncers directed us to the upstairs bar/function room, which was now being used as an overspill as the downstairs bars were packed with Birmingham fans. There was a big sign welcoming Blues fans as we entered the pub which had two large bars downstairs with large screens showing the Arsenal v Sunderland game. We headed upstairs into a massive room with a small bar and another large screen showing the same match as downstairs. There were about 20 Blues fans already in there with others coming up the stairs behind us as directed by the bouncers.

I obtained a pint of cider for myself and a coke for Nicola as she is only 15 and we went over by the large bay windows to watch the Blues fans having fun in the car park below us. There was a big Birmingham City flag draped over the wall of the car park which was being held in place by two very large rocks. Nicola and I had a good laugh at that. The Blues fans outside were drinking and singing and generally enjoying themselves as the mounted police looked on nearby. I had a few drinks upstairs, watched the fans and had a chat with the barmaid who kept coming over to chat to me and to enquire about the Blues fans. She was telling me a bit about the Manchester City fans from the week before, who didn't sound a friendly lot at all by all accounts. They had been fighting amongst themselves in the car park when the pub was about to stop serving because of trouble in the ground.

The Blues fans, on the other hand, were just enjoying the day and having a good drink and sing song. As we had got to the pub at just after one o'clock, I was able to have a couple of drinks before we left the pub at about twenty five to three to walk the short distance to the ground. We had electronic tickets which took me a couple of minutes to work out how to use, by which time Nicola had used hers at the next turnstile and was waiting for me inside. There was already a lot of Blues fans in the bar area underneath the stand and I saw a few people I knew and said hello to.

We headed up to our seat behind the goal and the Blues fans were already in good voice and singing abuse towards Robbie Savage. The teams were already on the pitch warming up and Blues were playing in our third kit of red shirts, red shorts and red socks. There were a lot inside the ground but also quite a few empty seats amongst the Blackburn fans. This led to Blues singing 'your grounds to big for you' which was quite funny. They also sang 'it's just like being in church' due to the fact that Blackburn didn't sing much. Blues sang 'you've only got one song' as well as ninety minutes of abuse to Robbie (Judas) Savage, which was highly enjoyable. Nicola and I sang loads, and enjoyed the atmosphere in the away end. Keep Right On was sang loud and proud as usual and when Blues sang 'Brucie – give us a wave', Steve Bruce waved across at us.

The game wasn't quite as entertaining as the Blues fans and when Blackburn took the lead it didn't stop us singing, in fact just the opposite, we burst into a rendition of 'were Birmingham, were Birmingham, were Birmingham City!' loudly. Then, not long after half time we had a perfectly good goal by McSheffrey disallowed. Larsson crossed it in from the goal line and with a player lying at his feet, thereby playing the other onside, McSheffrey tapped it in. NOTHING WRONG WITH IT. Brucie was raging afterwards, especially as Blackburn then went straight up the other end and won a penalty. At 2-0 down it looked daunting, but give Blues credit, we really came at them and it wasn't long before the ball fell to Jerome in the area and he hit a cracker into the top corner right in front of us. Fantastic, the Blues fans went wild and Nicola and I jumped all over the place. It should really have been 2-2, but somewhat unfairly, it finished 2-1 to Blackburn despite all our attacking. Their keeper kept them in it in injury time by tipping over a Jerome header that was heading for the top corner.

At one point, four Blackburn fans in the end next to us started singing and the whole of the Blues end started singing 'there's only four of you singing, four of you singing, there's only four of you singing'. This gave us a laugh and despite losing it had been an enjoyable trip with the entertainment

Amongst the blues fans being perhaps the best part. So, game over, but not too despondent, we headed back to board the coach to head back the Birmingham.

Nicola said she had really enjoyed the trip and would defiantly come again. She was a great little singer and great company and is more than welcome to come with me each time I watch the Blues. The trip back was uneventful, Nicola listened to her iPod for a while then we chatted and had a laugh as we got closer to home. As the coach passed the vile ground we all sang 'shit on the villa' and had another laugh and before long we were back at the car park at St. Andrews. My brother Neil and his wife Sue came to pick us up and we spent the journey back telling them what a fabulous trip we had just had.

I arrived back in Abu Dhabi and the first game I watched was away at Manchester City which we lost 1-0 but we soon bounced back by beating Wigan 3-2 at St. Andrews. Next up was a trip to Everton which we again lost 3-1 before losing against the Vile 2-1, and Portsmouth 2-0. Things were not looking too good and Steve Bruce had left us to take over at Wigan.

Blues soon got a new manager though in the form of Alex McLeish who left the Scottish national team to come and join us. His first game was away at Tottenham and my two new friends Trish Kennedy and Tracey Rawnsley had come round to watch the game with me. This was to become a ritual between us on a match day as we would gather at mine with Blues flags, scarves etc, down a few beers/Vodka's and watch Birmingham play every week.

The game proved to be great and Larsson scored an absolute cracker in the last minute for a 3-2 win that sent Trish, Tracey and I running round the living room and jumping on each other. McLeish was over the moon with his first win in charge of his first game, and I was over the moon to win at Tottenham.

Somewhat unluckily Blues lost the next game away at Newcastle 2-1, followed by a draw against Reading 1-1, a defeat at Bolton 3-0 and then a win against Middlesbrough 3-0. Next up was a 1-1 draw at St. Andrews against Fulham followed by an away defeat at Manchester Utd 1-0 and an embarrassing exit in the FA Cup at Huddersfield Town as we lost 2-1. Then we were off to the new Emirate Stadium to take on Arsenal and a great result was obtained as O'Conner scored in at 1-1 draw and as the cameras showed the celebrating Bluenoses I spotted my mate Julie right in the middle of them going mental. 'There's my mate!' I screamed at Trish and Trace as they burst into laughter at me pointing madly.

Blues lost the next game against Chelsea 1-0, then Sunderland 2-0 and then drew with Derby and West Ham Utd both 1-1. Things were not looking good this season and we were one place off a relegation place. I couldn't stand the thought of going back to the Championship so quickly.

Trish, Trace and Carolyn came around to watch the next game against Arsenal at St. Andrews. Everyone wanted us to win this game and my hopes began to fade when Taylor was sent off in the first couple of minutes. Much to our utter surprise though, Blues then took the lead through a brilliant goal from a free kick by James McFadden. Trace had said 'he's going to score from this' and he did and we jumped about madly – even Carolyn was cheering (probably because she is a prawn sandwich though and supports Man Utd). Only having 10 men made it really hard though and Arsenal scored twice to take the lead 2-1. I was shouting abuse at the screen by now and the girls were laughing. They fell about laughing when Zarate was brought on as a sub with 20 minutes remaining and I shouted 'you've fuckin had it now!' Trace said 'you really meant that didn't you'

I was right though, as one of our players was brought down in the penalty area with minutes remaining and the referee awarded us a penalty. The room went quiet as McFadden stepped up to take it and I could barely watch as he smashed it into the Arsenal net 2-2! My room erupted as we all celebrated wildly, running around the room and jumping on each other. What a brilliant result!

There was just time for us all to watch the home game against Tottenham which we won 4-1 before it was time for me to head home again to get my fix of live football.

CHAPTER TWENTY-SEVEN – End of season heartbreak!

It was great to be back in England again and I was really excited about getting to see live football again and my beloved Birmingham. I was to be home for just over two weeks and already two of my planned matches had been rearranged for weekdays. Typical, I thought!

I was really looking forward to the trip to Portsmouth and as it was a night game Stephen and I booked to travel on the St. Andrews Tavern coach. It was a long trip and we had been supplied with refreshments by my mom as always. Once we arrived in Portsmouth we disembarked and headed in the general direction of the ground where we bumped into Alan and his mates. I asked him if he was going to the pub and he said he wasn't but his mate Bob was so I headed off to the pub with Bob. There were loads of Portsmouth fans in the nearby pub so I kept my shirt covered up until a load of Bluenoses turned up. We were still hopelessly outnumbered though but we enjoyed our drinks in peace and chatted about the game. It was funny being in a pub with Stephen now that he could drink and I think this was the first time I had bought him a pre match pint! It doesn't seem that long ago since he was 5 years old and I was holding his hand on the way to the matches, now he is so tall that I am only shoulder level to him!

As kick off time approached we headed off into the ground and took up our seats. Once the match got underway the Blues fans had decided to remain standing for the game and the atmosphere and singing amongst our lot was great. Before long though, Blues were losing 2-0. What a disappointment! Then we started to play better and we pulled a goal back 2-1. Just before half time we scored again 2-2 and the Blues fans began singing '2-0 and you fucked it up!' to the Portsmouth fans. It was really funny and the atmosphere was great even if it was freezing. The half time whistle went and Stephen and I headed off to get a sausage roll. I telephoned the girls, Trish and Trace back in Abu Dhabi to tell them what a great atmosphere it was and what a great time I was having. They were pleased to hear from me and wished the Blues well for the second half.

Unfortunately the second half was not as good as the first and we conceded two more goals which inspired the Pompy fans to sing back to us '2-2 and you fucked it up!' I admit to finding that a bit funny though, but the game ended in a 4-2 defeat and if was off out into the cold for the long journey home.

It was another cold night game when we took on Newcastle Utd and St. Andrews a week later. I was just happy to be able to see Blues play at St. Andrews to be honest although I was in a bit of u sulk because I had just learned that I would not be able to get a ticket for the Reading game just before I flew back as it was sold out. The match against Newcastle finished in a 1-1 draw and it was really two points dropped as we really should have won this game.

So, after my trip to Portsmouth for the midweek game and my visit to St. Andrews for the Newcastle game, I was eagerly awaiting what would have been my last match and an away trip to Reading on the Saturday. My sister's boyfriend Steve always manages to get me tickets for the games but on the Monday before the Reading game my sister Annette got a text from him saying that the Blues end was sold out and he could not get tickets. I was absolutely devastated! I could not believe it, and I could not bear the thought of being in Birmingham and not being able to get to the game. I had looked forward to this game for ages. It would have been a new ground for me too as I had only been to the old Reading ground.

After running around in a panic I finally sat down and thought about any friends who may be able to help me. I even rang the Blues commercial department, explaining that I had travelled 3,500 miles for the game, but they were unable to help me and advised me to ring the Reading ground to see if they could help.

Once I calmed down a bit I thought of Alan, who I have known for many years following the Blues and I still see him at the games when I get to away games. I gave Alan a call and he said he would try to help me but if he couldn't get one then did I want one in the Reading end as he had a friend in London who may be able to get me a home ticket. I said yes, I would settle for anything just to see the game.

The next day Alan called to say that his friend had got me a ticket for the Reading end and was really kind, saying he would take my ticket in the Reading end and I could have his ticket amongst the Birmingham fans. What a fantastic gesture! I was over the moon and was so grateful to his friend. Annette looked up from her magazine in amazement as I was dancing around the house and she said 'how are you going to get there?' I sang back 'how am I gonna get there I don't know, how am I gonna get there I don't care, all I know is I am on the way!'

I booked a ticket for the train to Reading for the Saturday and arranged with Alan that I would call him when I was on the way. Alan was dropping the lads in the city centre, so I said I would meet up with them for a drink before meeting Alan at the ground to get my ticket.

I was so excited on the Saturday, my mom had made me a packed lunch for the train and Steve had left me a small bottle of wine, also for the journey and my brother Neil had agreed to drop me at New Street station. So after picking up a can of cider, I was soon on board the Reading train and on my way. There were loads of Blues fans on the train chatting amongst themselves, also enjoying a few cans and looking forward to the game. As the train left Birmingham it began to snow! It looked really nice out of the train window but had stopped by the time we got to Reading. Lots more Blues fans got on in Oxford, also loaded up with beers.

As we arrived at Reading station I called Alan's friend who told me that Bob would be in the pub just outside the station, so that was where I headed. The pub was easy to find and was called The Three Guineas. It looked pretty packed with Bluenoses and as I met up with Bob, who was standing outside, he suggested that we head off to Wetherspoons instead. There were two other people meeting up with Bob, a bloke called Paul and his daughter Chelsea, and I soon got talking to them too.

We went into Wetherspoons and Bob and I got a drink, only to discover that they wouldn't serve Chelsea because she was underage – even though she only wanted a soft drink. As the rest of the lads were in a small pub just around the corner, Paul and Chelsea headed off there and we said we would join them when we finished our drinks.

It was quiet in Wetherspoons and as soon as our drinks were finished we headed around the corner and caught up with all the others in a small pub (can't remember the name) which was also full of Bluenoses. A few drinks were downed here and then Bob ordered a taxi to take us to the ground as it was getting very close to kick off time. I hadn't realised the time and when we arrived at the ground Alan was waiting patiently with his nephew in his car outside the ground to give me my ticket. I would be sitting away from my mates in the second row, but after a few beers I didn't really care where I sat so long as it was with the Bluenoses.

I had a great view, although I did think the atmosphere was a bit subdued for Blues. Where have all the singers gone? I think we should go back to having terraced areas again to bring the atmosphere back. However, Blues did give a few loud renditions of 'Keep Right On'. As the match got underway Blues had a few good chances to take the lead, but of course the inevitable happens and Reading scored. Once again, if only we had taken our chances, especially the one that McSheffrey missed when he was through on goal! I felt our defence was at fault for their goal, but

Blues launched into a rendition of 'Keep Right On' to try and lift the team. The game continued and very soon Forssell crossed the ball into the penalty area and Mauro Zarate smashed the ball into the net right in front of the Blues contingent! We went wild in the Blues end and Zarate ran to celebrate in front of the fans and it was right in front of where I was standing – about two feet from pitch! He was being mobbed by the other player's right in front of us and we were all jumping all over each other in celebration. It was brilliant. I could feel my phone vibrating in my pocket so I pulled it out to answer in and it was my mates in Abu Dhabi, Trish and Tracey, who were watching the game live. 'We just saw you on the telly!' they screamed at me, 'and it stayed on you for a good 30 seconds, unbelievable'. They said I was celebrating like a mad thing, but they know that I always do! Trish is a Bluenose and Tracey is a secret Bluenose cos she is a Leeds fan really but hasn't missed watching a Blues match yet this season, watching the games with Trish and me, and celebrating every goal Blues have scored!

The Blues fans had come alive and found their voices as we danced and celebrated. Blues were by far the better team – surely a winner must come! And come it did, but against the run of play and Reading again took the lead due a poor defence at a set piece. This is certainly becoming a habit this season and I think that McLeish needs to have a serious look at our defence!

The final whistle sounded and the thousands of shocked Bluenoses headed outside for the waiting special buses put on to take the Reading fans back to the city centre. There were a few seats being kicked and gates being kicked on the way out as Blues fans let out their frustrations. We all know how hard it is at times being a Bluenose! I met up with Paul and Chelsea and we boarded one of the buses. As we headed upstairs the whole bus broke into a loud rendition of 'Keep Right On' which I joined in with. I got into a conversation with some Bluenoses about our away support this season and how I was finding that the Blues were becoming a bit subdued at matches lately and a couple of the lads agreed saying it was shocking at White Hart Lane considering we won. We have always had good away support and have been famous for our humour and support for years. One of the lads said that it was because we had a poor team this year, but I disagreed – how often have we had a poor team? And we have still sung our hearts out! If we can't win on the pitch then the fans have certainly always won their singing battle off it! Let's hope our vociferous support returns again soon.

Before long we were back outside the station and headed to the Three Guineas which was fast becoming full of Bluenoses in full voice. Keep Right On was belting out loudly and the beers were flowing as we all enjoyed the banter before we headed home. One side of the pub was singing 'we hate villa more than you!' to the other side who were also singing 'we hate villa more that you!' back to them. I had a right laugh with the lads and Chelsea and must admit to starting a few songs off myself. In fact, I was enjoying myself so much that I missed my train back! I even got talking to a Reading fan that thought our supporters were great.

So, after a really good time with the Bluenoses in the pub, I headed back to Birmingham on the next train with Paul and Chelsea. The train was full of Bluenoses and after obtaining a few ciders we sang a few songs all the way home. As we came up the steps into New street station we all sang 'Keep Right On' loudly and it echoed impressively around the station. We passed a couple of villa fans that were quickly put in their place and I was soon meeting up with Annette (my sister) and Steve before heading home via the Stores in Harborne.

I must admit, the day out itself was a lot of fun, as it always is following Blues away from home, but the defeat was disheartening as it seems to be the story of our season. All we can do is 'Keep Right On' and have faith the Blues will still be playing Premiership football next season! Whatever the outcome we will continue to support them unconditionally as we have been born to do!

My first game back in Abu Dhabi was against Manchester City at St. Andrews and once again my adopted Bluenoses mates Trish and Trace came round to watch it with me. It was a cracking match as well as Blues put on a great display and Zarate scored two brilliant goals – I just love him and hope we can stay in the Premiership thereby having a chance of signing him. He is one of the most exciting players I have seen at St. Andrews for a long time. His two goals helped Blues on to a good 3-1 win and although we were still one place off relegation it gave us hope again.

However, that was to be dashed again in the next game away at Wigan as the 5,000 travelling Bluenoses witnessed an awful display as Blues lost the game 2-0 and it was getting nervy as the end of the season approached with only 5 games to go. We put on a better display against Everton in the next game at St. Andrews as Zarate scored again but this time we were very unfortunate just to draw the game 1-1. Then it was the local derby against Villa at Vile Park.

My mom was visiting at this time so we left her sunbathing at the Sheraton and Trish, Trace and I headed to the social club to watch it. We all had on Blues shirts and I had my large Blues flag, which I stuck up on the wall in the social club, and I had the Blues Crest painted on my face. However, at the time when we were due to kick off Francis could not get it on any of the channels and they all reckoned I had the time wrong. I was sure I hadn't and after quite a while of trying to get the game on I texted Annette who informed me that I was right and Blues were losing 2-0 already. I was gutted and said I was heading home where I knew the game would be on in my flat and the girls said they would come with me. Only problem was I had told mom to come round the social club to meet me when she finished at the Sheraton so after trying her mobile which was switched off, I asked Francis to tell her I had gone home. It was quite funny when my mom arrived at the social and Francis said I had gone home – she wouldn't believe I had left her there and she said 'she wouldn't go home and leave me" until he told her Blues were losing and she said 'oh, yes she would then' and she came back in a taxi.

It was even worse by the time we got back and was now 3-0. I sat in silence with Trace as Trish chatted to mom in the kitchen, it was now 4-0 but when Forssell scored to bring it back to 4-1 Trace and I did jump up and celebrate. Trace is a big Leeds fan and she understood how bad I felt as we lost the game 5-1 and I stated it was the worst day of my life. I couldn't mope too much though as my mom was there but if I had my way I would have sacked every player in a Blue shirt that day with the exception of Zarate and Forssell. They committed the worst crime imaginable by not showing any passion in a Blues shirt against the Vile from across the park. That in itself is unforgivable!

The next game was against Liverpool at St. Andrews and mom and I set out for the Brit Club to watch the game clad in my Blues shirt, scarves and my flag. Trish and Trace were a work but were going to join us just before half time hopefully. They did arrive before half time and Blues were winning 1-0 which was great. The atmosphere in the club was awful though and they seemed to frown on anyone making any noise or celebrating. Now this is something I MUST do so I decided that at half time we would leave and head over to the social club. We waited ages and could not get a taxi so we were forced to go back inside to watch the second half. Despite twice being in the lead Blues were held to a 2-2 draw and we were in the bottom three. I was really worried, even as Lee told me not to worry as Blues were too good to go down. Famous last words I thought.

The last but one game that could take us out of the bottom three was against fellow relegation rivals Fulham away. I watched the game in despair as we played totally crap and lost such an important game 2-0. It was more or less inevitable now that Blues would be relegated apart from a last day miracle on the final day of the season which would involve other team's results. We had done it before but I was extremely worried. Then I had very bad news from home as my uncle Sid had sadly passed away and I was heading home for his funeral and to be with my family at this sad time.

Well, here I was back in England for the last game of the season and our last chance to avoid relegation. Having seen so many relegation battles over the years my nerves were shot to pieces. Memories of avoiding relegation by winning at Coventry on the last day of the season and winning at Southampton also on the last day of the season back in 80's sprang to mind. However, I kept also getting flashbacks to Tranmere in the 90's when we were relegated despite winning 2-1 because the other results went against us. I had a terrible feeling that this could happen again, especially as Blues were relying on the outcome from two other games.

Like most Bluenoses I was awake early with nerves. I was up around 7am and tried to keep myself busy until it was time to head to St. Andrews. My sister Annette's boyfriend Steve was picking me up to take me to St. Andrews and I was waiting nervously when he arrived at quarter past one. Annette was working an early shift at Selly Oak Hospital where she is a nurse and wouldn't finish until after 3pm so couldn't make the match. My friends Tracey and Trish (Bluenoses) had sent texts from Abu Dhabi wishing the Blues luck. I asked them to keep me informed of the Fulham and Reading scores during the game as they would be out on the town watching the game.

Steve arrived in his new Blues hat and I was hopping about with nerves in my Blues home shirt and we were soon on our way. It was a lovely sunny day – no need for jackets and there were Bluenoses waiting for buses everywhere. It wasn't long before we were parking near to the ground and we headed to the 'Wagon & Horses' for a pre match drink or two!

There were loads of Blues fans outside the pub enjoying a pint in the sunshine. Most looked a bit nervous though. With a nice cold pint of cider in my hand we spotted some mates of Steve and stood chatting with them. Like me, the others were also nervous. One of the blokes had been up since 7am and had cleaned and washed the front path before washing his neighbour's car in order to take his mind of the match. We discussed previous great escapes and heartbreaking relegations that we had been through over the years. One lad was wearing the new away strip for next season, and I must say it looks really nice. I would have got one myself today but nerves dictated that I was in dire need of a pre match drink to help settle them.

So, with a couple of pints of cider downed, we headed up towards the ground in the bright sunshine. It was just like the old days with Blues fans everywhere heading towards the ground. Steve stopped off to get something from Dave Thomas, the Made In Brum bloke and then we were entering St. Andrews. I was a bit disappointed as I could only get a restricted view ticket at the back of the Kop at the side of the executive boxes, but after a couple of minutes Steve turned up to inform me that there was a spare seat next to Lee, an old friend of mine from following Blues since the 80's. Lee's son had got chicken pox so I was able to take his seat, which meant I had company and a great view. I was right next to the Blackburn fans so I was able to give them some stick too.

The atmosphere inside was brilliant! The ground was buzzing and Keep Right On was ringing out loud and proud. We were not going to go down without a fight! St. Andrews looked full. I couldn't see a single empty seat apart from next to the visitors. Blues had handed out 20,000 clapper type posters with Come On Blues on them and these were being waved or held aloft and looked very impressive and added to the noise level. Unfortunately I didn't get one of these! Oh well, I was still going to make plenty of noise! Blues were now singing 'we're Birmingham, we're Birmingham, we're Birmingham City!' all around the ground. It was very impressive, the atmosphere was brilliant!

The players ran out onto the pitch amid a sea of blue and white and a noise level that was reaching fever pitch. As soon as the game got under way I could see that the Blues players were up for the battle. Blues were kicking towards the new railway stand in the first half which was great for me as I was sitting on the corner of the Kop by the Railway stand. The Blackburn fans were taunting us about going down, but we just sang our Blues go down song – come back up, win the cup and all that! Blues fans were singing our hearts out even when word got out that Reading were 1-0 up at Derby. Our lads were up for the fight and we were still in with a chance. I turned to Lee to say that I wished Zarate was playing as I think he is brilliant, only for him to point to a player with his head shaved and tell me that he is in fact playing! That cheered me up no end. I preferred the long hair look though!

When Murphy hit a shot from way out and it flew into the net the ground erupted. We were all jumping on each other and dancing about and making appropriate gestures at the travelling fans. Maybe we could do it. Not long before half time people at the back of the family stand started cheering and word got around that Derby had in fact equalized against Reading. The rumour soon spread around the ground and before long the entire ground was singing 'staying up, staying up, staying up!' and everyone was partying. The Blackburn fans looked stunned and the Blues players seemed to rise up even more. I rang my sister to see if this was true because I remember at Tranmere in the 90's when a rumour went around that West Brom were losing which would have meant we were safe, only to find that it was just a false alarm and we went down. Annette said she would find out and call me back and as the half time whistle sounded we all became aware that the rumour was in fact false and Reading were now 2-0 in front. I was shattered, as were all those around me. It was looking grim.

Blues came out for the second half and Blackburn seemed to raise their game for the first ten or fifteen minutes and it wasn't long before our shaky defense conceded an equalizer. I was now feeling really disheartened and when I heard that Reading were now 3-0 up I knew it was all over. Although my heart was breaking once again I got behind the team as did the rest of the St. Andrews faithful and Blues did not disappoint us and a good goal by Cameron Jerome, who had just come on as substitute, put us back in the lead 2-1. It wasn't long before some of the 'so called fans' started yelling abuse at David Sullivan and his family in the executive seats and I have to say that I was deeply ashamed. I had never seen fans turn on the board in this manner before and despite the lack of money being spent I remember how the current board saved us from bankruptcy and the Kumar's years ago. I know the Hong Kong Phooey disaster in the middle of the season did not help but they have done us a huge service over the years. It wasn't long before the whole Kop was singing 'where's the money gone?' and I had to agree that this was a good point, perhaps if we had spent more then we may have stayed up? Mind you, I think that the transfer window has a lot to answer for and should be scrapped! It only serves the big teams like Man Utd, Chelsea, Arsenal and Liverpool (who we are all completely bored with anyway!). If we didn't have a transfer window system then we could have bought defenders when we needed them and stayed up!

Blues were playing great now and before long we were 3-1 up, although the atmosphere had changed a little with the knowledge that we weren't playing for anything now and we were down. The Blackburn fans were still attempting to wind us up but when the fourth goal flew in from Muamba the Bluenoses started baiting them back by singing '4-1 to the championship!'. That left the Blackburn fans lost for words!

The final whistle blew and rather than be downhearted the Blues faithful sang 'Keep Right On' loudly to our devastated players who had just realized we were down. Some players threw their shirts into the crowd for the fans and were about to embark on a lap of applaud when supporters ran onto the pitch in their thousands and put a stop to it. What a shame, it would have been nice to applaud the players at the end of the season. The fans then turned their attention once again to the board and began singing 'sack the board' – which I must say, was started by the Blackburn fans in irony. When the fans were bored with this they turned their attention towards the Blackburn fans, who were being very brave behind three rows of police and stewards protecting them and were attempting to antagonize the situation. With thousands heading towards the police line they began swiftly leaving.

So, after taking a few pictures of the pitch invasion on my mobile and leaning over the wall to inform the Blackburn fans what I thought of them, Steve and I headed back towards the car to head home.

Once we got back to my mom's house it was decided that Annette, Steve and I would head off to Harborne for a couple of drinks to commiserate. So, a taxi was duly ordered and we were soon downing beers in 'The Stores' pub with a few of Steve's mates. I was disappointed to see that the pub is fast becoming a vile pub and the entire time I was there was spent informing vile fans what I thought of them, although in their favour they have become used to my abuse and all admitted that they were sad to see Blues go down.

Apparently the 'vile' barmaid told Steve's brother Eddie to take his Blues hat off! Lucky I didn't hear that because it would have worth a ban and I had to be led away by my sister. And so another season was over and with a heavy heart we all headed back to my mom's where she had cooked a lovely Sunday roast to cheer us up. There was not much that could cheer me up to be honest but we will be back and as Championship next season. Come On!!

The Premier League Championship was won by Manchester Utd and Chelsea were runners up. Reading, Birmingham City and Derby Country were relegated and the FA Cup was won by Portsmouth who beat Cardiff City 1-0. The League Cup was won by Tottenham who beat Chelsea 2-1 after extra time but for Blues it was back to the Championship and hopefully a successful promotion battle.

CHAPTER TWENTY-EIGHT – Promotion!

So far I had not had a good year and was hoping the new season would bring me some cheer at last. After losing my Uncle Sid in May I then lost my lovely Nan in July and had once again flown home for a funeral and to be with the family. My Nan was in her 100th year and we will all miss her along with my Uncles Sid and John who are all together once more.

I was looking forward to the 2008 – 2009 season in the hope that it would be a good one and that Blues could regain our place back in the Premiership where we belong. I would have to get used to having to listening to the games via live commentary and I would miss watching them play every week. Luckily though, the first game of the season at home against Sheffield Utd was to be shown live so I was able to watch Kevin Phillips, our new signing, score the winner in the last few minutes as he came on as substitute. The game finished 1-0 to Blues and we were up and running.

Then it was midweek cup action as Blues travelled to Wycombe Wanderers in the first round of the League Cup and earned a good 4-0 win to send us into the next round and a another away trip to Southampton in round three. Before that though, we took on Southampton away in a league match and came away with another good win this time 2-0 and we were in 3rd place in the Championship. We went one better in the next game by moving to the top of the table after a good 2-0 home win over Barnsley and I was really happy.

Blues then had a slight hiccup in the next game by losing at Southampton 2-0 but this time it was in the League Cup so I wasn't too upset. Our 100% record was lost as we only drew our next match in the league against Norwich City away 1-1 and we were in 3rd place but still unbeaten in the league. And then I was heading home and looking forward to watching the boys live again.

I was home in the UK again but this time for ten days only. Not to worry though, I was determined to make the most of it and planned on getting to all of the three Blues games that were due to take place while I was home. Two of the games were at St. Andrews against Doncaster Rovers and Blackpool and sandwiched in between was a nice trip to Bristol to take on Bristol City at Ashton Gate. I was really looking forward to this game, as I have never visited the Home of Bristol City so it would be a new ground for me to visit. Also, I always love away games the most, as this is when you get to mix with the true Bluenoses who travel away and the atmosphere is always brilliant amongst the Blues support. Especially lately with the atmosphere not being what it used to be at St. Andrews.

It was a nice sunny day when I travelled with Stephen and Steve to St. Andrews for the Doncaster game and once we had obtained our beers in the Wagon & Horses, we stood outside in the sunshine chatting to each other and a few other Bluenoses. It was a great being back at St. Andrews and although the atmosphere is not as good as it used to be these days it was a lovely feeling being back. The game got underway and I though Doncaster gave a really good account of themselves but Jerome scored a good goal and it was a 1-0 win to Blues that I was celebrating at the end of the game. Brilliant. Blues had made the best start to a season for many years and I was enjoying it. Then it was off to Bristol for the next match against Bristol City and I was really looking forward to it.

I was travelling to the game with my sister Annette, her boyfriend Steve (known to his mates as Stegga), my nephew Stephen and Lee Pitman who has been a friend for many years of following the Blues. Lee was driving us there and he arrived at my mom's house to pick us up at around 4.30pm. Annette had worked an early shift as a nurse at Selly Oak Hospital, but had managed to shower, change into her Blues shirt and was ready for the trip. My mom had picked up Stephen and she was now cooking sausages to make sausage and tomato sandwiches for us to eat before we go. Stephen managed to eat his but Annette and I asked for them to be wrapped up for us to eat on the journey. Mom had also made up a bag of goodies that were also for the journey.

It was good to see Lee again as I have known him for a long time and we remember travelling away regularly during the good old days of the eighties. We have shared some fun times including the train incident away at Grimsby and getting arrested at Chelsea before the match. It was great fun in those days and the atmosphere was fabulous.

So we all got into the car and we set off for Bristol in the hope of arriving early and getting a pre match drink. It was a fun drive as we were in good spirits and Steve had bought a bag of bottled beers as it was his birthday. After a bit of cajoling Annette and Stephen managed to get a bottle of beer each off him. Luckily for them I don't like beer and would much rather have a cider which was noticeably absent. Oh well, I decided I would entertain the others with my singing instead. Lee had remarked that the kids were quiet in the back! I replied 'are we there yet?' several times imitating donkey in Shrek! I then proceeded to eat my sausage buttie and then broke into song. I did several Blues songs, driving Lee mad in the process. I even sang 'front end, front end give us a song'. Lee told Steve to sing something but the front end remained silent despite my taunts.

On the way we passed several Blues coaches which we cheered, and we had Steve's Blues On Tour scarf across the back window on display. The traffic wasn't too bad either and just before six we arrived in Bristol. Steve was navigating and had about a hundred pages of instructions from the Internet by which he directed Lee to a nice little pub set back off the main road just next to the Ramada Hotel. As we drove up a small road to the pub at the top I couldn't help but notice all the parked cars were facing us. I pointed this out and asked if perhaps it could be a one way street. Steve replied that it wasn't as he had walked up the road previously! We all burst into laughter at his words – WALKED up this way! Lee dropped us at the pub and then went to park the car just down the road.

It was a lovely little old pub with just a few locals inside and no Bristol City fans to be seen. There was a small beer garden out front, to which we headed before deciding it was too cold and heading back inside just as Lee arrived from parking the car.

We had a great time in the pub chatting amongst ourselves and downing several pints – except Lee who had to stick to water due to the fact that he was driving. I sent Lee my 'shit on the villa' ring tone via Bluetooth. It took ages to send though as the only phone my Bluetooth was picking up was called 'Andy', but after about ten minutes of trying and switching my Bluetooth off and on Lee realised that this was in fact his phone that he had bought it from someone called Andy!

At just after seven o'clock we drank up and headed for the ground, which was about two miles away. As we got close to the ground the traffic became heavy but luckily we spotted a parking space outside a boarded up pub not too far from the ground. We arrived in the ground about five minutes before kickoff and the Blues end was buzzing! The visitor's area just behind the goal was unreserved seating, which is brilliant because then you can sit where you like, and all the singers can sit together. Although all the Bluenoses were singing at Bristol that night, around 2 – 2,500 I reckon. Only problem was the seats have no backs to them but no problem tonight as the entire Blues end were on our feet throughout the game.

It was a brilliant atmosphere and after only five minutes Larsson put the Blues in front and we erupted in wild celebrations. I jumped on Annette and Stephen and we danced about madly. Then to our delight Jerome put us 2-0 up after about 25 minutes to more wild celebrations! This was more like it after the dire show against Doncaster last Saturday. The Bluenoses were in full voice and 'Keep Right On' rang out loudly on a number of occasions and also several renditions of 'were Birmingham, we're Birmingham, we're Birmingham City!' The Bristol City fans were silent and it wasn't too long before Blues began singing 'no noise from the tractor boys'.

It was a brilliant first half and at half time I spotted Alan (who I have known for many years travelling with Blues) and went over to chat to him. Alan is a brilliant Bluenose who has taken me to several away games over the years and we began reminiscing. He informed me that he has now been to 3,000 Blues games, what a fantastic achievement – he should be given a medal! He has only missed a couple of games and that was when he had his hip operation. Even when he could hardly walk when his hip was bad, I would still see Alan struggling up the steps at away grounds. What a hero and what a Bluenose! He has my utmost respect. What can I say Alan, you are one of the games characters and I am forever in awe of you.

As the second half kicked off we had moved to the corner section and had seen several other Bluenoses that I know. I was surprised by the arrival of two Osama Bin Laden's, a horse and Rodney from only fools and horses. I love when Blues fans come in fancy dress to away games; they looked brilliant and stood behind us. Dave from Made In Brum took a quick picture of them, which included Steve, as he does resemble Del from only fools and horses!

Blues didn't play quite as well in the second half but could still have been further ahead but for a bit of luck before we made a mistake leading to the ball dropping to a Bristol player who planted it straight into the empty net 2-1. With ten minutes to go the Bristol City fans began heading out and the Bluenoses began singing 'time to go, time to go, time to go' song. The game was never in any doubt, though and it finished with another away win for Blues and still in second place in the table. Brilliant.

Back to the car and we were soon on the way back to Birmingham. I sang all the way back home much to the amusement or perhaps annoyance of the others? I did several renditions of 'were Birmingham' a few 'Keep Right On's' and several other old ones. I thing Lee was probably relieved when I got out at my moms, although he did say it was a top night and he had forgotten how much fun travelling away could be.

It had been a brilliant night out and a great win and I was more than happy when I arrived home. Unfortunately my last game before I headed back was one I wanted to forget against Blackpool as we played awful and lost at home 1-0. The only enjoyable part of the day had been the pre match pint outside the Wagon & Horses in the sunshine. This brought our unbeaten run to an end in an unlikely manner but we were still sitting in second place in the table.

Back in Abu Dhabi the next Blues game was away at Cardiff City and I had to make do with listening to the live radio commentary again as Blues achieved a very good away win 2-1 which we followed up with an away draw at Derby 1-1. On 4th October Blues beat Queens Park Rangers 1-0 at St. Andrews to go top of the table and I was getting really excited about a possible quick return to the Premier. Unfortunately Blues dropped back to second place after a 1-1 draw away at Burnley. The rollercoaster ride continued as we Blues then defeated Crystal Palace at St. Andrews to back top and stayed there the next week thanks to a good 3-1 win over Sheffield Wednesday, again at St. Andrews.

I began to worry again after Blues lost the return game at Queens Park Rangers 1-0 and then lost somewhat unluckily against Coventry 1-0which I watched live. Blues had a very good goal disallowed and the replay showed that they ball had well crossed the line for a goal but the referee didn't give it and we were robbed. The Coventry fans celebrated like they had won the FA Cup which just showed how much all the other teams in the league feel that Birmingham City are the team they want to beat. It makes it so much harder for us.

I was getting really frustrated listening to the live commentary, especially the next game against Nottingham Forest away and I was happy to come away with a 1-1 draw at the end. Blues were still in 2nd place though and then went on a three match winning run against Charlton 3-2, a good away win at Swansea 3-2 which ended their unbeaten home record and a home win against Ipswich 2-1. The next game was on live and it was a top of the table clash against leaders Wolves. Trish and Trace came round to watch this game and we celebrated madly when Jerome scored to put us in the lead. Blues played brilliantly and we all agreed that if we played like this all season then we would get promotion back to the Premier League. Then Wolves snatched a scrappy equaliser and the game finished 1-1 much to our disappointment as I thought we had done more than enough to win the game. Still, it was a good result against the top side in the championship.

Good wins against Watford 3-2 and Plymouth 1-0 followed before we crashed down to earth losing 1-0 at Preston. They do seem to be our bogey team. Then it was another top of the table clash as Blues took on Reading at St. Andrews and it was on live again. Trish and Trace came round again and we got the vodka out which did little to dull the pain and disappointment as we lost the game3-1. The only highlight was a cracking goal scored by Kevin Phillips which levelled the scores and gave us great pleasure as we once again ran around the flat celebrating. It was not to be though and I was getting a little worried again. Blues were now out of the top two for the first time since the beginning of August as we dropped to 3rd. I would be so gutted if we missed out on automatic promotion after everything.

Blues got back to winning ways against Ipswich 1-0 and then drew 0-0 against Swansea before the big freeze hit us and the FA Cup game against Wolves was postponed. It did get underway though on the 13th January and 22,232 saw Blues robbed by a pass from the referee straight to a Wolves player who scored and we lost very unluckily 2-0. Knocked out of the FA Cup by the dingles was quite a blow but now we had to concentrate on promotion.

Next up was Cardiff City and a 1-1 draw, followed by a shocking 2-0 defeat at Blackpool! I couldn't believe it but I hid my disappointment and was soon cheered up again with a 1-0 home win over Derby. I could feel the end of the season getting closer and closer as Blues drew the next two games against Sheffield Wednesday 1-1 and Burnley 1-1. Then the rollercoaster ride went upwards as Blues won against Nottingham Forest 2-0 and then downwards as we lost 1-0 away at Coventry – again somewhat unluckily. Blues then drew away at Crystal Palace 0-0 and I was on my way home again for the next game away at Sheffield Utd.

It was 26th February 2009 and I was about to embark on another trip home to see my family and my beloved Birmingham City. I had planned the trip meticulously with the help of Annette and her boyfriend Steve. I had chosen these two weeks due to the fact that I would be able to get in five matches in total and they would include three away games, one of which would be Doncaster – a new ground for me and a trip that I relished. It was so very nice to be back on English soil again and to see everyone again.

My first game was a trip to Sheffield to see Blues take on Sheffield United at Brammall Lane. I had arranged to meet my nephew Stephen in Sheffield as he was coming across from Leicester where he is currently attending university there. The game was an early kick off at 12.15, another example of football being spoilt for the fans in aid of the revenue from the televised games as this game was scheduled for live viewing. This meant that I would have to leave early and meant that, according to Steve; I would not be able to get a train but would have to travel on the Blues supporters coach.

And so, on a lovely sunny morning, Annette and Steve dropped me off early at St. Andrews to board the coach to take me to Sheffield. I had a packed lunch made by my mom as usual and as I was travelling alone I made my way to the last available window seat near the back of a rapidly filling coach. I was on the second coach and before long a young boy with his dad sat next to me and his dad sat across from him. The coaches got underway and before long I was chatting to the boy and his dad about the coming game and the Blues in general.

It seemed to take a long time to get to Sheffield as I think we took the scenic route to prevent us getting there in time to go to the pub first and we encountered quite a bit of traffic at one point. As we arrived on the outskirts of Sheffield we were met by a police escort. This motivated the already noisy Bluenoses to break into song and to stand up and bang on the windows whilst in full voice. I was on the phone to Stephen at the time checking his process and he could hear the singing really loudly. 'Sounds great where you are!' he said. Stephen had in fact arrived at the station and was making his way to the ground to meet me.

As we pulled up outside the ground with about 25 minutes to kick off, I called Stephen and asked him where he was. He informed me that he was nearby and he could see the coaches but not me. I told him I was on the second coach and would walk to the front and that was when I spotted him. I could see a sea of red and white coming down the road and right in the centre of them was a lone Blues shirt coming towards me. I had to laugh; he has definitely inherited that from me!

We went into the ground, which was a new ground for Stephen, and went for a quick drink before kickoff. To my surprise I discovered they sold Vodka Blue so I got a couple of bottles for me and a pint of Carlsberg for Stephen who was amused by the lad in front who commented on the price of the beer. '3 pound fifty for a bottle of Carlsberg!' he commented 'it's only a pound in snobs!'

The game was another important match as were all the games at the moment with Blues sitting in second place in the championship and Reading breathing down our necks. The Blues fans were in good voice as usual, apart from a couple of moaners standing behind me in the second half. The whole of the Blues contingent were quite content to stand and as I took my place with Stephen I bumped into Brendon, an old friend and whom I would be travelling to Barnsley with the following week. As the game got under way it soon became clear that it was not going to be our day and a very disputable penalty cost us the game as Sheffield Utd ran out 2-1 winners. It was a really unjust result but we sang our hearts out and despite the result it was a great day out.

I said goodbye to Stephen and gave him some of the sandwiches that mom had made for his journey back to Leicester and told him to enjoy the trip and that I would see him again soon for the Southampton game when he would be back in Birmingham for the weekend.

Next up would be Bristol City at St. Andrews and would be a double for me this season as I had travelled to Bristol for the away match back in September on my last trip home. It was on Wednesday evening on the 4th March and I was going to this game with my sister Annette. Because Steve was working and would meet us at the game, Annette and I decided to go out for something to eat before heading to the game, so after deciding on Jimmy spices on Broad Street, we made our way there. We had a great meal, washed down by a bottle of wine and then jumped a taxi to St. Andrews. Annette laughed when I jumped in the taxi and asked the driver to take us to 'Stan's, please mate!'

I must admit it felt pretty cold to me, which was probably because I am now adapted to warmer climates, and I was too cold to have a drink in the bar in the ground before kick off! Our seats were at the back of the corner of the Kop/Tilton and the atmosphere was great. It was much better that the silent Kop that I had become used to on the last occasions I had been to Stan's. I had begun to wonder if we would ever get the old atmosphere back that was so envied around the country by other teams and their supporters but tonight it was back. It kicked in just after a great tackle in which Lee Carsley showed the other players just how it should be done – with passion, and the other players duly followed suite, which really lifted the Bluenoses and the atmosphere was the best I have known for a long while.

Blues played the best I have seen for quite a while too and

when we scored the roof seemed to get lifted off the stadium. The ground erupted, just like old times and Annette and I celebrated like we always do by jumping around like mad people. Well, you just have to don't you! It's in the blood. Our promotion push was back on track and we came out of the ground very happy indeed by our 1-0 win.

A few days later on the Saturday, I was again off to St. Andrews, this time with Stephen to watch Blues take on Southampton. Steve picked us up and as usual we went to the Wagon and Horses, not far from the ground, for a pre match pint or two. Steve said he wasn't drinking, but that didn't stop Stephen and me as we downed a couple of pints whilst discussing our chances. As it was still a bit cold we opted to stay inside the pub and not venture outside with our drinks as we had become used to on the previous occasions I had been there.

As kick off approached we headed to the ground and stopped off to talk to Dave – Made In Brum whereby I obtained a couple of badges for my collection. Programmes were obtained and Stephen and I headed to our seats on the corner of the Kop/Tilton whilst Steve headed for his seat in the family stand. Once inside we soaked up the atmosphere and joined in the singing as the team came onto the pitch. The game got under way and I noticed a familiar face standing behind me. I was surprised to see Shyla who I have known from way back in the 80's when I travelled everywhere with Blues and it was always the same faces such as myself, Julie, Pam, Debbie, Shyla, Lee Pitman and Brendon Anderson amongst others. Shyla had been on the tour of Holland that I went on in the 80's and it seemed really funny seeing him again. We exchanged a couple of words and arranged to have a chat in the bar at half time.

By the time I had queued for the beers at half time I couldn't find Stephen anywhere and when I called his mobile I discovered he had returned to his seat. He soon joined me after I informed him I had a beer for him and I mulled over old times with Shyla and arranged to meet up with them at some point at Doncaster in a week's time. Then it was back to the game and another great goal and another home win 1-0 to keep us in second place in the table and keeping the pressure on the Dingles from across the road.

I was really looking forward to the next game as it was away and I was travelling with some of the lads. I had arranged to meet Brendon and Ron at the Cricketers pub by St. Andrews as we were travelling by the Blues supporters coach again due to it being a Tuesday night game and no way to get home afterwards if we had gone by train. My brother Neil dropped my at the Cricketers at 2.30pm as the coach was due to depart at 3.30pm giving us time for a few pre match pints. Brendon was already waiting for me inside and I was soon downing cider and showing him my new mobile phone screen saver which was a photo of a seagull reading a paper titled 'Guide to Shitting on the Villa' excellent. Of course I then blue toothed a copy to Brendon's phone after passing it around for the others to see and nod their approval.

Then it was off to get the coach which, due to the fact that there was only one, was quickly filling up and we all had to split up, apart from Brendon and I who managed to get aisle seats next to each other. As I have already said I have known Brendon for many years and we were soon reminiscing again and I was enthralled by many of Brendon's stories from years back and it didn't seem too long before we were arriving in Barnsley, via a stop at the service station. As far as I try to remember back, I cannot remember going to Barnsley before so this could well be a new ground for me. The coach pulled up in the car park in the ground and we were soon disembarking in search of a pub.

Brendon had planned to take us to the local leisure centre next to the ground where, he informed us, there was a very nice pub inside. He was correct and the pub itself was quite big really and very nice. There were a few red shirts already inside when we arrived and as the pub quickly began to fill up with Bluenoses, the red shirts promptly left. I made the mistake of ordering a pint with the lads and then had to keep up with them, although, I'm proud to say I did! We all had a very pleasant time in there and I met some new people, including a dad and his now grown up son and another bloke who travels to all the England games. We had a chat about Germany 2006 and all in all I had a really nice time.

Then it was off to the ground via a shortcut through a load of bushes and thicket. Brendon got stuck as he caught his coat on a bush, which gave me a bit of a giggle. And then it was into the ground, of which Blues had been given half of one end behind the goal with the other end being kept empty. This was great as we just headed to the bars at the empty end and got served immediately. We bumped into other Bluenoses that I knew including Graham and Fiddler from Harborne. Then we went to find a seat and as Brendon headed for empty seats towards the front, I redirected him to the centre of the singing fans as I wanted to sing! And sing I did, encouraging Brendon to join me in full voice, which he did as we belted out 'keep right on' proudly.

Blues played really well, but I was dismayed when Barnsley scored against the run of play. Just our luck, I thought as I headed to the toilets in disgust. I was just returning to my seat when Blues scored and I ran along our row jumping madly on everyone. Brendan and I jumped all over the place in celebration. The atmosphere amongst the Blues contingent was brilliant, although a couple of idiot stewards tried to spoil the party by moving in and trying to drag out anyone who looked to be enjoying themselves too much. Blues promptly broke into song and sang 'get a proper job, get a proper job' to the tune of Chirpy Cheep Cheep. I smiled and joined in, and before long the local constabulary had a camcorder trained on the singing Blues hoard. Must have been for their collection of all time greats! Blues broke into another chorus of 'you can stick your fucking camera up your arse!' which, again, I found really amusing. So, apart from only getting a draw as the match finished 1-1, I had a really good day out.

On the journey back I had a good chin wag with Brendon and an old guy sitting behind him. The old guy was worried about the upcoming game at Doncaster, but I reassured him that I had a really good feeling about the game and was sure Blues would win. The only down point of the day was as I was in a taxi on the way home with Brendon who was dropping me off at my moms, when I realized I have left my programmes on the coach. I was gutted as I collect my programmes. Of course, no one on the coach was honest enough to hand them in and despite calling the coach company I never got them back. The next day Brendon called me and offered me his programme which was really nice and a big sacrifice by him as I know he also collects them as I do. He passed by my moms and dropped it in for me and I must admit it was really nice of him.

The last game of my trip was fast approaching and it was the trip that I was looking forward to the most. I was travelling to this game with Steve, my sister's boyfriend and we were travelling on the train. I really love going by train as I always enjoy the trip and you get there early enabling us to meet up with the other Bluenoses and see a bit of the town before having a pre match pint or two.

On my last Saturday before I went back, I was up early and really looking forward to the day ahead. My mom had packed a bag of food which could quite possibly have fed the amount of people on the train itself. This was probably because she knew I would be travelling with Steve! Mind you, Steve duly arrived armed with some sandwiches of his own as well as a few beers for the train. His son James dropped us at New Street Station in his new car and we were soon in the off license obtaining more drinks for the train. I got a couple of cans of cider and a newspaper and Steve got a couple of small bottles of wine. I was beginning to wonder whether he would arrive in Doncaster sober!

There were quite a few Bluenoses on the platform waiting for the train which soon arrived and we boarded and found our seats. Beers were duly opened and just before the train departed, one of Steve's mates and his son got on our carriage and sat not far from us. Then we were on our way and the party began. Just before we got to Derby it was announced that there would now be some Derby County fans boarding on their journey to Sheffield. I wondered whether this was to tip off the Blues fans or in the hope of avoiding trouble. There were quite a few Derby fans that got on armed with beers, but there was no trouble and they even asked us who we were playing and wished us well. I suggested that they do us a favor by beating Sheffield Utd, who were also now closing in on us, and we would return the favor by beating Doncaster. This was happily agreed as the Derby fans disembarked and waved farewell to us.

So, following a good journey, we arrived in Doncaster and I promptly zipped up my jacket to hide my Blues shirt and enable us to slip unnoticed past the waiting police presence at the station and out into the town. Steve was busy on his mobile trying to find out where the others were as the four of us set off into town. Steve's mate and I just wanted to stop at the first pub we saw for a drink but Steve insisted on finding his mates in a pub which proved to be quite elusive. Anyway, we eventually found our way to this pub which was packed with fans of many descriptions watching Liverpool's demolition of Manchester Utd at Old Trafford which was being shown live. It was 2-1 to Liverpool when we arrive but it soon became 3-1 and then 4-1 much to the delight of the neutrals and the odd scousers in the pub. The prawn sandwich brigade left with their heads bowed. Excellent.

We were now sandwiched in a corner of the pub with the many Bluenoses and Steve's mates and I once again saw people I knew such as Fiddler, who apparently had not had a very good night the previous night. Like a true Bluenose though, he was at Doncaster, and I got chance to catch up with him.

The pub was really hot and a bit packed for me and I managed to persuade Steve and some of the lads to head for a pub nearer the ground. Steve had spoken to Brendon who was at the Beefeater near the stadium and he said it was a big pub and there were loads of Bluenoses there. This sounded just my cup of tea and so we ordered two taxis's and before long we were on our way to the Beefeater to join the others.

On arrival at the pub, I was delighted to see it was full of Bluenoses and the atmosphere was brilliant with singing constantly breaking out. There were loads of people I knew in there and I was soon chatting to Brendon near the bar whilst downing another pint of cider. There were also a load of Blues who had drifted outside and I even saw Shyla to say hi to. I sang quite a bit too and even started a few songs going. It was great and before long it was time to walk the short distance to the stadium which could be clearly seen as we left the pub. As we approached the ground we saw a group of Blues fans who had decided to 'take' the local hill to which the new stadium is named after. They were holding aloft a massive Birmingham City St. George's flag and singing 'Keep Right On'. All the passing Bluenoses, including myself, joined in and it was quite funny.

The stadium itself was quite nice for a new stadium even though it was a little bit small and the atmosphere inside was good. Once inside the Blues end it was free seating, which I really love because it means the singers can all be together and makes the atmosphere even better. I led the lad's right to the centre of the singers as usual the Blues contingent were situated behind the goal and were already in good voice. Blues played really well and before long Jerome scored right in front of us Bluenoses and our end erupted. I was jumping about madly as usual as were all the other Bluenoses.

With still some time left to half time Steve decided to go the toilet and said he would get the drinks in and meet me downstairs at half time. Not long after he had gone, Blues scored again and the bluenoses went wild in celebration. 2-0! We were on our way! My phone was vibrating in my pocket and it was Steve asking what I wanted to drink as they didn't have cider. 'Anything vodka based' I replied –'oh by the way Steve, its 2-0!'

So at half time it was 2-0 and I headed down to the bar with Brendon and friends to find Steve who had called about 5 times the say where he was. However, he got his left and his right mixed up and it took a while to find him and get the glass of wine he had gotten for me. When I found him he was with fiddler. After a brief chat I headed back to the other lads and handed out a few sandwiches to keep everyone going, and then it was back to our seats for the second half.

The second half was a cruise really as we never looked in any danger of losing and a group of Blues fans did a conga before heading down to the front of the stand to wave flags and sing "Keep Right On'. The stewards looked on in amazement and clearly had no idea what to do. These stewards were not mini-Hitler's though and left the Blues fans to celebrate which was currently being shown live by SKY. Apparently the cameras showed the Blues fans doing the conga and celebrating. It was a great day and we were soon heading to the buses which would take us back to the station where our train would very soon be leaving. I thought we would miss it to be honest, but when we arrived we found that the police had held it back to accommodate us.

We obtained beers for the train in the station and boarded for our journey home. There was a heavy police presence on the train and as much as I tried I could not persuade Steve to sing. No surprise really though as he is not a singer. I decided to venture into the next carriage and see if they would sing and to my delight I managed to get them all singing 'Keep Right On'

On return to our carriage a big group of the lads sang to me 'we love you Blondie, with your long Blondie hair, we love you Blondie, cos you love the blues' it was great, and I immediately decided to go and join them and get them singing. I had a right laugh with them but Steve texted my sister to tell her that I was about to get myself arrested! Mind you, it was quite funny cos she immediately called me and my mobile ring tone is the crowd version of shit on the villa and everyone cheered when it rang.

Once we got back to Birmingham and jumped into a taxi, Steve decided he wanted to stop for a quick drink in the Green Man in Harborne to catch up with the other Bluenoses who had driven back. There were a lot of Blues in the Green Man and we were soon chatting to Brendon and Graham again. Then it was off home and I was left to reflect on what a brilliant day I had had and what a brilliant win for Blues. I had thoroughly enjoyed my trip home as usual and was quite sad at the thought of leaving again. Till the next time, I thought sadly

Back in Abu Dhabi again I felt that I was really missing out on the run in to promotion. I was more nervous than ever, I think when you are able to go to the games you at least feel part of it, almost like you can have an effect on the outcome. Listening to the next game against Norwich City was painful, especially as we only drew 1-1 and I felt that every point was import at the minute as there was only six games to go to the end of season and the last game could end up being massive as it is against Reading and they are the other team challenging with Blues and Wolves for the two automatic promotion places.

The next game at St. Andrews was massive as it was against Wolves who were currently occupying first place in the Championship with Blues second but 6 or 7 points behind them. It was a chance to catch up some ground and the match was once again being screened live. I was so nervous as I draped my flags and scarves over the sofa and chairs. Trish and Trace arrived just before kickoff and my nerves soon rubbed off on them too. When Blues scored my flat became a wild celebration of blue and white as the three of us ran around hugging each other and waving our arms in the air. I think it made me even more nervous though as I knew I would be gutted if they equalized. Then the second goal went it – queue more wild celebrations and when the final whistle blew with the score at Birmingham City 2 Wolves 0, I was in heaven! I couldn't wait to see my dingle mate Dale to give him some stick as he had to me when they knocked us out of the FA Cup. Revenge was sweet and Blues were well on track for a quick return to the Premier league.

With only five games left Blues dropped valuable points in draws against Charlton 0-0 away and against Plymouth 1-1 at home as Blues were reduced to ten men. It was getting extremely nerve wracking and was not a time for the faint hearted. Then Blues travelled to Watford and won 1-0 meaning that if we won our next game against Preston at St. Andrews Blues would be promoted back to the Premier League where we belong. The game was also due to be screened live. Unfortunately my match day buddies Trish and Trace would be unable to watch it with me as they would be in Dubai, but asked for updates via text messages.

I was so nervous because I really expected Blues to cock it up like we always seem to do and to take it to the last game of the season at Reading which would be awful, it not a great climax for the neutral supporters. As always I draped flags and scarves everywhere and wore my Blues shirt and had a couple of ciders to calm the nerves a little. The game got underway and I just don't know how I survived it. Blues were the better team by far but Preston (our bloody bogey team) scored a spectacular goal to take the lead. Blues never gave up though and soon equalised but then Preston scored an even more spectacular long range goal and we were beaten and shocked. I was gutted, even though I half expected Blues to make it difficult as they so often do. Being a Bluenose we know that nothing is ever made easy for us and we always do it the hard way. It would go to wire and the last game of the season which would be a daunting away trip to Reading. I even debated flying overnight to London to catch the game and then fly straight back, but I knew I had to work and it would be too expensive, plus I may even yet have to fly home for the play off final. I though how unfair it would be if Blues missed out after being in the top two for all of the season.

And so it all came down to the last game of the season away at Reading which would be screened live. Wolves had already been promoted to the Premier league and so it was just second place that was up for grabs or a consolation place in the play offs. Depending on results it was possible for Blues, Reading or Sheffield Utd to finish in 2nd place and gain promotion to the Premier League. It Blues won at Reading then it would be Blues who would be promoted as no one would be able to catch us, but if Reading won then they could be promoted, or if the Reading v Blues game was a draw and Sheffield Utd won their game then Sheffield Utd would be promoted. To say I was nervous was a vast understatement on the day of the game.

Trish and Trace had to take the cat (Doug's) that they had been minding for Carolyn, to the vets in preparation for his flight to

Jersey to rejoin Carolyn, therefore they would not be able to join me to watch the game until around half time but said they would get there as soon as they could. I had flags and scarves everywhere and was downing cider dressed in my Blues shirt as the game got underway. I was more nervous than excited as I was absolutely terrified that we would miss out and end up in the play offs, and miss out again. Only a win would be enough for Blues and I was a wreck!

The atmosphere was brilliant and the Blues fans could be heard loud and proud as usual. They away end was absolutely packed with Blues with not an empty seat to be seen, which is more than could be said for the home support which was littered with empty seats. Perhaps their fans had lost faith in the run in. It was an exciting match and the Bluenoses were getting behind the team and when we scored the away end erupted! I went crazy and ran around the flat on my own celebrating like a mad woman. I texted my sister who was at work in Birmingham and I sang and sang on my own, not caring what the neighbours thought! Mind you, they should be used to me by now! So half time arrived with a score line of Reading 0 Birmingham City 1.

Just as I was refilling my drink at half time the doorbell rang and I opened it to Trish and Trace in Blues shirts asking what the score was. I was too busy singing 'we're Birmingham, we're Birmingham, We're Birmingham City!' to reply. "You're winning then!" said Trace, as I danced around in celebration. "Yes!' I said. So joined by the girls we sat down for the second half, all of us a bundle of nerves. Then the doorbell rang again and this time it was Trish's sister Shannon who was visiting her from Australia, and she too was wearing a Blues shirt. I was so impressed, they all looked brilliant and Trish even had a Blues scarf and her Blues teddy with her. We were all so excited.

All I wanted was for Blues not to concede a goal and keep it safe but when Kevin Phillips scored our second I was ecstatic and jumped on the girls as we all celebrated by screaming, jumping on each other and running round the room and kissing the TV screen! Fantastic, I was beginning to believe we could do it! Then

Reading scored almost immediately bringing the score to 2-1 which was still great if we could hold on to it. And hold on to it we did, in fact we came close to getting a third when O'Conner unleashed a shot from outside the penalty area that hit the post as we all jumped to our feet and let out a chorus of 'ooohhhhh'.

The Blues fans were singing 'Keep Right On', 'shit on the Villa' and 'we are Premier League, say we are Premier League' as Trish, Trace and I joined in.

When the final whistle sounded with the score at Reading 1 Birmingham City 2, I was out of my seat and celebrating with the girls as the Bluenoses at Reading celebrated on the TV screen. We watched in Bliss as the Blues players ran across to the celebrating Blues fans and joined in the celebrations. I was over the moon; it is times like this that it makes it all worthwhile being a Bluenose. Oh how I wished I was there with them and my heart ached to be part of it. We have our ups and downs but we never give up and we celebrate like no other set of supporters know how. To see all the Blues fans in fancy dress and face paint etc, with looks of pure joy on their faces it is hard to describe how we feel when we achieve something. We are part of a family like no other family and every one of us is proud to be part of it. Those of us that were together in the late seventies and early eighties know what a fabulous group of supports we are and we won't let the Premier League take that away from us by attracting glory hunters who do not know how to support a team unless they win everything.

This meant that Blues finished in second place and we are back in the Premier League after only one season away! The final table finished with Wolves as Champions, Birmingham City in 2nd place and promoted and Burnley were promoted in the play off final after scraping into the play off places on the last day of the season. Relegated from the Championship were Norwich City, Southampton and Charlton. The League Cup was won by Manchester Utd on Penalties after a 0-0 draw against Tottenham. The FA Cup was won by Chelsea who beat Everton 2-1 at Wembley.